"Having panic disorder has taught me how little most of us know about anxiety disorders in general. And working with Jerilyn Ross has shown me how committed she is to helping patients and their families through improved education."
—Earl Campbell
Heisman Trophy, 1977
Pro Football Hall of Fame, 1991

"The best investment any one of us can make is to know everything we possibly can about an illness we are suffering from. *Triumph Over Fear* provides the critical information succinctly and with great clarity. It is a superb contribution."
—Thomas Detre, M.D.
Senior Vice Chancellor for Health Sciences
University of Pittsburgh

"In this timely and very useful book, Jerilyn Ross presents in a clear and lucid manner the most current information on anxiety and its disorders, and describes exciting and effective new treatments now available for these serious conditions."
—David H. Barlow, Ph.D.
Distinguished Professor, Department of Psychology
State University of New York at Albany

"This is a breakthrough in the understanding and treatment of panic and anxiety. It provides the most up to date information on these troubling disorders."
—Aaron T. Beck, M.D.
President
Beck Institute for Cognitive Therapy and Research

"Jerilyn Ross is an outstanding national leader for better understanding of the problem of anxiety disorders. Her book is recommended reading for professionals, people who suffer, and people who want to understand."
—Herbert Pardes, M.D.
Vice President for Health Sciences
and Dean of the Faculty of Medicine
College of Physicians & Surgeons of Columbia University

"An essential book. With hope and encouragement, *Triumph Over Fear* takes the stigma out of anxiety and shows the way towards recovery from one of society's most common and impairing disorders."
—Jonathan R. T. Davidson, M.D.
Director
Anxiety and Traumatic Stress Program
Duke University Medical Center

"An invaluable resource. It enlightens as well as educates family members who are often baffled by the strange complaints of their loved ones. It's enormously popular among our patients."

—James O. Wilson, M.A., L.P.C.
Director
Phobia & Anxiety Center of the Southwest
Dallas, Texas

"Collecting her own personal and vast professional experience, Jerilyn Ross has produced a highly readable and user-friendly description of a psychological approach to the treatment of the most common psychiatric problem, anxiety disorder."

—Myrna M. Weissman, Ph.D.
Professor of Epidemiology in Psychiatry
Chief, Division of Clinical Genetic Epidemiology
College of Physicians & Surgeons of Columbia University

"A wonderfully informative book . . . In a warm, gentle, and compassionate way, Jerilyn Ross discusses her own personal struggles and describes the treatment approaches she used during her recovery process and with her clients."

—Sherry Byer, Ph.D.
Director
Panic/Anxiety Recovery Center
Chicago, Illinois

"*Triumph Over Fear* is well balanced in its presentation of the subject and written with immense attention to detail in the reconstruction of cases and with a sense of comfort and hope. It will appeal to and inform lay person and professional alike."

—Shirley A. Hibbein
The National Alliance for the Mentally Ill Newsletter,
The Advocate

"In writing *Triumph Over Fear,* Jerilyn Ross has made an outstanding contribution to both our understanding of and our ability to overcome phobias."

—Manuel Zane, M.D.
White Plains Hospital Phobia Clinic Newsletter,
PM News

"*Triumph Over Fear* is the most fascinating, the most readable, and the most informative book on anxiety, panic and phobia that I have read."

—Robert M. A. Hirschfeld, M.D.
Titus Harris Professor and Chairman
Department of Psychiatry and Behavioral Sciences
The University of Texas Medical Branch at Galveston

"Wonderful. The everyday language and clinical vignettes make this superb reading for individuals suffering from anxiety disorders."
—Charles K. Billings, M.D.
Acting Chairman
Department of Psychiatry
Ochsner Clinic

"An excellent book that will do much, not only to destigmatize phobias and other anxiety disorders, but also will be helpful to the many people who suffer from them."
—Carolyn B. Robinowitz, M.D.
Associate Dean
Georgetown University Medical School

"Jerilyn Ross has a wealth of experience in the treatment of phobic patients and shares it with the reader. This is a practical, useful book for those of us who treat these patients."
—James C. Ballenger, M.D.
Chairman, Department of Psychiatry and Behavioral Sciences
Medical University of South Carolina

"*Triumph Over Fear* is a splendid demonstration of Jerilyn Ross's expertise in the treatment of anxiety disorders and her commitment to help those who suffer from this illness. It offers great encouragement and help, as well as invaluable information."

—Mary Guardino
Founder and Executive Director
Freedom From Fear, New York

"Extremely well-written and very useful. Many people with anxiety disorders believe they have a much more serious mental illness because the symptoms can be so frightening. *Triumph Over Fear* provides clear and concise information that is easily understandable."
—Martin B. Keller, M.D.
Mary E. Zucker Professor and Chairman
Department of Psychiatry and Human Behavior
Brown University

JERILYN ROSS

BANTAM BOOKS

NEW YORK • TORONTO • LONDON • SYDNEY • AUCKLAND

TRIUMPH
OVER FEAR

A Book
of Help and Hope
for People with Anxiety,
Panic Attacks, and Phobias

To my parents,
Carolyn and Ray Ross,
and my brother, Richard,
in loving gratitude
for the love
and support they have always
given me.

TRIUMPH OVER FEAR

A Bantam Book

PUBLISHING HISTORY

Bantam hardcover edition/May 1994
Bantam trade paperback edition/May 1995

Published simultaneously in the United States and Canada

Bantam Books are published by Bantam Books, a division of Bantam
Doubleday Dell Publishing Group, Inc. Its trademark, consisting
of the words "Bantam Books" and the portrayal of a rooster, is Regis-
tered in U.S. Patent and Trademark Office and in other countries.
Marca Registrada. Bantam Books, 1540 Broadway, New York,
New York 10036.

PRINTED IN THE UNITED STATES OF AMERICA

BVG   20   19   18   17   16   15   14

Contents

Foreword by
Rosalynn Carter

DURING THE PAST DECADE, there has been great progress in the recognition and treatment of anxiety disorders, the most common of all psychiatric disorders, affecting over 23 million Americans.

National public and professional education campaigns, spearheaded by the Anxiety Disorders Association of America, the National Institute of Mental Health, and other key organizations, have helped ensure that these disorders are now more frequently and accurately diagnosed by those in the medical community.

People with an anxiety disorder, particularly that 1 percent of the population who suffer from panic disorder, typically see many physicians searching for an explanation for the distressing physical sensations that are symptomatic of the problem—only to be labeled as "high strung," "nervous," or hypochondriacal, and dismissed without obtaining an accurate diagnosis or being told that they have a treatable condition.

Within the past decade, progress in understanding the biology of the brain has been nothing short of amazing. Through careful clinical trials we have used this knowledge to significantly improve treatment of all psychiatric disorders, including the anxiety disorders. Special kinds of psychological therapies, such as cognitive-behavioral therapy, and new medications have enabled 60 to 90 percent of people suffering from an anxiety disorder to experience dramatic relief of symptoms and resume normal lives.

When an anxiety disorder is not recognized or appropriately treated, the toll is great, not only to the individual, but to his or her family and the community at large. Many people with panic disorder, for instance, have markedly constrained lifestyles because of fear of traveling any distance from home, which often leaves them unable to fulfill family responsibilities, career functions, and social obligations. In addition, one third of people with an anxiety disorder abuse alcohol, leading to an additional and separate set of problems. Many also have concurrent depression. Treating the underlying disorder will not only decrease a great deal of personal suffering, but will also have a positive effect on families, communities, and the workplace.

Triumph Over Fear is an important addition to existing educational efforts. People suffering from an anxiety disorder need to know that they have a serious but treatable problem. They need to know that they are not alone, that their condition is not trivial and that, with appropriate care, they can expect to lead normal, productive lives.

I began my work as an advocate for people with emotional and mental illnesses while I was First Lady of Georgia. I quickly came to realize that the great stigma against these people—a stigma that causes blindness about the genuine suffering of many—held back progress in all I was trying to accomplish.

Today, while I feel we are still fighting many of the myths and stereotypes we were fighting twenty years ago, I have seen great progress in the knowledge of the brain, the development of new medications and psychosocial services, and the opportunity to effectively care for people with emotional and mental illnesses and dramatically improve the quality of their lives. This progress presents an unprecedented opportunity to finally eliminate the historic discrimination against mental illness in our nation's health-care system.

There are key principles that must guide all our activities in this regard:

We must end discrimination against those with mental disorders. Discrimination has denied those who need care access to appropriate services for far too long, and it continues to limit resources available to pay for care.

We must recognize that mental health is an integral part of every person's health. Awareness of mental health problems needs to permeate the health-care system. Primary-care physicians, nurses, physicians' assistants—all must have sufficient knowledge about the interdependency between mind and body to know when intervention is necessary and who is best able to intervene.

Unfortunately, not many people outside the mental health field understand mental disorders or how treatable they are. Yet, not only those in medicine, but policy makers, other health-care providers and the general public need to know more about advances in treatment. Those of us in the mental health field have a responsibility to bridge that gap. We need more celebrities like Willard Scott, Patty Duke, and William Styron speaking out about their treatment and their recovery. And we need more mental health advocates like Jerilyn Ross keeping the public, health-care professionals, and legislators informed about the treatability of psychiatric conditions.

We must recognize the need to direct our resources in new ways. We know that the lack of appropriate mental health care has great emotional and financial consequences. Investing in early intervention, treatment, and follow-up care will prevent far more costly disability, and even death.

It is time for everyone to unite behind a common vision which transcends individual interests and offers hope and help to those who are suffering. The mental health community has a critical role to play in promoting a society whose individual members are healthy in both mind and body.

We cannot waver in our support of people with persistent and disabling emotional and mental disorders. We must ensure that these individuals have the comprehensive coordinated services they need in the community and the resources to obtain more intensive care in times of crisis.

And we cannot turn our backs on the millions of other Americans—young and old, rich and poor, of every race and ethnic origin—who at some point in their lives need some kind of psychiatric treatment.

You and I know these people. They are our friends, our neighbors, our colleagues at work. They are members of our families. They are ourselves.

Preface: The Most Common Mental Health Problem

AT THE Anxiety Disorders Association of America, the calls and the letters pour in.

"I saw you on that program," says a woman who is calling from California. "The person you were describing—the one who couldn't sign her name in public—that's me! I began crying—I couldn't stop—I had to call you."

"I've been terrified to leave my house," writes a man from New York. "I was so afraid. I couldn't tell anybody." (His handwritten letter goes on for twelve pages.)

"When the attacks first began, I was in terrible shape," another letter begins. "I didn't know what was happening to me. I tried to explain my feelings to my doctor; he didn't understand and told me I was fine. I truly thought I was losing my mind."

Another writes: "My phobias have been a very serious problem for the last fifteen years and have progressively gotten worse as the years go by. I have gone to all kinds of doctors and have even spent some time in the hospital to try and find out what the symptoms are or what is causing them. The frustrating part is when I am told that it is only nerves. . . ."

"No one could tell me what was wrong," says a caller. "I'm one of those people who has to keep checking. It sometimes takes me two hours to leave the house in the morning; I check the stove, the lights, the doors. I have to keep going back. . . ."

And almost everyone says something like "No one understands how I feel. I feel so frightened. I'm missing out on so much. I have no self-esteem left."

Their symptoms differ, but all of these people suffer from an anxiety disorder. Over the past fifteen years I have worked with several thousand men and women with similar problems. They are some of the bravest people I have ever met. Every day they face situations that feel as physically and emotionally terrifying and draining as walking in front of a speeding car, jumping from an airplane without a parachute, or being trapped in a burning building.

To someone who has not experienced an anxiety disorder, the terror, discomfort, and irrationality associated with these conditions will seem incomprehensible. Having lived through it myself, I can say that there are few experiences in life more terrifying or baffling.

After overcoming my own debilitating phobia—the most common of the anxiety disorders—my dream was, and continues to be, to give others the new lease on life that I was given. Whether I'm working with an individual patient, talking to a self-help group, conducting a training seminar for health-care professionals, or appearing on television, my goals remain the same: to make sure that every American who suffers from an anxiety disorder knows that he or she is not alone, helpless, or hopeless; and to see that all who do need help have access to effective treatment.

Approximately 23 million Americans, 13 percent of the population, suffer from an anxiety disorder, according to the National Institute of Mental Health (NIMH). Although anxiety disorders are among the most treatable of all psychiatric disorders, fewer than one quarter of those suffering from an anxiety disorder receive treatment. Millions of others suffer in silence, or go from doctor to doctor, many having no idea what is wrong with them. And even if they do know, many are too embarrassed or frightened to ask for help.

But anxiety disorders are not costly only to those who suffer from them. As great a toll as they take on their victims, the toll they exact from society is perhaps even greater. Robert L. DuPont, M.D., president of the Institute for Behavior and Health in Rockville, Maryland, found in a study completed in 1993 that anxiety disorders are the most expensive of all mental illnesses.

Drawing on a new statistical analysis of a major survey of mental illnesses done in the early 1980s, DuPont and his team determined that anxiety disorders as a group cost an estimated $46.6 billion in 1990, almost one third of all costs for mental illness.

Almost three quarters of the total costs of anxiety, some $35.5 billion, were considered indirect, due to reduced or lost productivity. Treatment costs are comparatively low compared to those for such mental illnesses as schizophrenia or manic depression. However, the lost potential of those with an anxiety disorder, excluded from the cultural, economic, or social life of the country through fear and ignorance, cannot be quantified in dollars, and even the most conservative estimates can barely scratch the surface.

Those of us involved in anxiety-disorders research, treatment, and public and professional education are all too familiar with the gaps and frustrations in our health-care system: the inability of even some of the best health-care professionals to recognize the symptoms of an anxiety disorder and either to apply the appropriate treatment or to make an appropriate referral; and the lack of access for people with anxiety disorders to publicly funded mental-health facilities and to adequate health insurance to cover private treatment.

Over the years I have been repeatedly saddened by the stories of wasted years, wasted lives—real tragedies that could easily have been avoided. And yet the myths persist, principally the general misunderstanding that people with anxiety disorders are the "worried well," people whose problems are "all in their heads" and who should simply pull themselves up by their bootstraps.

There are the people with agoraphobia who spend years avoiding places where they have had panic attacks until they are afraid to leave their houses, or a single room in their house. Or they cling to a "safe" person who seems to offer protection against panic attacks, or who at least will be there "if the worst happens," whatever the worst is—often something that cannot even be expressed. Social phobics experience shyness that becomes a shackle, holding them back from any but the most minimal relationships, professional or private. These people spend lifetimes watching colleagues—often less talented, less able—surpass them professionally, watching potential friends, lovers, mates go off, never knowing what might have been had they not been effectively imprisoned by their inability to relate socially.

Then, too, there are the victims who turn to alcohol or drugs to temporarily ease the terror or the shyness or the flashbacks and become doubly afflicted. And, finally, there are those who see no hope, who sink into a chronic depression and perhaps eventual suicide. The National Institute of Mental Health has estimated that some 70 percent of individuals suffering from one or another of the anxiety disorders has at least one other condition requiring psychiatric attention—including substance abuse—in addition to the anxiety disorder itself. Scientists call such conditions "co-morbid" conditions.

THE MOST COMMON MENTAL-HEALTH PROBLEM

The disorders that are currently considered by specialists to belong to the broad category of *anxiety disorders* encompass panic disorder, phobias (including agoraphobia, simple phobias, and social phobia), obsessive-compulsive disorder, post-traumatic stress disorder, and generalized anxiety disorder.

Their true extent did not become known until the early 1980s, when the National Institute of Mental Health conducted the first-ever survey of mental illness in this country. Known as the Epidemiological Catchment Area (ECA) survey, it collected information from approximately 20,000 people in five cities: Baltimore, Maryland, New Haven, Connecticut, St. Louis, Missouri, Durham, North Carolina, and Los Angeles, California.

The survey interviews were lengthy and detailed and generated data that became our most reliable source of information on incidence, prevalence, family history, age of victims, treatment, and costs related to mental illness. The survey continues to provide researchers with an ongoing source of information about mental illness and substance abuse.

One of the survey's findings was that anxiety disorders are the most common mental health problems in the country.

A more recent study, the National Comorbidity Survey (NCS) found the prevalence to be even higher than estimated by the ECA. One in every four survey respondants reported a lifetime history of at least one anxiety disorder. The NCS study's findings also suggest that anxiety disorders are more chronic than either depression or substance abuse.

Yet it was not until October 1991, at a National Institutes of Health consensus conference, that panic disorder, one of the most terrifying yet most treatable anxiety disorders, was officially recognized as a "real" and serious condition that can be effectively treated.

During the past decade a proliferation of newspaper and magazine articles, TV and radio talk shows, and books—both academic and self-help—has been tremendously helpful in raising our consciousness about the seriousness and the treatability of anxiety disorders.

Yet, as is evidenced by the more than fifty thousand letters received each year by the Anxiety Disorders Association of America (ADAA), a national nonprofit organization dedicated to improving the lives of people suffering from an anxiety disorder, the surface has barely been scratched. Millions of Americans remain in the dark about their condition.

Ignorance on the part of both doctors and patients, together with a widespread misunderstanding about the relation of mind and body, have been among the chief barriers to getting treatment for most of those who need it. These barriers are compounded by a tendency on the part of physicians (mostly male) and other professionals to ignore or belittle many complaints that affect primarily women, as do anxiety disorders. A wall of ignorance—and to some extent injustice—has separated those suffering from an anxiety disorder from those who could treat them.

To be fair, much of the knowledge about the disorders has only emerged in the past two decades, and much is still to be discovered—about genetic predisposition and about emotional and environmental factors that precipitate the disorders. The stigma that comes with mental illness in our society has yet to be dissipated. Indeed, many victims of agoraphobia cite "fear of going crazy" as one of the symptoms of a panic attack.

One of my chief aims in writing this book is to shed light on anxiety disorders, dispel some of the myths about them, and break down some of the prejudices. In Part One, I introduce you to five people (in addition to myself) whose stories illustrate each of the major disorders. These chapters focus on the problems of correct diagnosis and on outlining an initial treatment plan.

Part Two introduces another seven patients, including two children. Their stories will give you a fuller picture of the treatment process for panic disorder and phobias. It is now estimated that up to 90 percent of people with these disorders can be effectively treated.

If you, the reader, have an anxiety disorder, I hope the example of these courageous individuals will encourage you to reach toward recovery. With this in mind, Part Three is a self-help program that can be used alone or in conjunction with professional treatment. Like the people you will read about here, you too can triumph over fear.

Acknowledgments

FIRST AND FOREMOST I want to thank the thousands of patients with whom I have worked over the last fifteen years. It is truly a privilege to have been permitted to enter their emotional worlds as they shared their fears, disappointments, dreams, and triumphs with me. Many of the most creative and helpful therapeutic interventions I use in my practice and subsequently incorporated into this book emerged through the pain, the tears, the laughter and, oftentimes, the raw guts of the very people whom I have had the pleasure of helping.

I am greatly indebted to the following experts in the mental health field (listed alphabetically) who have generously read and provided critical review on all or parts of the book: Hagop S. Akiskal, M.D., Senior Science Adviser, National Institute of Mental Health (NIMH); James C. Ballenger, M.D., Chairman, Department of Psychiatry and Behavioral Sciences, Medical University of South Carolina; David Barlow, Ph.D., Distinguished Professor of Psychology, State University of New York at Albany; Robert Bernstein, Ph.D., Professor of Psychology, Marymount University, Virginia; James W. Broatch, M.S.W., Executive Director, Obsessive Compulsive Foundation (OCF); Dennis Charney, M.D., Professor and Associate Clinical Researcher, Department of Psychiatry, Yale University; Paula Clayton, M.D., Chairman, Department of Psychiatry, University of Minnesota Medical School; George Curtis, M.D., Professor of Psychiatry, University of Michigan Medical School; Jonathan R. T. Davidson, M.B., FRCP Psych., Associate Professor of Psychiatry, Duke University Medical Center; Thomas Detre, M.D., Senior Vice Chancellor for Health Sciences, University of Pittsburgh; Robert L. DuPont, M.D., Clinical Professor of Psychiatry, Georgetown University School of Medicine; James Finley, Director of Government Relations, National Community Mental Healthcare Council; Edna Foa, Ph.D., Professor of Psychiatry, Medical College of Pennsylvania; Abby J. Fyer, M.D., Associate Professor of Psychiatry, College of Physicians and Surgeons, Columbia University; Benjamin D. Greenberg, M.D., Ph.D., Senior Staff Fellow, NIMH; Mary Guardino, Director, Freedom From Fear; Robert M.A. Hirschfeld, M.D., Chairman, Department of Psychiatry and Behavioral Sciences, University of Texas Medical Branch at Galveston; Walter Kay, M.D., Associate Professor of Psychiatry, Western Psychiatric Institute and Clinic, University of Pittsburg; Donald F. Klein, M.D., Professor of Psychiatry, College of Physicians and Surgeons, Columbia University; Amos Korczyn, M.D., Professor, University of Tel Aviv; Michael R. Liebowitz, M.D., Professor of Clinical Psychiatry, College of Physicians and Surgeons, Columbia University. John S. Marsh, M.D., M.P.H., Assistant Professor, Division of Child and Adolescent Psychiatry, Duke University Medical Center; Jack D. Maser, Ph.D., Chief, Anxiety and Somatoform Disorders Program, NIMH; Norman E. Rosenthal, M.D., Chief, Section on Environmental Psychiatry, NIMH; Thomas W. Uhde, M.D., Chairman, Department of Psychiatry, Wayne State University School of Medicine; Sally Winston, Psy.D., Codirector, Anxiety and Stress Disorders Institute of Maryland; Barry B. Wolfe, Ph.D., Chief, Psychosocial Treatment Research Program, NIMH; and Richard Wyatt, M.D., Chief, Neuropsychiatry Branch, NIMH.

I am also extremely grateful for the time, wisdom, and encouragement of many of my friends and associates who critically commented on various portions of the book. I especially wish to thank Karen Akers, Jim Coleman, Paul Costello, Lisa Dallos, Judy Kramer, Allison Kullen, Ruth Link, Jan Ross, Burt Rubin, J.D., Hon. Claudine Schneider (R., R.I.), Fran Sidney, Sally Walther, Ann Wasserman, and David Wasserman. And I thank my many patients, who wish to remain anonymous, for reading sections of the book and giving me invaluable feedback that was essential to my knowing what was helpful and what was not.

My sincere appreciation and thanks to the professional staff at the Ross Center for Anxiety and Related Disorders—Judy Barth, R.N., Jeanne Marks, L.I.C.S.W., Marvin Oleshansky, M.D., and Joyce Robbins, L.I.C.S.W., each of whose outstanding and creative clinical skills contributed to the therapeutic successes of many of the patients whose cases are discussed in *Triumph Over Fear*.

A very special thanks to Peg Fagley, my personal assistant and dear friend, who helped me in every possible way. Peg's unremitting efficiency, outstanding editorial skills, and personal warmth and support assisted me in every task necessary to complete the book. I am deeply grateful.

I am also very grateful to the staff at the Anxiety Disorders Association of America (ADAA) for their ongoing and generous support of my efforts. Ivey Farber was there for me in many ways, especially in the beginning when I didn't have a clue as to how to use my word processor. Stacy Garfield, Carrie Devaughn, and Esme Frensilli were extremely helpful, particularly with the huge task of compiling the treatment resource list for the Appendix. And I am especially grateful to Joel Klaverkamp, ADAA's Executive Director, for giving me the peace of mind that, while I was frantically trying to meet my book deadline, ADAA was running smoothly and productively.

I owe a debt of gratitude to Diane and Allan Kullen for convincing me to move south; to Jean Carper, author of *Food: Your Miracle Medicine,* for her insights and advice about the trials and tribulations of becoming an author; to Ellen Kingsley, whose sensitively produced five-part television series on anxiety disorders inspired the title of this book; to Robert L. DuPont, M.D., for giving me the gift of opportunity; and to my precious niece and nephew, Andrea and Justin Ross, whose smiles never let me forget what's really important in life.

During the past several years, it has been both an honor and a privilege to work closely with former First Lady Rosalynn Carter in her extraordinary and tireless efforts to end the stigma and discrimination against people with mental health problems.

My agent, Jane Dystel, believed in this book from the beginning and helped in every way to see it through. Her support has been invaluable and I am extremely thankful to her.

Ed Claflin was instrumental in helping to initially organize the book—not a small task and one for which I am most grateful.

A heartfelt thanks to *Washington Post* health and science writer, Sandy Rovner, who so graciously helped me with the challenging task of incorporating complex scientific information into various sections of the book in an understandable and meaningful way.

And I am deeply grateful to Toni Burbank, my editor at Bantam, and to her assistant, Alison Rivers, for their untiring dedication to this project. Every aspect of the book was greatly enhanced by Toni's knowledge and insight, scrupulous attention to detail and insistence that this book become the best it could be. I could not have done it without her.

PART ONE

The Many Faces of
Anxiety

1

Anxiety Beyond Reason

ONE GRAY SEPTEMBER MORNING, a woman I'll call Gail who suffers from repeated panic attacks visits my office for the first time. She is accompanied by her husband, Mike. She couldn't have come without him. He is her "safe person."

Gail is a small woman with bright, darting eyes and a quick smile. She has two beautiful, healthy children. She seems full of energy—someone who should be in love with life.

Instead, she tells of terrors. She describes what it's like when she's having a panic attack:

"I feel like I'm losing my mind, going crazy. My heart starts pounding. I feel dizzy, frightened, unreal—as if everything is just slipping away. I become overwhelmed with a sense of impending doom, afraid I'm going to lose control and do something embarrassing or harmful, like scream uncontrollably or jump out of the car while it's moving."

Gail has visited numerous doctors. Fifteen years ago, when she had her first panic attack, she had just entered college. She went to the infirmary and tried to describe her symptoms to the college physician. He couldn't find anything physically wrong with her.

"It's probably just nerves," he said. "Lots of freshmen feel anxious. You'll get over it."

He gave her a prescription for Valium.

The panic attacks continued. They would happen while she was grocery shopping, driving, or sometimes even sitting quietly in the comfort of her own home. They were baffling and terrifying. Over the next five years, Gail visited several internists, a cardiologist, an endocrinologist, and a neurologist. She underwent extensive and expensive medical tests: an electrocardiogram, treadmill test, and angiography to check for heart disease; a glucose tolerance test for hypoglycemia; tests of thyroid function; and even a PET scan to rule out temporal lobe epilepsy.

After each doctor's visit or test she would brace herself for the all-too-familiar words "I can't find anything wrong. It's probably all in your mind."

Afraid of being perceived as a hypochondriac, Gail stopped going to doctors and suffered silently, as her world gradually narrowed. She began avoiding any place or situation she thought might bring on one of the dreaded panic attacks: shopping malls, highway driving, restaurants, and theaters.

At the urging of a close friend, she agreed to see a psychiatrist, who encouraged her to talk about her family background. She felt hopeful for a while, believing that perhaps something from her childhood was causing the attacks and that once they figured out what it was she would be better. She learned a lot about herself but the panic attacks continued.

As she tells me this, she begins sobbing. "No one seems able to help me. No one understands."

"I think I do," I say to her. "I've been there."

My first panic attack happened when I was twenty-five years old. I was traveling through Europe with my friend, Ann.

Ann and I arrived in the ancient, picturesque city of Salzburg, Austria, in the midst of the annual music festival. At night the city was lit up like a fairground. Crowds bustled through the streets;

the cafés were jammed with Austrian vacationers and foreign tourists.

Perched on a mountaintop high above the city, Salzburg Castle was illuminated by spotlights. It looked like something out of a storybook.

The evening of our arrival, Ann and I decided to go to the Café Winkler, which was on the top floor of a mountainside building. With floor-to-ceiling panoramic windows, the café seemed to hover above the gleaming lights of the city. Inside there was the glow of candlelight, the soft strains of Viennese waltz music. Couples glided across the floor.

It wasn't long before two handsome young Austrians came to the table where Ann and I were sitting and asked us to dance. I remember thinking, "This is perfect." I was so happy. I could easily have danced the night away.

Then something happened. Suddenly I felt as if a magnet was pulling me toward the edge of the room. The pull was so strong I thought I was going to jump out of the window. Everything started to spin. I felt as though I was on the verge of completely losing control of myself.

"My god!" I remember thinking, "I certainly don't want to commit suicide! What is going on?"

I felt I was in terrible danger. Everything in my power was fighting that magnetic pull. The feeling was so seductive—it was like being in a vacuum or in the middle of a tornado, holding on for dear life. It took all my energy to prevent myself from running across the room and jumping out of the window. I broke out in a cold sweat. It felt as if my heart was pounding out of my chest.

And yet, at the same time, I remember being very conscious that *this made no sense*. I didn't *want* to jump out the window, but I was overwhelmed by the conviction that if I stayed a moment longer, I would be *compelled* to jump—I wouldn't be able to stop myself.

I had to get out of there, off the dance floor, out of the building.

In the midst of my panic, much to my amazement I heard myself speaking calmly to my partner.

"Excuse me," I said. "I have to make a call." I felt disconnected from myself as I spoke, almost as if I were watching myself in a movie. I was going through the motions of functioning normally, but inside I felt as though I was coming apart.

My handsome Austrian dance partner gave me a quizzical look; I quickly turned away. I didn't *want* to leave—I just *had* to. I caught Ann's eye and frantically signaled to her that I was leaving and wanted her to come with me. Then I made my way out of the dining room, leaving my dancing partner totally perplexed.

By the time I reached the elevator, the rush of terror was gone.

The elevator doors were just opening. I squeezed through the crowd and got on, feeling as if I had just awakened from a terrible nightmare.

As the elevator started down, my mind was racing. The feeling of panic had lasted a very brief time—not even a minute. But in the aftermath, my head was spinning. Baffling thoughts of what had just occurred kept racing through my mind.

When the elevator doors opened on the ground floor, I walked out of the building, still trembling.

I tried to explain to Ann what I was experiencing, but it was difficult. There didn't seem to be words to adequately describe what I was feeling. It just felt so horrible. Ann tried to understand and comfort me, but she, too, was frightened. We were alone in a foreign country and something terrible was happening.

I stood on the sidewalk for a moment, catching my breath, watching the passing cars, the normal nightlife in the crowded street of a magical city. I remember thinking: This place is so beautiful—it's almost surreal. Could that be it? Had I simply been overwhelmed by the magic of the moment?

I was exhausted, depleted and drained, convinced some life- or sanity-threatening disaster had just occurred. Where did that feeling come from? Was I sick? I had never felt anything like it before. Would it happen again?

Turning the experience over and over in my mind—reliving the nightmarish sensations—I knew that whatever it was that had happened to me that night in Salzburg would in some way change my life forever.

■ ■ ■

While I did not have another "attack" during the remaining two weeks of our European vacation, I became acutely aware of a strange and constant sense of anticipation and preoccupation with the fearful thought "What if it happens again?"

I had been home for three days when I went for dinner at my boyfriend's spacious seventeenth-floor apartment. I was sitting in the dining room, barely in sight of a window, when suddenly the sensations came flooding back: the dizziness, the pounding heart, the beads of sweat, and, most terrifying of all, the sense that I was going to panic and jump out the window. I desperately tried not to leave, to tell myself that everything would be okay, but the evening was ruined. I couldn't concentrate on anything my boyfriend was saying to me. All I could think of was, "I want to get out of here." In a few minutes the feelings of terror subsided. But, this experience had reinforced my worst fear: "It" *could* happen again.

A week later my heart sank when I opened my mail and read the invitation to a dear friend's wedding. The reception was to be held in the elegant penthouse restaurant of a New York skyscraper. A wave of terror shot through me as my mind focused on one thing only: How could I get out of going to this wedding?

Within six months I found myself unable to go above the tenth floor of any building. I was fine on the eighth or ninth floor, but for some unexplainable reason, even if I simply thought about going above the tenth floor, my palms would begin to sweat and I'd become overwhelmed with anxiety about what might happen. I have no idea, even to this day, why the tenth floor became my danger zone. But I do now know that if it made sense, it wouldn't be a phobia.

The phobia began spreading to other areas of my life, and that further scared me. One morning I was waiting for a train and suddenly I began to feel the by now all-too-familiar sensations—only this time I was afraid of panicking and hurling myself onto the tracks. I tried to reason with myself, saying, "This is ridiculous, I have absolutely no desire to hurt myself. I'm as happy and together

7

a person as anyone I know, and yet these bizarre experiences are beginning to take over my life."

I began to avoid the subway—and to dread where the sensations might strike next.

During the next five years, Ann and my then ex-boyfriend were the only people who knew about my panic attacks and my fear of going to high places. I didn't even tell my family. My parents and brother didn't know anything about my phobia until many years later.

I didn't understand what was happening, so how could I expect anyone else to? How could I say to someone, "I can't come to your house because I'm afraid I'm going to jump out the window"?

My fear of having a panic attack and losing control began to affect every aspect of my personal and professional life. What floor someone lived or worked on became the priority factor in selecting friends, boyfriends, jobs.

I went to extraordinary lengths to hide my "problem." When I met someone for the first time and was told where they lived, I would say, "Oh, I know someone who lives in that building. What floor are you on?" If the person lived above the tenth floor, I would find an excuse to meet them someplace else or invite them to my apartment. (To this day, I know the floor on which every one of my Manhattan friends lives and works.)

If a friend or colleague wanted to meet me for lunch and suggested, "Why don't we meet in my office and walk over to the restaurant together," I'd make up some excuse about my only having an hour for lunch so it would be best if we met right at the restaurant. I'd feel awful when I would have to break up a pleasant luncheon because I thought the person would notice that I really did have more time.

Some situations were simply beyond my control.

In New York I lived in a fourth-floor apartment in a twenty-story building. One of my friends, Chuck, lived on the twelfth floor. Chuck and I never dated, but he was a close friend and confidant, although I was too embarrassed to share this problem with him.

Chuck was a very social person. "I'm having these people over," he'd say. "Why don't you come on up?"

The twelfth floor!? "No thanks," I would apologize, "I'm afraid I have other plans."

Or I'd say, "Why don't you come to my apartment? I've already started dinner. I'm trying out this great new recipe . . . you'll love it . . . plenty for everyone . . ."

My evasion *had* to hurt my friendship with Chuck, and eventually it did.

I was teaching in the New York City public schools at the time, so I got home during the afternoon. One day about four o'clock I received a call from Chuck. His mother had died. He was leaving work early and taking the next train to Philadelphia to be with his family. But he'd left his laundry in the laundry room in the basement that morning and would need it for the trip. Would I mind bringing it up to his apartment so he could pack quickly? I could get his apartment key from the superintendent.

Such a simple thing.

And I couldn't do it.

I told him I would bring the laundry up to my apartment. All he had to do was ring me when he got back, and I'd have it ready for him to pick up.

Hearing my own words echo loudly in my head, I felt like the most selfish human being on earth.

"I don't understand," he said. "Why won't you go to my apartment?"

I had no explanation for him. I was willing to let down a dear friend in his time of grief, rather than face my own terror or expose my humiliating secret and risk having my friend think I was weak or weird.

In the mid-1970s I was teaching math in an inner-city school while studying for my master's degree in psychology at the New School for Social Research in New York City.

During the first semester I took an abnormal psychology course and remember anxiously reading through the entire textbook in one weekend, hoping to find some explanation for what was happening to me. Like most psychology students, I was convinced at the end of each chapter that I had whatever mental illness I had just read about. One moment I was sure I was schizophrenic, the next, manic-depressive, and so on. But as I progressed through the course I began to feel confident that I really didn't have any of the mental disorders I had read or heard about; yet I was baffled by the fact that whatever it was that was wrong with me wasn't in the book or ever mentioned by my professor during the class.

During study breaks I searched through the library, trying to find anything I could on fears, phobias, irrational thoughts and impulses. I did find some interesting analytical interpretations of phobias, like Freud's famous Little Hans case. But nothing I read offered me any insight as to why, at the age of twenty-five, I had suddenly developed a totally irrational fear of going above the tenth floor of a building. I had come from a wonderful, loving family, had had a happy childhood and a seemingly normal life in every other way.

One morning in 1977 I was home in my apartment reading *New York* magazine when I came across a story about people who had phobias that interfered with their lives. With rapidly growing excitement, I read on. The article described an attorney who was unable to drive on major highways, an executive who could no longer fly, a nurse who lived in fear of the next panic attack. This was *it*, I realized! I'm not the only one with these strange symptoms. The only difference was that these people were getting help and I wasn't; they were all enrolled in a phobia clinic at Roosevelt Hospital in New York City.

I couldn't stop rereading the article. I was overwhelmed with emotion; it was the first time anyone had described what was wrong with me. I rushed to the telephone, dialed the number for Roosevelt Hospital . . . and got a recording.

"Of course . . . Sunday afternoon . . . no one is there" . . . frustration and disappointment. I left a message.

After five years of misery, it seemed as if there might be a glimmer of light at the end of my terrifying tunnel. I could hardly sleep that night.

The next morning, unable to wait for someone to return my call, I dialed the hospital number promptly at nine o'clock.

By noon I was sitting in the office of Dr. Harley Shands, the medical director of the Roosevelt Hospital Phobia Clinic.

"What is it that you're afraid of?" Dr. Shands asked me.

"I don't know." I burst out crying, struggling for words that might make sense. "I feel so ridiculous—it's gotten to the point where even if I just *think* about going up to a high floor I begin to feel panicky. I'm not unhappy; I'm certainly not suicidal . . . Why do I have these horrible thoughts and impulses?"

I wasn't alone, he assured me. And I wasn't crazy. Nor would I do anything harmful to myself.

Under Dr. Shands's supervision, a phobia treatment group was forming the following week, and he was sure it would be helpful for me to join the group. In addition, he recommended that I meet weekly with a "contextual therapist," someone who would accompany me into anxiety-provoking situations and teach me how to deal with my anxiety at the time I was experiencing it.

There were eight people at the first meeting, men and women of all ages, including a lawyer, a teacher, and a businessman. The woman who addressed the group had been phobic herself.

I quickly discovered that I could talk about "the secret" I had never revealed to anyone. It didn't take long for those of us in that small but empathetically connected group to establish a very close bond with one another.

The therapist who was assigned to me for contextual therapy was named Joe. As I approached the high-rise building that was to be our meeting place, I looked up, as was now my habit, to play out in my mind what I was about to face. The familiar sense of terror swept over me as I anticipated what lay ahead.

As agreed, we met in the building's lobby. His warm smile and nonjudgmental manner helped to ease my feelings of embarrassment and uneasiness.

The goal of our first session was for us to go to the tenth floor and remain there for fifteen minutes. It seemed like an impossible mission, but reason told me I had to start somewhere—and I *so* wanted to gain control over my avoidance behavior.

Joe's reassuring comments eased my self-criticism about feeling foolish. He also assured me that I was in control of the situation. He told me I could stop the process and leave at any time. (As I later learned, if I had made that choice, he would have worked with me until I had been able to go back into the same situation and try again.)

This first intentional anxiety-provoking situation was not without its share of moments in which I experienced the same feelings of fear and confusion I had learned to recognize as panic, but the hope and assurance of gaining control were strong enough to get me through it.

In each subsequent session, we would "up the ante" and set a higher floor as a goal. When my anxiety predictably began to soar, Joe assured me that by staying in the situation and refocusing my thinking, the feelings would pass. He was right.

Each time this happened, it increased my confidence that, indeed, nothing would happen to me. *As frightening as the feelings are,* Joe kept reminding me, *they are not dangerous.* Of course he was right, but I had to be able to see that for myself.

I tried a number of techniques to refocus my thinking when I felt my anxiety rising. Some people in my group found it helpful to chew gum; others carried soda or juice with them. For some unknown reason I discovered that cracking and eating dried pumpkin or sunflower seeds, and at times furiously "popping" them in my mouth, relaxed me. Weird, I thought, but as Joe said, "Anything that helps you get into a situation is perfectly okay!"

I also kept a rubber band on my wrist and snapped it, while repeating to myself, "Stop!" when I found my thoughts running off with frightening images.

Counting backward from one hundred by threes was another helpful technique. It's pretty difficult to think through that mental exercise and focus on the fear at the same time. Inevitably, by the time I got to around seventy, I'd start laughing, the feelings would pass, and I'd feel "safe" again.

I can still recall standing on the fifteenth or eighteenth floor of some building, eating sunflower seeds, snapping a rubber band, and frantically counting backward by threes while waiting for the panicky feelings to subside—and hoping against hope that no one would step off the elevator or out of an office and see me!

But I *was* on that fifteenth or eighteenth floor, and that was the more important motivating force.

I diligently practiced on my own, each time going up one floor higher, convinced that I couldn't possibly go another. But I did, often having to remind myself as the all-too-familiar terror would show its ugly face, "You've survived these feelings before; you'll survive this time."

Each time I succeeded, I imagined myself building a muscle, and then making it stronger.

For my "graduation gift," ten weeks after I began treatment Joe invited me to have a drink on the top floor of the Gulf & Western Building. The restaurant, forty-four stories up, overlooked Central Park and Midtown Manhattan.

We got on the elevator and rode to the top. When the door opened, I froze and exclaimed, "I *can't!*"

Joe said, "Take the 't' off 'can't.' You *can*, but you don't *want* to—not just yet."

"Yes, I *do*," I insisted, and then burst out laughing. "You got me!" And without allowing myself time to change my mind, I stepped out of the elevator, shakily walked to the nearest table and plopped down onto a cushioned couch.

I was about twenty feet away from the window, yet it felt as if I were sitting on the window ledge. I dared to look out the window and vividly remember thinking to myself, with tears running down my cheeks, "It's magnificent." I loved New York with a passion, and it looked beautiful. Was I really looking *down* at it? Could it be that

I was *really* sitting on the forty-fourth floor of a building and looking out a window, in spite of waves of fear, dread, and panic?

I felt as if I had just won an Olympic Gold Medal.

▪ ▪ ▪

I told some of this story to Gail to assure her that she wasn't alone. I also explained that it was easy to understand why so many of the doctors she had seen were unable to diagnose her problem. Until recently, little was known about how to recognize and treat anxiety disorders. People who suffer from them usually appear perfectly normal. And someone who has never personally experienced any of the bizarre and frightening sensations of a panic attack could easily confuse the reported symptoms with some kind of malingering or imaginary syndrome.

The fact that I have experienced panic attacks gives me a credential that I certainly did not strive toward. But, ironically, it has become one of my greatest strengths as a clinician.

As I told Gail, I now work closely with physicians who know a great deal about anxiety disorders. Their specialized skills and knowledge are essential to many of my patients' treatment plans. And while it might take some trial and error to find exactly which treatment or combination of treatments would work best, I was able to assure Gail of my own confidence in her recovery.

2

The Work Begins

BY 1977 I had received my master's degree in psychology from the New School for Social Research in New York City, and I was a graduate as well of the Roosevelt Hospital Phobia Clinic. I had at last gained control of my height phobia.

The therapy that worked for me was at that time called "exposure therapy," or "contextual therapy," which meant facing the fearful sensations *in* real life in the *context* of the actual fear-provoking situation. It has been refined over the last fifteen years, and today it is more widely known as cognitive-behavioral therapy.

I was spending that summer in Washington, D.C., when one day, quite out of the blue, I received a call from a local psychiatrist, Robert L. DuPont, M.D.

Dr. DuPont, who had been director of the National Institute on Drug Abuse, had become interested in the treatment of phobic patients and had visited the Roosevelt Hospital clinic. Therapists there mentioned my experience and the fact that I had an academic background in psychology.

"Would you be interested in working with some of my phobic patients?" Dr. DuPont asked. *Would* I? I couldn't imagine anything I'd *rather* do!

Less than a week later, we met to talk, and he invited me to sit in on his phobia group that very evening. As the group session came to a close, Dr. DuPont handed me a piece of paper with four names on it. "These are your patients," it said. "Call me if you have any questions."

I was shocked. I was also ecstatic. And I was terrified. Did Bob DuPont realize that my experience with patients was limited to one—me? He later assured me that this was probably more experience than most of the psychiatrists and psychologists then treating phobic patients had had. So, bolstered by his confidence in me, I set out the next day to meet my first patient.

Her name was Mildred, a sixty-eight-year-old woman who had been unable to ride an elevator for the past fifty years. She had been to one psychiatrist after another over the past half-century and still she stuck to the stairs.

Yet only three weeks after we started working together I watched her step out of an elevator just down from the top floor. The joy and triumph in her grin were catching. She very nearly glowed with victory. It was then that I knew that helping people with phobias would become my life's work. She had been eighteen years old the last time she'd ridden in an elevator. I thought to myself, "If I can do *that* for Mildred, whom else might I be able to help?"

Hers was the first of a series of dramatic recoveries of patients with whom Dr. DuPont and I worked. A few other pioneers around the country were also becoming aware of the new technique and using it with success.

As personal stories of these seemingly miraculous cures began trickling out, reporters began to call and articles appeared at first in local newspapers, and then in national publications. TV and radio appearances with patients and therapists became common. As the word got around, phobia programs sprang up all over the country. Most gratifying, thousands of people with anxiety disorders learned for the first time that they were not "freaks," that there were others, many others—and, what is more, *there were finally places to get help*.

In 1979 I was invited by the prestigious American Psychiatric Association to present a paper about phobia treatment at their annual meeting in San Francisco. A few months later it was published in the *American Journal of Psychiatry*. It established me in the profession as an expert in this new treatment approach that often had such dramatic results. I was deluged with requests for assistance in setting up programs, in teaching the therapy, and simply for information on phobias. As a result, in 1980, Bob DuPont and I and several other mental health professionals, together with recovering patients, formed the Phobia Society of America. It was a nonprofit organization designed as a clearinghouse for professionals and consumers, and as a source of public information about this disorder about which so little was then known.

THE MISSION EXPANDS

Since the late 1970s, research on the brain and brain chemistry has revolutionized our understanding of human emotions and behavior. As this remapping took place, researchers and clinical workers began to understand phobias as part of a larger network of mental-physical disorders, ailments that are both psychological and biological.

Specialized committees of the American Psychiatric Association periodically hammer out new standards for the diagnosis and treatment of psychiatric disorders, which are then published in the *Diagnostic and Statistical Manual* (*DSM*). Today's professionals generally follow the *DSM*'s terminology and treatment guidelines, which define phobias as one of several related anxiety disorders. Reflecting this research, in 1990 the board of directors of the Phobia Society of America agreed to change the name of the organization to the Anxiety Disorders Association of America.

As defined by the *DSM*, the fourth edition of which appeared in early 1994, anxiety disorders comprise five distinct mental disturbances. There is, however, a significant overlap among them, and although each can occur separately, two or more are often found together.

Following are thumbnail sketches of the five: panic disorder, phobias, obsessive-compulsive disorder, post-traumatic stress disorder, and generalized anxiety disorder. As I introduce you to individual patients in the chapters to come, you will learn more about the varying symptoms, causes of, and treatments for each disorder. Every patient is unique, and every patient expands our understanding of the many faces of anxiety.

PANIC DISORDER

The human body evolved so that primitive people could instantaneously switch into "red alert" when physical danger threatened. Called the flight-or-fight response, this response is still part of modern humans' physiological—and psychological—makeup. In response to an image or some other kind of information conveyed by one of the senses, neurotransmitters—chemicals that brain cells use to talk to each other—trigger a series of physiological changes. As the messages cascade from the brain throughout the body, they may have the effect of sharpening the senses, setting the heart racing, and sending blood to certain muscles so that the body is prepared to fight or flee.

But nature is not perfect, and for reasons not yet understood fully by scientists, sometimes the brain receives images that set off what amounts to a false alarm. Although there is controversy as to whether a panic attack is actually a response to this false alarm, in many ways the experience feels as if one's fight-or-flight response is being inappropriately activated. Perhaps the brain misinterprets certain fleeting thoughts or chemical glitches as signs of danger in persons with a genetic vulnerability to panic attacks.

Most often, panic attacks first occur in late adolescence or the early twenties, but they can be found in children and sometimes occur for the first time in the elderly. For unknown reasons, women are twice as likely to suffer from panic disorder. Studies supported by the National Institute of Mental Health have estimated that up to 3 percent of Americans will have panic disorder sometime in their lives, and in any given year, there are at least 2.4 million who suffer from it. Women are more likely to seek treatment. It is speculated that many men who have the disorder hide it behind alcohol and other substance abuse in an attempt to self-medicate. Women often do the same.

Because the symptoms can also mimic those found accompanying various heart abnormalities, thyroid problems, or respiratory problems, panic patients often fear they are dying, about to faint, about to have a heart attack or a stroke, or about to lose mental control. One of the most common descriptions panic patients give is, "I felt like I was going crazy."

Physicians typically find nothing wrong with the heart, lungs, or other organs and tend to write off patients as neurotic or hypochondriacal. The patients are embarrassed and ashamed, and often become depressed in addition to the panic attacks.

But the fear during an attack is real, raw, crushing, and overwhelming. The urge to escape is irresistible. It is not imaginary. It is also not life-threatening.

The *DSM* definition of panic disorder requires that there be four episodes in a four-week period that include four of the following symptoms: sweating, shortness of breath, pounding heart, tightness in the chest, shakiness, feeling of choking, tingling, hot or cold flashes, faintness, trembling, nausea, sensations of unreality, and fear of losing control, dying, or going insane. Or there may be a single episode followed by a crippling *anticipation* of another attack. Even if it never recurs, the fear that it may can be as terrifying as the attack itself.

PHOBIAS

About one third of those suffering from panic disorder develop the potentially disabling condition, *agoraphobia*—the avoidance of public places and situations that are associated with the dreaded panic attacks. (In Greek, *agoraphobia* means literally "fear of the marketplace.")

It is almost impossible to accept the premise that such a powerful alarm can have no rational cause, so inevitably the individual attempts to find some kind of explanation for the danger he or she is being warned against. If a panic attack occurs, say, on a busy highway, the individual will ascribe the onset of panic to the highway driving. So in the future he or she may avoid highway driving and even become panicky at the thought. Or avoiding danger may lie in not going out at all, or at least not without a "safe" person.

A "safe person" is someone with whom the individual feels comfortable, someone who knows the secret, someone who will be there if disaster strikes. The person with the phobia is usually fully aware that there is no inherent danger in what is feared. The security felt in the presence of the safe person is, in effect, part of the "magical thinking" that accompanies the disorder itself.

Phobias are divided into three broad categories: *agoraphobia*; *specific phobia*, an irrational fear focused on a particular situation or object such as animals, closed spaces (claustrophobia), or heights (acrophobia); and *social phobia*.

Social phobia, a kind of malignant shyness, can chain an individual to a life of loneliness. Social phobics may fear any act undertaken in public—drinking a cup of coffee, writing a check, eating lunch. These people have a kind of massively exaggerated stage fright all the time. Some may have difficulty relating to others. They frequently have low self-esteem, and often imagine everyone else believes them to be objects of ridicule. They are generally agonizingly aware that these feelings are irrational. Yet, without treatment, they feel helpless to do anything about them.

Phobias have often been a subject of ridicule. But *funny* is one thing they are not. To be sure, a phobia about mountaintops will not significantly disrupt the existence of someone who spends his or her life in Ohio. But phobias about driving, elevators, insects, heights, eating in public, speaking in public, or relating to other people one-on-one are the destroyers of life's quality.

OBSESSIVE-COMPULSIVE DISORDER

To the outside observer, OCD is probably the most bizarre of the anxiety disorders. It is something like an emotional stutter. Its victims become hung up or stuck on certain thoughts, activities, or preoccupations. One such is cleanliness. They will compulsively wash their hands for literally hours at a time because they are obsessed about contamination by germs. Another behavior is called *checking*: a person will perhaps go back fifty times to check that a light is off or a door is locked before their anxiety is relieved. Some OCD patients must count incessantly—anything: tiles on the ceiling, specks of dust, windows in a building. Others live in terror that they will accidentally kill someone. Some spend hours returning again and again to a spot on the road where they saw a child on a bike, for example. They are compelled to satisfy themselves that they didn't hit the child with their car. Some collect things and will have rooms full of bottle caps or rubber bands or whatever—usually items of no consequence or value. Some develop complicated rituals that must be performed before anything else can be done, even in emergencies.

Many of these patients are painfully aware that their thoughts and actions are not rational and go to almost any lengths to hide their behavior. This is not in their best interests, however, and the earlier treatment is begun, the more likely the disorder can be controlled. Some new drugs are particularly effective with this disorder, especially when used together with cognitive-behavioral therapy.

POST-TRAUMATIC STRESS DISORDER

PTSD has emerged in the last twenty years as a much more common disorder than was previously believed. It came to light forcefully because of its prevalence among American servicemen and -women who had served in Vietnam, but specialists quickly perceived that it was a possible consequence of any emotional trauma, including rape, fires or floods, a car or plane crash, or captivity. Symptoms range from emotional numbness to nightmares and flashbacks. These are sometimes so severe that it is as if the trauma were being relived over and over.

PTSD can cause withdrawal from family or friends and sudden outbursts of temper with little or no provocation. Sometimes loud noises or other sudden events—even a word—can thrust an individual back into reliving the trauma. It can be associated with panic attacks, and it often leads its victims into substance abuse as a way of forgetting.

PTSD can emerge days, weeks, or months after the trauma, even if the victim has previously seemed to be coping well. Sometimes, as may be the case with childhood sexual abuse, the symptoms of post-traumatic stress syndrome do not occur until years after the precipitating event.

GENERALIZED ANXIETY DISORDER

Some people are "born worriers." But people with generalized anxiety disorder (GAD) make even these born worriers seem relaxed.

GAD sufferers worry unrealistically: about money, even though they are financially comfortable; about a family member away at school who is perfectly safe; about almost anything. They are consumed by these worries nearly all the time. They go around feeling shaky and, as patients say, "on edge." They are often at least mildly depressed. They may also be trembly, have muscle aches, be restless, be always tired, be short of breath, and suffer from heart palpitations, insomnia, sweating, abdominal upsets, dizziness, trouble with concentrating, and irritability. According to the *DSM*, the presence of at least six of these symptoms with no other apparent cause warrants a diagnosis of GAD.

TREATMENTS FOR EVERYONE

Despite remarkable success in treating these disorders with various psychotherapies and newly developed—or newly applied—drugs, data from the National Institute of Mental Health suggest that only about 23 percent of people with anxiety disorders are getting the treatments that can restore full quality to their lives. Yet the vast majority of those suffering from these common maladies can be made well enough to function effectively and even joyously.

In the next chapters you will meet some of my patients who will bring vividly to life the agonies of these disorders, the struggle to overcome them, their courage and persistence and, at the end, the sweet taste of victory.

3

Lorraine: Agoraphobia

UNDERLYING ANY PHOBIA is the overwhelming urge to flee an object, place, or situation that actually holds no real threat of danger. Although agoraphobia is broadly defined as "the fear of open spaces," the panic attacks associated with agoraphobia can occur anywhere. Even in a sales office . . .

Thirty-year-old Lorraine is a very successful marketing representative for a nationwide luxury-hotel chain. She often meets with clients to deliver presentations. "The amazing thing is that when I'm on the job, even as these waves of terror are rushing through my body and I'm convinced that I'm going to somehow lose control of myself, I manage to function. But I feel *so awful*."

Lorraine comes across immediately as a very likable person with a warm personality. On her first visit, while waiting in the reception area, she chats easily with my receptionist. By the second visit, my receptionist is looking forward to seeing her. Lorraine is one of those people who seem to radiate vitality, enthusiasm, and a lot of self-confidence—personality traits that are obvious assets in the job she holds.

But when the door closes and she begins talking about what has been happening to her, the picture that emerges is quite different:

"It all started about six months ago, shortly after my husband and I moved here from Detroit. We had really been looking forward to the move, even though we would be leaving our families and lots of good friends behind.

"A few weeks after we got here my father got very sick and I traveled back and forth to Detroit almost every weekend to help my mother take care of him. It was very difficult for me to be so far away from my family at a time like this. And I guess all of that emotional and physical strain, combined with setting up a new house, beginning a new job, and not having any friends here finally got to me.

"One morning, after a phone conversation with my father, who was now recovering from his illness, I was walking down the hall toward my manager's office when I suddenly felt as if I was going to be sick—a weird kind of sick. I felt dizzy and nauseous and I seemed to be unable to breathe right. My heart was pounding frightfully. But the worst part was these waves of terror that ripped through my body. I had no idea what was happening to me, but I had this overwhelming urge to run—anyplace, just run!"

But Lorraine didn't run. She *walked* into her manager's office, and, much to her amazement, was perfectly calm and composed as she discussed a highly technical issue with him—*as if nothing had happened.*

"But something *had* happened, and when I got back to my own office I burst into tears and dialed my doctor's number."

"Everything looks fine, Lorraine," her doctor reassuringly told her that evening, as she sat in his office after he checked her blood pressure and heart and asked her lots of questions. He suggested that perhaps she was under a lot of stress and simply needed some rest.

"I wanted to believe him," Lorraine tells me, "but somehow I didn't. And two weeks later, when those awful feelings returned while I was shopping for a new outfit with my husband—and again the following day while I was having lunch with a colleague—I knew something was very wrong. When I spoke to my doctor this time, he suggested that I get a neurological workup and referred me to a neurologist."

With total disbelief that she could even think this way, Lorraine described how while she was waiting for the test results, she found herself almost *hoping* that she had a brain tumor: "Then at least there would be an explanation as to what was wrong with me!"

The neurological tests were negative, but the frightening symptoms continued, more intensely and more frequently, in the weeks that followed.

"So I went to more doctors," Lorraine tells me with mounting frustration in her voice. "For the past few months it seems as if all I do is go from one doctor to the next. What is *happening* to me?"

Recently Lorraine has also begun to have terrible stomach cramps along with the pounding heart, nausea, and dizziness, and she describes how "the waves of terror pop up all over now"—at work, when out with her husband or friends, in department stores.

"I feel sick, and I keep seeing doctors, but they all say I'm not sick. I tell them that sometimes I get so nauseated that all I want to do is throw up, even though I'm not able to. I tell them that at times I can't breathe properly—can't get a full breath—and then I start to get lightheaded, dizzy. Very dizzy—like I'm going to pass out. Sometimes I feel like there's a tight band around my head and chest. I really feel as if I'm going to explode! I *hate* that. These are *not* normal feelings. I know there is something wrong with me. But I've been to my internist, a neurologist, a gastroenterologist, a cardiologist, and some others that I don't even remember. They all say I'm fine and make me feel like a hypochondriac. I don't even tell them everything that is happening to me because I'm too embarrassed. They'd think I was crazy. Maybe I am."

The fact that Lorraine's doctors have given her a clean bill of health, that her symptoms strongly suggest that she is suffering from panic disorder with agoraphobia—a treatable condition—and that she is personally motivated to get better allow me to confidently reassure her that her prognosis for recovery is extremely positive. However, it will be a while before she trusts that for herself.

Lorraine knows that people like her, and she has a basically strong self-image, but her feelings of impending doom strike her as irrational, and her fear of "going crazy" has added a haunting burden to her physical symptoms.

In recent weeks Lorraine has been leaving work early, taking days off, calling in sick. Sometimes when she goes to work she begins to feel a "tightness" all over and then the nausea and lightheadedness begin. She has trouble breathing. Her arms begin trembling. When it gets so bad she can't stand it anymore, she tells her manager she has to go home.

"What happens after you leave?" I ask her. "Do you feel better?"

"Sometimes. But then I begin to think, 'What if I can't go to the office anymore? What will happen if I can't work? What if I'm too sick to go on?' "

Sometimes Lorraine's frustration and anger are directed at herself, and other times her rage is projected onto those closest to her, like her husband. By the time she came to my office for that first visit, their relationship was becoming strained—and Lorraine had begun to feel doomed.

She remembers watching a TV interview with an agoraphobic woman who quit her job and became completely housebound. When she saw that show, more than two years ago, Lorraine thought to herself, "How weird. How could that happen to someone?"

Now, her greatest terror is that it could happen to her. She watches herself closely. She sees all the signs: the avoidance behavior, the excuse-making, the terrifying physical sensations and nightmarish thoughts.

Her world is narrowing. "I'm starting to think it can happen anywhere. Pretty soon, I won't be able to go anywhere at all."

And then what?

She pictures a lonely, frightened woman, huddled in one room of her house, afraid to step outside.

Once her panic was so overwhelming she was rushed to a hospital emergency room. The creeping feelings of disaster, her rapid heartbeat, her breathlessness—all these things convinced her she was having a stroke or a heart attack.

The hospital personnel were not at all sure she wasn't and kept her overnight, testing her for both cardiac and neurological problems.

Almost every agoraphobic will admit to a similar experience. Indeed, fully one third of individuals arriving at emergency rooms with heart attack symptoms are in the throes of a panic attack.

Nevertheless, until recently few emergency-room personnel, even cardiologists, were trained to spot panic attacks.

Lorraine's tests were all negative (although expensive), and the physician told her the next morning that she has "nothing to worry about." That, of course, made her worry even more.

Lorraine describes how she felt she had reached the end of her rope the day her internist sat her down and said, "Lorraine, you've got to get yourself together. There is *nothing* wrong with you. It's psychosomatic. It's all in your head!"

The first thing I can do for Lorraine is to reassure her that her symptoms were real.

"Your condition *is* partly in your head," I explained, "but not the way your doctor meant. There is mounting evidence that anxiety disorders, whatever their symptoms, involve one or another of the chemicals in the brain known as neurotransmitters. These substances act as messengers between certain neurons in the brain, and often in other parts of the body as well. When these systems are disturbed, they can cause different emotional or physical reactions in various parts of your body. It begins in your mind, and is certainly part of the brain all right, but that does not make it any less a biological entity. After all, your mind *is* a part of your body!"

"That certainly makes sense to me," says Lorraine, "but why then did my doctor say my symptoms were psychosomatic?"

"Well," I explain, "with the discovery of neurotransmitters, the meaning of the word 'psychosomatic' has drastically changed, but unfortunately not in the eyes of the casual observer or even in the eyes of some doctors. The term 'psychosomatic' does not mean the disorder is imaginary. It does not mean that it can be controlled by 'getting yourself together.'

"What it does mean," I tell Lorraine, "is that the mind and the body are inextricably linked and that what affects one will have some kind of fallout on the other. And so, even though these disorders are based in a malfunction of the biological processes of the brain, the kind of psychological therapy I will be doing with you, cognitive-behavioral therapy, will help to heal the malfunction."

Lorraine understands what I am saying and wants to believe me, but isn't quite convinced that she can be helped. I certainly empathize with her skepticism, given all she has been through. Like so many other patients I have seen, Lorraine has a nagging sense that "this treatment is my last hope. What if it doesn't work?"

I allayed some of Lorraine's anxiety by telling her that during the past decade a tremendous amount of information has been learned about how to treat anxiety disorders and that if one type of treatment doesn't work there are many options. In her case, we would begin with a cognitive-behavioral approach and if necessary add medication. If the first medication selected didn't work or had unpleasant side affects, the dosage could be adjusted or the medication changed until it was right.

Lorraine was confused by the fact that she could function fine in some situations, such as when she was around clients, and yet feel unable to function in situations that were far less threatening—department stores, friends' homes, restaurants. There didn't seem to be any consistency as to where, why, or even how the symptoms struck. "What am I afraid of?" she said. "It doesn't make sense."

I asked Lorraine to try a little experiment: to close her eyes and put her thumb out in front of her, focusing all of her attention on her thumb. I said, "Let me know when you feel some sensation, any sensation—throbbing, pulsing, tingling, heat—in your thumb".

Within about twenty seconds Lorraine told me that indeed she felt a slight pulsing sensation. I then asked her, "How often during the day are you aware of your thumb pulsing?"

She laughed. "Never. I don't normally think about my thumb!"

"Aha! But now think about what happens when you begin to feel your heart pounding and you focus *all* of your attention on your chest, or when you feel nauseated and you focus *all* of your attention on your stomach. If it is so easy to increase your awareness of sensations that you're not usually even conscious of, like pulsing in your thumb, just by focusing your attention on them, imagine what happens when you focus your attention on potentially *distressing* bodily sensations. What do you think happens then?"

"I guess they can get pretty exaggerated," Lorraine said reflectively. "It seems that when I was focusing on my thumb—even for those few seconds—I wasn't thinking about anything else. So probably, when my awful symptoms start acting up I zoom right in on them!"

"Exactly," I said. "And as you focus more on the symptoms, blocking out things around you, the frightening sensations escalate—often into a full-blown panic attack. If you happen to be in a store or a restaurant when the sensations begin to spiral, it's likely that you will associate that particular store or restaurant with the unpleasant feelings, even though what's happening internally has no real connection to your external environment. It only *seems* that way.

"Think about what would happen if right now a sabertooth tiger came charging into this room. As your body geared up its 'fight-or-flight' mechanism your heart would race, you'd probably break out in a cold sweat, feel dizzy and nauseated, and desperately want to get out. You wouldn't worry about the fact that you were feeling these symptoms, nor would you worry about where you were. You would simply want to escape.

"For some reason, certain people such as you have a 'fight-or-flight' alarm system that goes off for no apparent reason; it acts as if there is a sabertooth tiger in the room when in fact there is no real threat of danger. This reaction causes the same cascade of biological changes in the body that would occur if it *were* preparing to go into battle.

"A major part of the cognitive-behavioral therapy that we will be doing," I continue, "is my teaching you how to form new and more accurate perceptions of these distressing physiological and psychological sensations. Then, when your body's fight-or-flight alarm system goes off for no apparent reason you will recognize it for what it is and not become overwhelmed by the frightening sensations."

If Lorraine were in a group with other people with phobias, all of them would understand what the others meant by "panic attack," even though the situations that trigger those attacks and the specific symptoms might be quite different for the different group members. For some, only one or a few situations might be threatening. Lorraine's dreaded attacks could happen anywhere.

I explained to Lorraine that agoraphobia manifests itself in many ways. Some people with agoraphobia are frightened by the possibility of being "trapped" in a public place, and may stop using public transportation, going to the theater, or visiting shopping malls (which are purposely designed to entrap people!). Others may avoid wide open spaces such as fields, long corridors in buildings, or wide streets. Some people have difficulty being anyplace by *themselves*—including their own homes—but can travel freely with a trusted companion. Still others refuse to leave their homes, remaining behind closed doors for days, weeks, or even years, or venture out only in a fixed route between home and work.

All avoid situations where they fear becoming overwhelmed with anxiety and/or having a panic attack and not being able immediately to get to an environment in which they feel safe or to a person with whom they feel comfortable.

Some people have spontaneous panic attacks that seem to come "out of the blue," are not associated with any particular places or situations, and do not result in any avoidance behavior. These people have panic disorder *without* agoraphobia. Conversely, some people can have agoraphobia without having panic attacks. When questioned carefully, however, these people can generally recall having had at least one panic attack prior to the onset of agoraphobia. The fear of having another attack can lead those who are vulnerable to begin avoiding places and situations that they even *think* might bring on another one.

Whether or not someone's panic attacks lead to avoidance behavior, the *fear* of having a panic attack can become all-consuming, and each new episode reinforces the fear. In fact, fear of another attack often causes as much anxiety as the attack itself. Learning to deal with this *anticipatory anxiety* would be another major focus of Lorraine's treatment.

"Is all this stress-related, the way my first doctor said?" Lorraine asked me. "Will I have to cut back on my work? The pressure is incredible when we're doing a big presentation."

I was able to reassure Lorraine on this score. "Having an anxiety disorder doesn't mean you can't have a high-stress job," I told her. "What you are feeling is not the same as the normal anxiety everybody feels under job pressure.

"Stress might have been a trigger for your first panic attack," I continued, "but it didn't cause it. We all have certain biological vulnerabilities that can come out under stress. Another person might have responded to the same circumstances with migraine headaches or with colitis. You are biologically predisposed to panic attacks."

As I later explained to Lorraine, the strains she was under at the time of her first attack—a new city, a new job, her father's illness—combined to make her feel that her life was out of control. The stresses of separation, loss, and rapid change may be particularly difficult for people prone to panic attacks. But, to repeat, they are only part of the picture.

I did, however, have one suggestion for Lorraine's workday.

During our initial interview I learned that Lorraine was a coffee drinker, starting each morning with two or three cups and continuing throughout the day at the office. I suspected that that might be contributing to her problem: People with panic disorder are often excruciatingly hypersensitive to caffeine.

Caffeine is a drug, and in large doses it can cause symptoms *in anyone* of nervousness, anxiety, pounding heart, and difficulty in breathing. Patients often report that coffee, tea, and cola drinks, all of which contain caffeine, make them feel as though they were experiencing panic attacks. Researchers have demonstrated that individuals with panic disorder have significantly increased anxiety, nervousness, fear, nausea, restlessness, and heart palpitations in response to caffeine.

At the end of our first session I told Lorraine that there was something she could do immediately to help herself: eliminate coffee, tea, colas, even chocolate from her diet.

I outlined a treatment plan: Lorraine and I would meet weekly—sometimes in my office, sometimes "in the field"—for an estimated twelve to fifteen sessions, during which time I would teach her many anxiety-reducing techniques and coping skills. In addition, Lorraine would join my twelve-week therapy group, where she would meet others who share many of her concerns, frustrations, and hopes for recovery.

"Did any of the people who will be in my group have has much trouble as I did in trying to find out what was wrong with them?" Lorraine asked as she was getting up to leave.

"Unfortunately, some even have you beat in the number of doctors they visited before being told the name of their condition," I responded. In fact, until very recently, the average number of health specialists seen by someone with an anxiety disorder before getting a diagnosis was *ten*! Today, however, this situation is changing as more and more health-care professionals become educated about the signs, symptoms, and treatability of anxiety disorders.

4

Jerry: Social Phobia

HIS NAME IS JERRY.

He tells me this with great difficulty while his eyes dart around the room, as if trying to find a comfortable place for his gaze to land. Finally he looks down, steadily regarding his hands as he nervously rubs his palms together. His voice is barely audible. He smiles, and then quickly takes it back.

Outside in the reception area, Jerry's parents wait patiently—wondering, as I later learn, whether this is the last chance for their son.

Jerry has social phobia. At first glance, social phobia comes across as extreme shyness. But unlike ordinary shyness, social phobia is so severe that it interferes with daily functioning, at work, at school, and in almost all interpersonal relationships (except the immediate family). It is a shyness that is so emotionally painful that many who suffer from the disorder shun any kind of social contact.

Like most people with social phobia, Jerry lives with a persistent fear of being scrutinized by others and of humiliating or embarrassing himself in public.

Jerry is now nineteen. When his parents made their appointment with me, they told me that Jerry was always a bit shy, even as a young child. Until he got to high school, though, his shyness didn't stop him from making friends or participating in social activities. He was quieter than the other children, but otherwise seemed to be quite normal and happy.

When he reached his early teens his parents began to notice that he was becoming more and more withdrawn, but they attributed his behavior to "adolescent hormones." He was a serious student, well mannered and eager to please, traits any parents would be thrilled to observe in their teenage son. When Jerry turned down invitations to go to parties or concerts with his friends, using his schoolwork as an excuse, his parents were relieved: They felt lucky not to have to worry about his being exposed to drugs or alcohol or having to drive home late at night.

But they *did* have something to worry about. Left untreated, social phobia, which significantly affects at least 3 percent of the population, can lead to vocational limitations, social impairment, and financial dependency, as well as agoraphobia, alcoholism, and depression. Sufferers may also be haunted by thoughts of suicide, or may actually make suicide attempts. Affecting slightly more females than males, social phobia typically begins between the ages of fifteen and twenty. Jerry's parents recall how adamant he was about not wanting them to make him a party for his sixteenth birthday; in retrospect, all the signs were there.

Jerry's straight-A average earned him a scholarship to an Ivy League college. Although this would be his first time away from home, his parents were sure he would do just fine. Assuming that he would outgrow his shyness in college, they optimistically sent their only child off, never imagining that he might drop out. They were shocked when he called two weeks before the end of the first semester to tell them that he was coming home—for good.

"My parents were devastated", recalls Jerry. "My father is the chief financial officer for an international firm and my mother is the deputy director of a major government agency; they don't understand the words 'I can't.' It was incredibly frustrating trying to explain things to them. I remember once, on the phone, trying to get across how difficult it had become for me to be around my peers. My father, in his most 'empathic' voice, said, 'Oh, I was shy at your age too, but I just *made* myself get out there and meet people.' I don't ever remember feeling more alone and frightened than I did at that moment."

During his brief months in college Jerry didn't make a single friend. At first he could handle attending classes, but soon even that became too difficult and his attendance began to slip. By mid-December he stopped going altogether. He kept up with the reading assignments, but because he missed the class work his grades plummeted.

Finally, Jerry got into a pattern of rarely leaving his room except for meals. Usually he would slip into the cafeteria just before it closed and eat alone at a table by himself.

After he told his parents he didn't want to stay in college, they made arrangements for him to take a leave of absence. Now that he is home, he stays in his room and listens to music all day.

I ask him what he listens to, thinking perhaps he is a music aficionado who loves opera or some other classical music.

"The Top Forty," he says, as his face turns bright red. He struggles to find a comfortable place for himself in the chair.

Surprisingly, he is able to talk about his problem—even seems to welcome the opportunity to do so. He tells me that when he meets someone for the first time, his heart pounds so furiously that he can hear the blood rushing in his ears. He dreads not knowing what to say or, worse, not being able to speak at all.

He describes what it was like for him in college. "The worst thing for me was to be in a class where I had to interact with other students. For some strange reason, being around people much older than me was okay—but being in a classroom with people my age was torture. I have no idea why. Every time I walked into a classroom I would start sweating profusely, my mouth felt like it was full of cotton, and I didn't think I would be able to talk—even if my life depended on it. Then I would start to feel this intense heat rise up through my arms and legs and face and I would turn bright red—as if my entire body was blushing."

For a split second Jerry seems to forget I was in the room with him as he clenches his fists, sits up very straight, and almost shouts, "It was the most awful kind of embarrassment anyone could ever imagine!"

Catching himself he slumps back into his chair and begins playing with a loose thread on the sleeve of his sweater, seemingly deep in distressing thoughts. "When the professor started talking," he mumbles, almost as if talking to himself, "I couldn't focus on a thing she was saying; all I could ever think about was how awful I was feeling and how desperately I wanted to get out of there. It was impossible for me to learn any of the material taught in class."

Jerry understands "normal" embarrassment. "If you spill ketchup on someone's white tablecloth," he says, "that's embarrassing." And he knows the embarrassed feeling anyone gets if he's unintentionally rude to someone else.

"But," he asks, "what do you call an embarrassment so intense that it begins with the word 'Hello'? What kind of embarrassment is it when simply walking into a room with other people makes you feel like your body is on fire?"

Jerry has tried to help himself. He even once forced himself to take a public-speaking class when he was in high school, an incredibly brave thing for someone with a social phobia to do. The experience was agonizing, and although by the end of the class he was able to get through a speech, it made no difference; the next time he just had to introduce himself to someone, he blushed, stammered, and left the room quickly.

About three weeks after he first arrived at college, in response to the bullying of his roommate, Jerry tried to ask a girl out, but the words would not leave his lips. He acknowledged that he was as afraid of hearing "yes" as of being turned down.

Avoidance is always an alternative for someone with a phobia, although the consequences are usually undesirable. The person who is phobic about driving on major highways, for example, has the option of taking the longer side-street route, but then resents and regrets wasting precious time that could be spent with family or at work. Someone with agoraphobia may choose to shop in a small neighborhood store rather than go to a shopping mall, probably spending more money and having fewer choices. And someone with a social phobia may avoid eating lunch with colleagues, missing out on office friendships and goodwill.

Avoidance does "work" in the sense of eliminating the dreaded panic attack or irrational feelings of embarrassment—or at least it seems that way for a while.

But what happens next—when the person who is avoiding highways has a panic attack while driving on a side street? Or the agoraphobic person has a panic attack in the small neighborhood store? Or the person with a social phobia finds himself blushing uncontrollably while eating dinner in a restaurant with a close friend?

In fact, avoidance is a self-reinforcing trap. And every act of avoidance makes that trap easier to fall into the next time—until avoidance becomes an almost automatic response. It is often simply a matter of time before the driving phobic stops driving altogether, the agoraphobic become housebound, and the social phobic completely isolates himself from other people.

Finally at home in his room, with the sound of music to keep him company, Jerry did not have to worry about blushing or stammering. Or saying the wrong thing. Or not being able to talk at all. In his isolation, he felt safe.

But isolation has its own risks. Jerry tells me he has a Swiss army knife on his desk. From time to time he looks at it, wondering whether he should kill himself. He wonders whether anyone would miss him. He is sure no one would. But he has never attempted suicide.

It is not difficult to understand why approximately one third of those suffering from social phobia also suffer from depression.

Most people recognize the mood changes of depression: sadness and irritability, feelings of hopelessness and worthlessness, and loss of interest in activities once enjoyed. In addition, depression often causes distressing physiological symptoms. These include fatigue and loss of energy; unidentified aches and pains; and changes in weight (gain or loss); in appetite (either loss of appetite or overeating); and in sleeping patterns (either insomnia or oversleeping). And there may be cognitive symptoms, as well, such as difficulty in concentrating, remembering things, or making decisions.

People with a social phobia often develop symptoms of depression in response to a nagging inner voice: "You're no good"; "You'll make a fool of yourself"; "Everybody will laugh at you." Or "People will think you're weak."

As I explain this to Jerry he nods his head and says, "Sometimes I feel paralyzed by my sense of vulnerability—as if I wear all of my fears and anxieties right on my shirt pocket for everyone to see—and I become obsessed with the thought that there is nothing I can do to stop people from judging me adversely. I know I'm intelligent, but my feelings of shame and embarrassment make me feel inept and powerless—even when I know I'm smarter than the people I'm with."

Part of my work with Jerry will be to help him control his devastating self-criticism. We will work together to "reframe," or shift, those negative and destructive thoughts to ones that are more reality-based and productive. (Such direct work on thought processes is the "cognitive" portion of cognitive-behavioral therapy.)

To demonstrate how we will do this, I ask him for an example of a situation where his embarrassment stems from his being adversely judged.

"Yesterday, in my dentist's office," he quickly replies. "The receptionist wanted to check my bill, and I couldn't remember when my last appointment had been. The receptionist thought I was pretty stupid or something. I felt like a real jerk."

"What *evidence* do you have that she thought you were stupid?", I ask.

"Well, I sure *felt* stupid."

"Is your feeling stupid the same as someone.else thinking you are stupid?"

"I guess not," he said somewhat sheepishly.

I continue the questioning: "Can you find any rationale for your negative assumption? Did the receptionist say something critical to you? Did she look at you strangely?"

By the time we complete this little exercise Jerry realizes that he has no evidence for his faulty thinking—but that his mind and body are responding *as if* he had all the evidence in the world!

Most of us have some degree of social anxiety, or we have passed through a stage of life when we felt extremely awkward, shy, or embarrassed being around other people. Some teenagers have more problems than others in this developmental phase, but usually these problems begin to pass as a person gets older.

But Jerry is not just going through a phase. His morbid fear of publicly humiliating himself far exceeds concerns about "fitting in" socially or "making a good impression." Anxiety about his thoughts, feelings, and behavior has reached a level where even his self-image is distorted: A nice-looking young man with dark hair, fine-cut features, and an athletic build, he describes himself as ugly, awkward, and pudgy. Though many people would be charmed by his shy approach, soft voice, and frequent blushing, he is merciless in his judgments of himself: "I'm not like other people. Everyone else can find things to say and knows what to do in social situations. I'm awkward and clumsy."

Jerry has been to several psychiatrists, each of whom has prescribed a different medication or combination of medications. He was beginning to feel like a "human guinea pig," he tells me, "because none of these doctors had a clue about what was going on inside of me and I got the feeling they were just using me for their experiments."

There is probably some truth to Jerry's last comment; not that the doctors were "using" him in a negative sense—but the fact is that social phobia has only recently been recognized as a distinct disorder. Although there are several FDA-approved medications on the market that are helpful in treating social phobia, none has been approved specifically for the treatment of this disorder. So although the medications his doctors prescribed have been established as safe, more clinical trials are needed to find out what medications are best for people with social phobia. Until we have more specific information, Jerry and others like him may be subject to some trial and error with regard to medication.

Not surprisingly, when Jerry's mother first called me, she told me that in spite of having taken him to three or four doctors since he came home from college six months ago, it wasn't until she met the psychiatrist he was currently seeing—the one who suggested she bring Jerry to me—that she had even heard the term *social phobia*. None of the other doctors seemed to be able to put a name on his condition. One doctor said that his underlying problem was depression, although the symptoms didn't exactly fit. Another suggested that Jerry might be preschizophrenic. Again, this diagnostic ambiguity is not unusual because social phobia, often referred to as the "neglected disorder," is a relatively recently recognized and diagnosed disorder, even among mental health professionals.

Jerry's current psychiatrist is the principal investigator for a university-based social phobia clinical trial. "Jerry's case is complicated," he tells me over the phone. "While he definitely meets the criteria for social phobia, there is also a good deal of depression. And he does seem significantly withdrawn. I did an extensive psychiatric evaluation with him and did not find any evidence of major mood swings, delusions, hallucinations, or thought disorders, so for now we can rule out schizophrenia and manic-depressive illness. But I do want to keep a careful eye on his depression. I've put him on a combination of medications: Klonopin [an antianxiety drug] and Zoloft [a new type of antidepressant]. Judging from his early response, I'm optimistic that this combination will get some of his symptoms under control."

The psychiatrist goes on to say that he had explained to Jerry that while the medications may help lessen some of the unpleasant physiological and even psychological sensations, the drugs alone will not "cure" his problem. He needs to learn how to change his negative and nonproductive thoughts and behaviors as well as develop basic social functioning skills.

That's why Jerry is sitting in my office.

Toward the end of our session I describe the behavioral part of Jerry's treatment plan to him in detail. First I assure him that he would never be "forced" to do anything he didn't want to do.

"We'll begin the work here, in this office, at a pace at which you feel comfortable. When you're ready, together we'll venture out into real-life social situations; restaurants, lectures, even parties. Once you've developed some good coping skills, we'll talk about having you join one of my social phobia treatment groups."

Typically, phobia treatment groups include people who feel relieved to meet others who share their problem. But for Jerry, and others with social phobia, the very act of participating in a group—any group—is at the heart of their fear, so we'll wait a while before adding this component to his treatment.

In addition to teaching Jerry specific techniques for coping with his uncomfortable thoughts and feelings, I'll do some social skills training with him. This could be as basic as teaching him how to make small talk at a party or how to ask someone out on a date. Because he has avoided social life since the beginning of high school, he has a lot of catching up to do.

Jerry looks a bit nervous when I mention this, but I assure him again that we'll be taking one step at a time. "After all," I remind him, "this is only our first session. I don't *expect* you to even think about doing the things I'm mentioning—yet!"

He forces a smile and tells me that he really does want help, but is afraid of how difficult he thinks it will be. He has had so many bad experiences that he doesn't feel sure of himself.

But he is telling all this to a person he met for the first time less than an hour ago. And he talks calmly, without blushing or shaking. Before the end of the session I will point that out to him. Here, today, with me, he has already started practicing—and he has done well.

5

Doug: A Double Problem

WHEN DOUG MADE his appointment with me, he assured me that "basically I don't have a lot of problems." He just feels a little anxious in group situations when he might be called upon to speak.

In fact, Doug feels much more than "a little" anxious at the possibility of being required to give a talk or a presentation. He is *terrified*—afraid he will panic, lose control, and publicly humiliate himself. Like Jerry, Doug has social phobia. However, unlike Jerry, whose phobia permeates every aspect of his life, Doug's problem manifests itself only in public speaking situations. He has other physical and mental health problems that will complicate his treatment, but these are not immediately apparent.

Doug works in the research division of a large pharmaceutical company. He is thirty-eight years old; married twice and divorced twice. He has a warm smile and seems comfortable with himself.

Except for this fear of having to speak in public. He tells me that he is bored with his current job, but knows that for someone in his position, public speaking is a prerequisite for advancement. He dreads the day when he might be offered the promotion he really wants and deserves, because then he would be forced to stand up and speak at meetings, in conferences, in the boardroom.

"I know I couldn't do it."

Others might consider public speaking a golden opportunity to be in the limelight. Not Doug. Each time he thinks of standing in front of an audience, Doug relives his first panic attack, vividly recalling every detail.

"It happened for the first time about fourteen years ago. I started to give a speech—actually, just a short talk to a local citizens' group—and all of a sudden I broke out in a cold sweat. My heart was pounding. I was trembling, shaking. My throat felt like it was closing up, making it difficult for me to get the words out. It all happened so quickly . . . *I don't know where it came from.*" The terrifying feelings passed as quickly as they appeared, but he felt uneasy throughout the rest of his presentation.

Shaken, he wondered whether it was a one-time event, or whether it would happen again. Six months after his first experience, he had to face another audience, a group of colleagues to whom he would present some of his research data. He worried about it for weeks in advance, but for some reason—and much to his relief and surprise—he didn't have a problem. His confidence grew in the weeks that followed. So, when his boss asked him to deliver a brief report to a group of company executives at a bimonthly board meeting, he actually found himself looking forward to the challenge.

He came to the meeting well prepared, feeling comfortable with the material he planned to present—but he was *not at all* prepared for what happened as he began to speak. Halfway through his opening remarks, for no apparent reason, the terrifying sensations returned; the tremors, the sweats, the pounding heart. His throat tightened and he felt as if he couldn't get the words out.

The words did come out. But with a dry mouth and legs that felt like Jell-O, Doug felt as though he was hanging on for dear life. The more he focused on trying *not* to lose control of himself, the more he felt overwhelmed by a sense of unreality and feelings of impending doom.

Doug was sure that everyone in the room noticed what was happening to him. How could they not see his shaking hands and the beads of sweat that poured down his face? Certainly they could hear the stammering and trembling in his voice. Like his earlier "attack," the frightening feelings subsided after a while and he managed to finish his talk. He even vaguely recalls hearing someone tell him that he did a good job. But he knew, as he sat quietly listening to the next speaker, that he never wanted to put himself in that situation again—even if it meant giving up the chance for promotion.

As we speak, a family profile emerges. Doug's mother is "very nervous" and has trouble riding elevators; she has been taking Valium for years. His brother has repeatedly visited hospital emergency rooms thinking he was having a heart attack. The tests have always been negative. Doug remembers that his maternal aunt, who is deceased, never wanted to drive across a bridge.

It has never occurred to Doug that these problems faced by his family members have any relationship to his own problem, yet more and more research is demonstrating a genetic component in vulnerability to one or another of the anxiety disorders. It is unclear why one family member might be phobic about elevators and another about public speaking; certain environmental factors may interact with inherited susceptibility. It is clear, however, that family histories of anxiety disorders often span several generations.

This is a surprise to Doug, and it helps him to realize that there is a physiological basis for his symptoms.

To find out the probable reason Doug's panic became associated with public speaking, a psychoanalytic therapist might probe into Doug's early childhood experiences. With many people, underlying "causes" buried in childhood experiences can be uncovered. Doug, for instance, could recall being asked as an eight-year-old, to describe a school science project to his uncle, a professor whom he idolized. The uncle was fiercely critical of Doug's delivery and "cut him to the quick," as Doug put it, when his nephew gave the wrong answers to certain questions. Doug remembers running out of the room in tears, feeling totally humiliated.

Doug still fears criticism from those who are in a position to judge him. But uncovering this or some other event in his past, however accurate it may be as a precursor of his current problems, will probably have little impact on eliminating Doug's symptoms.

Insight alone is not effective in treating anxiety disorders. Knowing the origin of a phobia, like knowing that it is irrational, does not make it go away. By the time most people seek help, the phobic reaction has become deeply ingrained. Doug now experiences his distressing physiological sensations even when he is only anticipating a public-speaking situation.

In fact, Doug is so sensitized to the fact that getting up in front of an audience (or even a conference room full of colleagues) may trigger a rush of terror, that his body reacts to even the most mundane public-speaking opportunities as though they were threats to his life. Somehow, something in his brain misperceives his colleagues as ferocious tigers, ready to attack. Exactly what, why, or how this happens is still a matter of intensive research.

Fear of public speaking is not unusual. As a matter of fact, I have seen several national surveys that ask people to rank their greatest fears, and public speaking is always *number one*. Fear of *dying* is usually sixth or seventh!

Even the most seasoned veteran can be affected by a bout of "performance anxiety" or "stage fright." But Doug's fear is *not* the same as normal fear; he could handle that. Doug is afraid of having a panic attack in front of an audience. Panic attacks carry with them an overwhelming sense of doom and foreboding, a feeling that one is about to slip into insanity or is simply about to die. This is bad enough when one is alone. It is unbearable to think of having it happen in public.

And, because Doug and others who share his problem feel as if giving a speech is like being put into a life- or sanity-threatening situation, they cannot "prepare" in the normal way for a public-speaking engagement. Even if they spend hours memorizing and rehearsing a speech, they *still* won't feel protected from that horrible sensation of danger. To the usual and normal tension and nervousness that anyone would feel before delivering an important presentation is added a wild card: the question "Will I have a panic attack, lose control, and humiliate myself?"

As the interview continues, I ask Doug whether he has any medical problems and when he last had a full physical exam. These are routine questions I ask all new patients. Many chronic medical conditions, such as hyperthyroidism, cardiac arrhythmias, hypoglycemia, and temporal-lobe epilepsy can precipitate anxiety and cause symptoms similar to those that someone with panic disorder or a phobia might experience. Therefore, these conditions must be ruled out before making an anxiety-disorder diagnosis.

Doug tells me he has been under a doctor's care for moderate hypertension, which the physician has had difficulty controlling.

When I ask Doug about medications he has been taking, he mentions that early in his treatment for hypertension his doctor put him on Inderal (propranolol hydrochloride), a drug that slows and stabilizes the heartbeat. As an unexpected side effect, it also helped his speaking phobia. "It's the only thing that ever helped me at all," he tells me.

This is not surprising. Propranolol has a broad effect on the nervous system. Many hypertensive actors and musicians who were first put on the medication for blood pressure or cardiac problems suddenly found that their stage fright had disappeared. The drug became a popular underground backstage commodity for several years, and today many physicians prescribe it for performance anxiety.

"If Inderal helped you," I ask Doug, "why did you stop taking it?"

Doug tells me that it did not lower his blood pressure sufficiently, so his doctor prescribed a different medication. Much to Doug's and his physician's frustration, none of the other standard medications for hypertension had much of an effect, either.

I continue our interview, asking him about his eating and exercise habits. Then I ask, "Do you drink much alcohol?"

"Oh," he says casually, "about a bottle or so of wine a day."

"Bingo," I think.

Could Doug's drinking be the basis for his resistance to blood-pressure treatment? It would certainly interfere with his phobia treatment.

People with social phobia often find that alcohol alleviates some of their anxiety. Studies have shown that some 10 to 20 percent of people with social phobia also have a serious drinking problem. And one third of alcoholics have a history of panic disorder or some form of social phobia *before* they start drinking. When alcoholism occurs with an anxiety disorder, the drinking problem must be treated first.

Doug assured me that his drinking was limited to the evening and that he did not use alcohol as a means of self-medicating prior to giving a speech; nevertheless, consuming an entire bottle of wine every night constitutes a serious problem that requires treatment. Whether the excessive drinking or the public-speaking phobia started first for Doug was unclear at this point—I would probe a bit more later on. What was very clear was that his alcohol problem had to be addressed.

With Doug's permission, I phoned his doctor immediately following our session. "Did you know your patient has a pretty serious drinking problem?" I asked him. "What gives you that idea?" the doctor wondered, sounding a bit skeptical. I told him what Doug had said.

The doctor called Doug in for another examination and, taking the alcohol problem into account, settled on a medicine that began to control Doug's hypertension. Still nettled, the physician called and asked me how I had found out about his drinking.

"I asked him," I said.

■ ■ ■

During our next session I discussed with Doug some options for getting his drinking under control. I strongly recommended he begin by attending an Alcoholics Anonymous (AA) meeting.

"And have to speak in front of all those people?" he asked, turning bright red.

This is a real dilemma for people like Doug. It's probably a major reason that so many people with public-speaking or other types of social phobia who use alcohol to self-medicate are unable to get help for their alcoholism, even if they want to. Asking such people to attend an AA meeting is like asking them to face the tiger head on—without any ammunition.

Taking this into account, I offered the following suggestion to Doug: "Since the kind of therapy that will help you deal with your phobia is best done in real-life situations, why don't we use the AA meetings as a place to practice? That way you'll begin to deal with your alcohol problem and simultaneously get a jump start on treating your public-speaking phobia."

Sensing Doug's mounting apprehension, I added, "You don't have to speak at the meeting until you are ready to do so, and you can leave at any time. And I'll be right there with you to help you deal with any uncomfortable feelings that may arise."

Doug was determined to get better, and although he knew he would have many obstacles to face in the weeks ahead, he took his first step before leaving my office: He agreed to contact AA that evening and bring a list of local meetings to our next session.

6

6

Norman: Obsessive-Compulsive Disorder

SITTING IN MY office for the first time, Norman describes what it's like to pack for a trip.

"I tell myself that I'm going to plan carefully this time, so I won't leave anything out and I won't have to check. I lay out everything on the bed. I count the shirts I'm going to pack, and then I count again to make sure they're all there. I take out my underwear, and count. I do the same with my pants, shoes, belts, ties, toiletries. . . . Then I put everything in the suitcase and shut it. Then I think of something I've forgotten to pack. I try to remember whether I put it in—I think I did, but I can't be sure. I take everything out again, pile it on the bed, and count. If it's all there, I put everything back in my suitcase. I count each group of clothes or toiletries as I put them in. I close the suitcase. But a few minutes later I become concerned I've made a mistake. I *must* have left something out. I take everything out again . . ."

"The last time you went on a trip," I asked, "how long did it take you to pack?"

"Five hours."

"How many suitcases were you packing?"

"One."

■ ■ ■

For Norman, every day is fraught with perils.

A gentle-looking man of thirty-six, Norman is a researcher for a government agency. He wears a neatly pressed dark suit; his immaculate white shirt has a starched collar.

Norman is married but has no children, and he and his wife do not plan to have any; the very thought of introducing additional chaos and disorder into his life is beyond his imagination. Ever since he was seventeen, Norman has struggled with *obsessions*, persistent and repetitive disturbing thoughts, images or impulses, and *compulsions*, the need to perform some ritual or routine to help relieve the anxiety caused by the obsessions—although their content and intensity have changed over the years. Although he doesn't recall having any serious problems as a young child, in retrospect one can see that there clearly were some early signs of the disorder.

"How come most parents can't get their kids *into* the bath or shower and we can't get you *out?*" he remembers his parents complaining when he was in third or fourth grade. Never feeling quite satisfied that he was "clean enough," he would wash and rewash every single part of his body, sometimes taking an hour to bathe.

When he played with other children he always felt the need to run home and wash his hands—even if he hadn't had any direct physical contact with the other children. He firmly believed that if someone else's body sweat had gotten on him, he would somehow be contaminated.

"I would feel extremely anxious until I was convinced I had scrubbed all their 'germs' off my body."

Although his need to be perfectly clean interfered somewhat in his day-to-day routines and subjected him to some teasing from his parents and friends, it didn't have a major impact on his school work or on his ability to socialize, until the middle of his senior year of high school. He has no idea what precipitated the change, but *something* happened that year that vastly increased the scope of his irrational behavior. A previously avid reader, Norman suddenly found himself having a great deal of difficulty reading his assignments, sometimes rereading a sentence or paragraph several times to make certain he didn't miss a single word. It could take him hours to complete one page of a book. It's not that he couldn't concentrate or retain the information, he just had this nagging feeling that he had forgotten to read something.

And then the counting started. He recalls missing his stop on a bus one day on his way to a friend's house because he couldn't stop counting the seats—over and over, just counting them until he got it "right," meaning that he was satisfied he hadn't missed one. He made up a fairly plausible excuse to his friend about why he was late, but the next time that friend called him to get together, Norman said he was busy. This became his standard answer to any friend who called.

Relieving himself of his anxiety—by washing, counting and, later on, checking things over and over again—became all-consuming for Norman. Today there are many situations Norman must avoid if his life is to move ahead, even if only at a snail's pace. If he reads the front page of the newspaper, he will not be able to put it down until he is certain he has read every single article three times.

"Why?" I ask, knowing that won't be an easy question for him to answer.

"I'm not sure why I have to reread every article, or why I have to do it three times," he responds, knowing there isn't any logical explanation for his behavior. "But I'm afraid if I don't do it, my anxiety will be so overwhelming I won't be able to tolerate it. While I'm in the throes of my ritualizing, I truly believe that I *must* continue or I'll miss something important—or that I won't remember everything that I read. After I finish and am relieved of my anxiety, I realize how ridiculous my behavior was. But somehow that doesn't carry over to the next time I try to read the paper." For now, Norman has decided it is better to avoid the morning paper altogether, rather than risk being hours late for work.

He also gave up eating hot cereal in the morning because,

whether his wife cooked it or he cooked it for himself, he would waste twenty minutes checking and rechecking the stove afterward to make sure it was turned off.

The number nine recently became an element in his rituals. When he takes off his clothes at night, another ritual begins. He holds up his pants and counts. "One, two, three, four, five, six, seven, eight, nine." At the end of the count, he checks the pockets and counts again: "One, two, three, four, five, six, seven, eight, nine." He puts the pants on a hanger, straightens out the seams, checks the way they hang, checks the shape of the creases. Do they hang right? Will they wrinkle? He holds up the hanger again. "One, two, three, four, five, six, seven, eight, nine."

Finally, for some inexplicable reason, he feels satisfied, and can put the pants and hanger in the closet. But then, just when he is about to close the closet door, it occurs to him he may have forgotten to check the back pockets. He takes the pants out and reaches into the back pockets. There's nothing inside. But now the pants are no longer straight on the hanger. The seams are crooked. He begins to straighten the seams, then realizes he can't do it right. His irrational thoughts compel him to take the pants off the hanger and begin all over again. He repeats the ritual from the beginning, counting to nine at each stage: "One, two, three . . ."

Each morning Norman awakens to the day's barrage of anxieties. Just to get out of the house, go to work, and get through the day, he must overcome daunting obstacles. If he gets caught in the one-to-nine counting ritual when he is dressing, it may take him an hour or more to put on his clothes.

In recent weeks, Norman tells me, he has been setting his alarm earlier and earlier, sometimes getting up at four-thirty in the morning in order to get out of the house by eight-thirty. He does manage to get to work on time.

Up until a few months ago, he was able to keep his compulsions hidden from his coworkers. As a matter of fact, many of his traits—orderliness, meticulousness, attentiveness to detail—would normally be considered positive qualities, especially for someone in a research position. But when he missed an important meeting because he couldn't stop counting the keys on his computer, he knew it would be only a matter of time before his work performance began to suffer.

This is what finally prompted Norman to talk to his minister, the one person outside of his family whom he knew he could trust with his baffling and embarrassing secret. The minister had attended a talk I had given a few weeks earlier on obsessive-compulsive disorder and handed Norman the program with my name on it.

During our initial meeting, Norman brought out a notepad that he propped on one knee. Throughout the session he kept assiduous notes of our conversation. As we began our second session, one week later, he pulled out the notepad and showed me how he had organized his problem; he had created three "categories" for his obsessive rituals and compulsions: (1) checking *inside* the house, (2) checking *outside* the house, and (3) avoiding contamination. He gave me the following examples.

Checking his lunch bag fits in the category of checking *inside* the house.

First he has to place the lunch meat and the lettuce on the bread in a certain way and cut the sandwich at a certain angle. Then he must peel and slice one carrot and one piece of fruit, carefully placing them in separate plastic bags. When everything is ready and laid out on the counter, he examines his lunch to make sure he hasn't forgotten anything. Next he places the wrapped sandwich, carrot, and sliced fruit in a brown paper bag and neatly folds the top of the bag three times. Feeling anxious that he may have left something out, he must check once again. He opens the top of the bag and takes out the contents, placing them on the counter. He stares at them for a bit to make sure he is really seeing that they are all there and then puts everything back in the lunch bag, once again folding the top three times. Then he holds up the bag and shakes it to make sure he can "hear" that everything is in there. Unless his wife or the telephone interrupts him, he can easily repeat this ritual ten or twenty times. After he leaves the kitchen, he often returns later in the evening, takes the bag out of the refrigerator, and begins the checking ritual again.

Another problem *inside* the house is trying to balance his checkbook. The task is painfully prolonged. For Norman, balancing a checkbook is more than adding up outstanding checks and comparing the balance with his bank statement; this is only the beginning. Once he has accomplished that process, he must go through all the canceled checks again and make sure he has not missed any; then he must review all his figures. If he begins this process early in the evening, it may be two or three A.M. before he can finally put his checkbook aside and collapse, exhausted, into bed. Even then, he is not done. His first thought the next morning is likely to be "I missed a check. I made a mistake." And the following evening, as soon as he arrives home from work, he will repeat the procedure.

Norman's *outside*-the-house category includes his fear that he may have run over someone with his car. If he hits a bump in the road, or something that *feels* like a bump, he has to stop his car, get out, and walk around it several times, carefully checking to be sure there isn't a body underneath.

Norman was quite surprised and relieved when I told him that many people with OCD have exactly this symptom. I once worked with a man who, like Norman, knew intellectually that he hadn't hit anybody, but *felt* so strongly that he had that he would call the police and report himself—sometimes two or three times a week.

Norman's third category of fears involves contamination. For Norman, the simple act of shaking hands with a friend or colleague can leave him so riddled with anxiety that he feels incapable of functioning until he is able to wash off the imagined germs.

I told him about another patient of mine who also had a fear of contamination. I had asked her exactly what she felt if she didn't wash her hands after touching someone. She replied, "Imagine how you would feel if you stuck your hand in a pile of cow dung and were told that you couldn't wash it off for a week!"

"That's *exactly* how it feels to me as well," Norman said, "only I've never been quite able to say that to anyone—until now."

Like many others with OCD, Norman found it comforting to know that he was not alone with this problem. In fact, OCD affects approximately four million Americans.

"It's not that I want others to suffer," he said, "but it certainly helps to know that I can't be all that weird if so many other people have the same symptoms."

I told him that the onset of his illness was also quite typical. The symptoms tend to begin during the teen years or early adulthood, with about one third of the people having OCD showing the first signs of the disorder in childhood. As was Norman's experience, once the symptoms of OCD begin, they become increasingly more pervasive over time.

Although considerable progress in understanding, diagnosing, and treating the disorder has been made in recent years, we are still not certain of its cause. At one time researchers speculated that OCD resulted from family attitudes or childhood experiences, including harsh discipline by demanding parents. But recent evidence quite clearly suggests biological factors as the major contributor to the development of OCD.

People with OCD typically feel a compulsion to perform certain rituals. This compulsion is often accompanied by superstitious beliefs that if such rituals aren't carried out, tragedy will strike a loved one. The urge builds and builds, until the only way to relieve the anxiety is to perform the ritual.

The problem, of course, is that the rituals do not help: They provide a sense of temporary relief from the overwhelming anxiety, but it is *only* temporary. Each ritual must be repeated again and again and again, but the feelings of relief dissipate so quickly that the rituals themselves become increasingly demanding. A person with obsessive-compulsive disorder may have moments of tranquillity, when everything seems "taken care of," but these moments are all too fleeting. Almost instantly the need returns—to count, wash, check, hoard or repeat bothersome sayings or prayers to oneself.

Many people with OCD also suffer from coexisting problems such as depression, panic disorder, or an impulse-control disorder. Therefore, it was important for me to rule out any of these or other conditions that might affect Norman's treatment and recovery. Given the pervasiveness and intensity of his OCD symptoms, I was surprised that he didn't exhibit any signs of depression. As a matter of fact, he seemed quite well adjusted in many aspects of his life. He functioned responsibly at work, had a few close friends, although not many, and had a loving relationship with his wife— whom he jokingly says he met *because of* his OCD.

"I was waiting to board an airplane and couldn't break myself away from the Departures screen. I kept checking and rechecking to make sure I didn't miss my flight. Suddenly, this beautiful young lady interrupted my rituals and asked me if I would keep an eye on her luggage while she ran back to the ticket counter to exchange a ticket. Of course, I obliged and it later turned out that she was on the same flight with me. The rest is history!"

I invite Norman to bring his wife to our next session. Cheryl is a pleasant-faced woman, her prematurely graying hair pulled back in a tight bun. She wears pressed slacks and a brightly colored blouse. Her handshake is firm.

Although she knew that Norman had some "strange" habits before she married him seven years ago, Cheryl wasn't prepared for how much his habits would interfere in their daily lives. Nor did she know just how pervasive his problem was or that it would get progressively worse. To reduce the tension and delay caused by his obsessions and compulsions, Cheryl tries to make things easier for Norman. She packs his suitcase for him if he is going on a business trip, reassuring him several times that everything he needs is packed. Or she pays the bills at the end of each month, protecting him from the wasted hours he would spend obsessing over them. Sometimes she stands in front of the garage door after he backs his car out in the morning and demonstrates to him that the door is locked, so he can get to work on time.

Cheryl tells me she hoped that by participating in his rituals she would be able to reassure Norman that he didn't have to do those things or that he would see how nonsensical the behavior was, and be able to stop. But neither approach worked, and after a while she found herself so caught up in his disorder that she felt completely drained.

"Sometimes," she says, "I get so angry and frustrated that I just yell out, 'Stop! Don't do that anymore.' Then I feel guilty because I know he can't help himself."

I explain to Cheryl that both her anger and her guilt are normal reactions to the confusing and disruptive nature of OCD. She loves her husband and wants to help him, but just doesn't know how—yet.

"One of the first steps you can take to help Norman is to learn as much as you can about his illness. And the more you understand OCD, the less victimized you'll feel by it.

"There are a number of ways you can learn about OCD and participate in your husband's recovery; From time to time you can sit in on Norm's therapy sessions so that you become familiar with some of the coping skills he will be using to control his obsessions and compulsions. You can join an OCD family support group, and meet other people who struggle with the same issues that confront you. And you can help Norman practice what he learns in therapy at home."

After feeling helpless with regard to her husband's illness for so long, Cheryl seems to welcome whatever role she could play in his recovery—even if it means doing things that make *her* uncomfortable.

In order to give Cheryl an example of how she could help Norman, I ask her to describe a specific situation in which she participated in his obsessive-compulsive behavior.

"Just last night," she begins, "following a nice evening out with my sister and her husband, Norman and I went to bed quite late. Both of us were exhausted. Five minutes later Norman said he was going to go downstairs to check the door and make sure it was locked. I reminded him that he had already checked it several times after we came home. He asked me if I was sure. I said yes, I was sure—I had seen him put the lock on. We said good night and not even a minute later he asked me again, was I sure he locked the door. Shouldn't he just run down and check? Again I assured him that the door was locked. I was so exhausted I finally said I would go down and check if that would help him get to sleep. He said it would, so I went downstairs and checked the lock. I was barely back in bed when he began questioning me again, was I sure it was locked. I was ready to scream!"

"Okay," I say, "what do you think would happen if you *didn't* answer his questions or try to finish his ritual for him?"

"He'd keep asking me questions and drive me crazy until I *did* answer him or checked the door myself—and even then, he wouldn't be satisfied."

"Exactly. And not only does your responding in that way not stop the behavior, it actually reinforces it. Because he *knows* you're going to answer his questions. He *knows* you'll help him do his rituals. Intellectually, Norman knows that the door is locked and that his thinking is obsessive. But for some reason that researchers don't completely understand yet, people with OCD *feel* as if the action did not take place. It's as if their brain short-circuits and doesn't get the completed message.

"So no matter how many times you try to reassure Norman that a certain action did take place, his personal emotional experience is that it didn't. And to overcome that discrepancy of perception he has to learn to trust his actions—or the actions of those around him—rather than trust his thoughts."

Cheryl quickly understands where I am leading. "From what you're saying, it sounds as if the way I can best help Norman develop confidence that the door is locked or the oven is off—even though his faulty thinking tells him otherwise—is for me *not* to give in to his demands for reassurance."

"Exactly," I say. "You can answer a question *once* or demonstrate to him *one time* that a behavior has taken place, but after that, tell him that you won't answer obsessive questions or participate in rituals. I know that won't be easy for either of you, but it's crucial for Norman's recovery."

"You're right," Cheryl responds. "Nothing can be more difficult than the way things are now."

Norman wants to be able to hang up his trousers like a normal person without repeatedly checking them. He would like to be able to balance his checkbook and read the newspaper again without fearing that these acts will become all-consuming. He would like to be able to go for a drive and not have to stop the car and get out to check every time he goes over a bump.

"Do you think I'll *ever* be able to do these things?" he asks.

"Absolutely," I respond. "As long as you understand—which I believe you do—that the degree of progress you make in treatment will be directly related to how much you're willing to practice what you learn. That means exposing yourself *every day* to the very things that make you uncomfortable. And it means stopping yourself from doing the things that reassure you. This therapy is called 'exposure with response prevention,' and it is the most successful non-drug treatment for obsessive-compulsive disorder. But you have to be willing initially to tolerate the intense anxiety you'll feel when you prevent yourself from performing your rituals."

I then discussed a treatment plan with Norman.

"The most effective way to change a person's negative behavior patterns is to intervene rapidly and consistently. I'm going to recommend that next week we begin a three-week, three-times-a-week intensive cognitive-behavioral program. During this time I will teach you many techniques that will help you to rid yourself of unwanted thoughts, images, and beliefs. They will also alleviate your compulsions."

During the *exposure* part of his treatment, Norman will be asked to spend long periods of time in situations that make him uncomfortable, such as going to a party and shaking hands with everyone he talks to.

In *imagery practice* he will be guided to mentally visualize himself in distressing situations and vividly picture the consequences he fears will occur if he does not engage in his ritualistic behavior. He may, for example, be asked to describe in detail the image of his house burning down as a result of his not checking the stove.

When *ritualistic prevention* is added, Norman will be required to refrain completely from ritualistic behaviors. For example, he will be asked to leave the house without checking the garage door, and to hang up his clothes at night without counting. By facing his fears without giving in to his compulsions, he will gradually become less anxious.

"We may decide to add medication later on," I explain to Norman, "but most of your problems are related to ritualistic behaviors, which involve both actions *and* thoughts. These are very responsive to cognitive-behavioral therapy. Treatment would be more complicated if your condition manifested itself only as obsessive thoughts. Thoughts by themselves are more difficult to change and get under control. There are now several medications that can help with both the obsessive thoughts and the compulsive rituals, but I'd like to save the option of medication until we determine whether it's necessary."

Norman completed the intensive part of treatment and continued to meet with me once a week for about two months, attending a weekly local support group (Cheryl attended a parallel group for spouses), and practicing diligently on a daily basis. Then, one afternoon, Norman walked into my office with a huge smile on his face.

"Cheryl and I are going to Jamaica for a week," he tells me. "And guess what? I packed my suitcase in less than twenty minutes!"

Then he adds, "Cheryl took twenty-five. . . . You know how women are!"

7

Iris: Post-traumatic Stress Disorder

THE VOICE ON the other end of my phone sounded both hopeful and confused.

The caller, who identified herself as Iris, said, "I heard you on a
radio show last week. A woman called in wanting to know if you
thought she would ever be able to overcome her driving phobia.
Although she said her problem was so severe that she was not even
able to drive her car out of her driveway, you were very encouraging. You told her that with appropriate treatment her prognosis for
recovery was excellent.

"I was thrilled to hear this," she went on, "because I too have a
driving phobia. I recently gave up hope of ever being able to get
into a car again. But as I listened to more of the discussion I
realized that my problem is very different than what the woman
who called in to the show was describing. Her fears seem to have
come out of nowhere and don't make any sense. I know where my
fears came from. And they make a lot of sense."

As Iris briefly described her problem to me, it was clear that she
had indeed developed the avoidance behavior that is commonly
identified with a phobia. But I suspected from what she told me
that she was more likely to be suffering from a different anxiety

disorder—Post-traumatic Stress Disorder (PTSD). Avoidance behavior is one of several possible symptoms of PTSD.

I suggested to Iris that she come in for a diagnostic evaluation, and I assured her that even if her problem was different from that of the woman on the radio show, it was also a treatable condition. She too could look forward to the day when she could get back into a car—both as a passenger and as a driver.

Many of the symptoms of PTSD are not easily identifiable, and avoidant behavior is not always reported in the course of a routine physical or psychiatric evaluation. Yet once the avoidant behavior is identified, it is not clinically difficult to differentiate between the avoidance behavior of someone with PTSD and the avoidance behavior of someone with a phobia.

For example, if I asked someone with a driving phobia to describe what she was afraid of—why she avoided driving—she would most likely say something like "I don't know. I just have these horrible feelings—lightheadedness, difficulty breathing, feelings of impending doom—that come over me for no apparent reason every time I even think about driving." Or "My heart beats so fast every time I try to drive that I'm afraid I'll have a heart attack and die." Or "I'm afraid I'll lose control of myself and purposely drive into oncoming traffic." The person would recognize that her feelings are irrational and have nothing to do with any real threat of danger.

But when I asked Iris—a stylishly dressed, single forty-five-year-old college professor who came to my office two days after our phone conversation—to describe why she stopped driving or even riding in a car, her response was quite different. It was chilling.

"I'll be riding in a car—just sitting in the passenger's seat, since I stopped driving after the first episode. As the car goes through an intersection, suddenly, without warning, my mind will be overtaken by these vivid, nightmarish images: Out of the cross-street comes a huge truck, heading right towards my car door—and it won't stop! I'll see it careening wildly, out of control.

"Without thinking I curl up in self-defense, I clutch my hands to my ears to block out the sounds. But they won't stop. I close my eyes and start screaming at the top of my lungs. But no matter how tightly my eyes are closed, my fist is clenched or my ears are covered, I won't be able to blot out the sight of the oncoming truck, the screams of the passengers, the shock of impact. . . ."

Post-traumatic stress disorder was identified as a distinct psychiatric disorder in the early 1980s. It gave a name to Vietnam veterans' reports of horribly vivid, nightmarish flashbacks of combat experiences. In earlier wars, the disorder was known by other names. Civil War doctors called it "soldiers' heart." Following World War I, World War II, and the Korean War, soldiers reported similar distress, then called "shell shock" or "battle fatigue."

But PTSD, which affects between 2 and 9 percent of the population, is not restricted to war veterans. It can follow any unusually distressing event such as rape, a fire, a flood, sexual abuse, captivity, or a plane or car crash—which is what triggered the onset of Iris's illness.

"My friend Carrie and I were returning home from a party," she began. "Carrie was driving. I remember seeing a green light turn yellow just as we came to an intersection. Carrie sped up to beat the light—a sensation I can still feel in my bones. Out of the corner of my eye I saw the massive bumper and grill of a tractor-trailer truck. The truck was heading, at full speed, straight towards my door.

"The last thing I remember was hearing loud roaring sounds, the screech of brakes, the blast of the horn, Carrie's scream and the crunch of steel. Then everything went black."

Iris suffered massive injuries. She was in a coma for nine days, and it was three months before she was finally released from the hospital. Her friend Carrie, the driver, was dead.

The accident happened in 1987. After a year, Iris had almost completely recovered physically, but she had frequent nightmares and was nervous whenever she rode in a car. Then, gradually, although she still had some difficulty falling asleep at night, the nightmares eased, and the memory of the accident began to fade from her waking consciousness. Then, in January 1991, Iris was involved in another accident. It was a small one, a rear-ender. She had stopped at a traffic light and the driver of the car behind her didn't brake in time. Alone in the car, she was shaken but uninjured.

However, this second accident triggered something. A few days later, she was riding with her friend, Alan. They were driving at low speed through a wide intersection, when Iris's "mind's eye" suddenly glimpsed a huge truck. It came from nowhere, bearing down toward her side of the car at enormous speed. Just before the moment of impact, she felt her heart slamming against her ribs. She screamed, clutched her hands to her head, and crouched in a fetal position.

Alan pulled over to the side of the road, stopped the car, and stared at her. Iris was sobbing.

There had been no truck. There wasn't an accident. No one was in any danger.

Iris had experienced a "flashback"—a mental reliving of a traumatic event as if it were actually occurring. Sometimes, as in Iris's case, a flashback can be so severe that the individual unconsciously begins acting as he or she did at the time of the trauma.

Terrified to think about what would have happened if she had been driving when the flashback occurred, Iris refused to get behind the wheel of a car after that incident. Then the living nightmare repeated itself just a few weeks later as her sister was driving her to a grocery store, and it continued to occur in subsequent outings with family members and friends. Iris felt that it had become too painful and no longer safe for her to ride in a car at all, even as a passenger. Those who witnessed her alarming outbursts could only agree.

People suffering from PTSD may have a wide variety of symptoms, and the specific symptoms and their intensity may vary quite considerably. But a diagnosis of PTSD is rarely made unless an individual has at least one symptom from each of three distinct categories: (1) nightmares, persistent, unwanted memories or thoughts of the event, or flashbacks; (2) avoidance behavior (specifically, avoidance of activities, circumstances, or thoughts that might revive memories of the traumatic experience); and (3) hyperarousal responses, including sudden, unprovoked anger, marked anxiety symptoms (such as sweating or racing heart), jumpiness, an extreme sense of being "on guard," poor memory or impaired concentration.

It was immediately clear to me that Iris experienced symptoms from the first two categories, and as I began asking her about her moods, emotions, and relationships, symptoms from the third category surfaced as well.

"I used to be a fairly calm, even-tempered person. It took a lot to set me off. But now that we're talking about it, I'm beginning to realize that for the past few years I've had a constant feeling of being on edge—startling easily and sometimes snapping at people for no apparent reason. I think I may even have lost some friends because of some of my inappropriate outbursts of anger."

Iris suddenly became very quiet. Her eyes welled up with tears. "What makes me so sad is that I've alienated myself from some of the very people who gave me the courage and support to go on when I was lying in my hospital bed, refusing to go to physical therapy because I didn't think that I could endure one more ounce of pain."

Iris went on to describe her personality prior to the accident. "I was considered a very warm and caring person—sometimes, my friends teased, to a fault." But in the past few years she had had difficulty feeling and displaying her emotions (other than her unexpected outbursts of anger), particularly to those closest to her.

"Last year Linda, one of my dearest and closest friends, lost her job and turned to me for emotional support. She wasn't asking for much, just an ear to listen and a shoulder to lean on once in a while. I wanted desperately to be there for her, but I couldn't. I stopped returning her phone calls and didn't want to spend time with her.

And it wasn't because her problems brought me down. I just didn't seem to care. I felt like such a terrible person."

Iris was somewhat relieved when I explained to her that it is very common for victims of PTSD to experience a sense of emotional numbness. Very often, people exposed to a traumatic event feel detached and estranged from those with whom they previously had close, intimate relationships. This kind of "emotional anesthesia" is a way of avoiding some of the psychic pain.

Although PTSD symptoms typically appear within a few weeks of the trauma, sometimes there can be a long gap between the triggering event and the onset of the disorder. Months—or even years—may go by after the initial shock has worn off and life appears to have returned to normal. Sometimes a patient seeking treatment for what appears to be an anxiety problem or depression has completely blocked the incident from his or her memory. Or he or she fails to tell the therapist about it in the belief that it is not important. This can make the diagnosis of PTSD difficult.

Iris had full recall of the precipitating trauma. But until the flashbacks began, an untrained observer might not have connected her more subtle symptoms with PTSD. Yet, as I continued my diagnostic evaluation, it became clear that Iris actually began experiencing symptoms within a few weeks of the accident.

She remembers, for example, having tremendous difficulty concentrating or falling asleep for several months, even after she left the hospital. She also refused to talk about the experience.

"When people around me, including my doctors, asked me questions about the accident or about Carrie, I would start sobbing hysterically and tell them I didn't want to talk about it. Not wanting to add to my emotional pain, they would back off. After a while, they didn't bring it up anymore—and I didn't either."

No one can say for sure whether an early intervention would have warded off any or all of the psychological problems Iris faced as a result of the crash. However, we do know that people involved in a traumatic event are less likely to develop PTSD if they are treated immediately following the trauma. Treatment should include psychological interventions, in which the victim is given the opportunity to debrief and ventilate feelings and emotions. It should also include, when appropriate, medication to help with distressing symptoms such as insomnia and severe anxiety. Newly emerging data show that severe trauma can cause changes in the brain and that those not treated at once are most likely to develop a chronic condition that's difficult to reverse. In the long run, Iris might have had fewer subsequent problems if the people around her *had* encouraged her more to talk about the accident or about the loss of her friend—even if it was upsetting for her to do so.

For a long time experts were puzzled as to why some victims of trauma develop PTSD and others do not. And they didn't understand why about 50 percent of those who do develop the disorder recover—often on their own—within a few months of the onset of their symptoms, while others suffer for much longer periods of time. However, it has now been demonstrated through research that the more severe the trauma, the more likely one is to develop PTSD. And, someone exposed to a prior trauma (but not necessarily the same trauma, as in Iris's case) will be more sensitive to traumatic events later in life and, therefore, more vulnerable to developing the disorder. But, as I assured Iris, the good news is that there are now a number of effective treatments for those whose symptoms persist.

A portion of Iris's therapy would include the primary therapeutic intervention I use with my phobic patients: accompanying them as they gradually confront the feared situation while applying anxiety-reducing techniques. But in this case we would be taking even smaller and slower steps, so as not to retraumatize her.

Like other PTSD victims, Iris would need help in restoring her sense of control, so she could begin to feel safe again in the distressing environment. We planned to do cognitive-behavioral work together to teach her specific techniques for changing the way she thought and acted about her problem. We would also spend some time doing traditional talk therapy. This might possi bly help Iris to "process" the traumatic experience and better understand—and therefore more effectively deal with—her confusing and upsetting feelings and emotions. In addition, Iris needed help to reduce her inappropriate bursts of anger, jumpiness, and flashbacks. I told her that I would teach her some relaxation exercises for this purpose, but also suggested that she meet with the psychiatrist on my staff for a medication consultation. Medication can help lessen the intrusive and avoidant symptoms. This, in turn, may make therapy easier, because it becomes possible to talk about the recurrent thoughts and emotions without such intense distress.

Toward the end of our first session I handed Iris a booklet on PTSD published by the Anxiety Disorders Association of America. After quickly glancing through the list of symptoms and related problems she looked up and said, "Except for the fact that I never sought comfort in drugs or alcohol, it looks as if I'm a pretty typical case. It feels good just to put a name to what I've been going through. But I have a question for you:

"When you were on the radio talking to the woman with the driving phobia, you said that you're not frightened to drive with people who have panic attacks, you said you know that, no matter how scared they are, they won't lose control or do anything dangerous. But when I'm having a flashback I *do* lose control and my behavior *can be* dangerous. Are you really willing to get into a car with me?"

Iris was right: I have no fear about getting into a car, as a driver or as a passenger, with someone who has a driving phobia. As a matter of fact, when I'm training therapists to work with phobic patients, I tell them that unless and until they feel comfortable riding with a driving phobic, they're not ready to do exposure therapy. People who have panic attacks think they will lose control and do dangerous things, but they do neither. For a therapist to be able to assure a patient of this, he or she has to believe it himself or herself.

A flashback, however, is different from a panic attack. "Yes," I told Iris. "I am willing to get into a car with you. But while some of the work we will do is similar to what I do with my phobic patients, there is a fundamental difference in how we will confront the feared situation.

"When I'm working with a patient who is phobic, I am constantly encouraging the person to move into the 'discomfort' zone and to let go of trying to control his or her feelings. When I work with you, I will be helping you to find a way to *restore the sense of control* that you had before your accident. So by the time I ask you to get behind the wheel again, or even to sit in the passenger's seat, you will have regained your confidence."

Iris set up an appointment with me for the following week. She was on her way out of my office when she turned back, smiled, and said, "I didn't tell you that I let my driver's license lapse. I couldn't get myself to even think about renewing it—until today."

I knew our work had begun.

PART
TWO

Portraits of Recovery

8

A Therapy Revolution

WHEN I FIRST started working with people who, like me, suffered from an anxiety disorder, new patients came into my office weighted down with medical records. I soon discovered that this was par for the course. Even today, patients often wander from doctor to doctor, specialist to specialist to try to find answers to "this weird thing I have."

In fact, it has been estimated that before patients are diagnosed with an anxiety disorder, they will have seen an average of ten doctors. My patients had usually seen family practitioners, cardiologists, neurologists and/or gastroenterologists. Some had also entered traditional forms of psychoanalysis or psychotherapy. Occasionally they had been in analysis for years. These patients often achieved considerable insight into their lives—but their anxiety disorders were still disabling them.

It is widely accepted today that anxiety disorders are complex manifestations of brain chemistry, yet they often respond to what seems like the simplest, most common-sense therapies. Still, no two patients are the same, and whereas one patient may respond to a certain approach, something quite different may be called upon for another.

When I began working with Bob DuPont, what we called contextual therapy—the kind of therapy that had helped me so much—had not been scientifically tested and was, to most of the mental health community, rather suspicious. DuPont was a well established and highly respected psychiatrist, but the idea of a psychiatrist actually going out with patients to help them face their fears was barely short of scandalous. How dare we treat their anxiety without going back and looking at their early histories, determining what childhood traumas caused their problems, how they were toilet-trained, whether their mothers loved them?

But the fact was, our treatment worked. Little by little the word began to spread. Several months after I began working with him, one of DuPont's colleagues at a big teaching hospital in the area invited us to come and talk to the psychiatric residents there about our new techniques.

We might as well have been invited into a lion's den.

We arrived to face a roomful of psychiatrists-in-training who had recently completed medical school. We described one of our first success stories—the case of Grace whose agoraphobia had kept her housebound for thirty years. (I tell her story in Chapter 9.) I described how I went to her home and helped her take her first steps outside. Bob confirmed that within five months she was able to go out and shop and make new friends, things she'd previously been too frightened to do. Then we opened the meeting to questions. I thought we were going to be drawn and quartered on the spot.

The young doctors were especially outraged by DuPont, who was supposed to be one of their own. "What do you mean you could do this in five months, without probing her mental history, without resolving the childhood conflicts that obviously underlay her symptoms?" They dismissed our successes, charging that our treatment merely suppressed symptoms, and that the underlying problems would soon manifest themselves in other, possibly more dangerous, forms.

Bob DuPont stayed remarkably cool. "When I went to medical school," he said, "I took an oath, the Hippocratic oath, to do

74

everything in my power to make patients better. When I see a patient getting better because we are going out with him or her, and because we're doing things that are not conventional, then I believe it is my duty to pursue that kind of treatment with that patient." Pointing our that Grace was out working and shopping and functioning, he said, "Obviously we did treat the problem."

The young doctors remained so hostile that I found them almost threatening. The next day we got a phone call, followed by a letter, from the chairman of the department apologizing to Bob and me for our rough reception.

About a year later, the same chairman invited us to return—but with a difference. The first time we had been asked to report on our therapy. This time, the invitation stated, the residents had heard so many good things about our work that they wanted us to come back and *teach them how to do it*!

What we then called *contextual therapy*—desensitizing patients *in the context* of their fears—had been pioneered by two psychoanalysts, Manuel Zane on the East Coast and Arthur Hardy on the West Coast. They were traditional Freudian analysts, but each found himself with patients who were unable to leave their homes to come for therapy. So these two analysts flouted dogma and began to make housecalls. Although Zane later said that his initial goal was simply to make the patients brave enough to come to see him in his office, he found that if he could gentle them into leaving their houses, they would make great progress in other aspects of their psychiatric problems as well. Help was not always a matter of understanding where the psychological issues came from. Help was sometimes just walking to the mailbox on the corner.

Contextual therapy is not, however, simply a matter of exposing people to their fears and showing them how unfounded they are. It is not like the everyday wisdom that if you fall off a horse you must get back on again immediately or you'll never be able to again. People with phobias have to contend not only with the fear-causing situation, but also with the negative thoughts and misinterpretations of bodily sensations that have become associated with it. By the time they come for treatment, they have built powerful habits, both thoughts and behavior patterns, that function almost automatically to keep the phobia in place. Some patients could go back into the fear-causing situation over and over again without getting better, but simply reinforcing their negative learning. That's what we had to get at.

During the 1970s, Aaron Beck, M.D., a psychiatrist at the University of Pennsylvania, became famous for his pioneer work in treating depression by examining the thought patterns associated with negative mood. Later, he and his colleagues applied comparable techniques to the treatment of anxiety disorders. Beck's approach, named "cognitive therapy," gave new precision to therapists' attempts to break the imprisoning cycle of panic.

Basic to cognitive therapy is the observation that many feelings that appear to arise spontaneously actually originate with a thought. For example, "I'm trapped, I can't get out of here!" is a thought, one that can trigger powerful feelings and actions. In some cases, the feeling or reaction may arise so quickly that we are unaware of the thought. But if we can change or stop the thought, we can change the feeling or stop the reaction. Increasing conscious awareness and control of such thought processes are a central goal of cognitive therapy.

In other cases, the thought is fully conscious—but mistaken. If our heart races during exercise, for example, we can say to ourselves either, "I'm really getting a good workout," or "I'm having a heart attack." If it starts to race "out of the blue," as many people experience during a panic attack, we are even more likely to think "I'm having a heart attack." Teaching new ways of interpreting experiences (called *reframing*) is also basic to cognitive therapy.

Behavior therapy, as its name implies, focuses on identifying and changing negative behavior patterns. It draws on much modern research into how a behavior is first learned, how habits are formed, what causes a behavior to continue, and what interrupts or stops it. Behavior therapists have developed many techniques to directly modify a person's behavior. They also stress the importance of practice in learning or relearning. Many of the therapeutic techniques we teach patients—from progressive relaxation and breathing retraining to Manuel Zane's "Six Points"—are based on behavioral-learning techniques.

Fifteen years ago a student of Manuel Zane's approach took me by the hand and helped me conquer my height phobia. His system of helping me "prove" to my brain that I really didn't want to jump out of a window, combined both cognitive and behavioral techniques. My personal success with this kind of treatment, the subsequent successes of my patients, and the scientific evidence of its effectiveness have led me to become a devoted and passionate disciple of cognitive-behavioral therapy.

During the 1980s, new research led therapists to focus more on the physical aspects of anxiety disorders. David Barlow, Ph.D., of the State University of New York at Albany, demonstrated the value of teaching patients about the physiology of panic attacks and hyperventilation, retraining their breathing patterns, and correcting misconceptions about the physical symptoms of anxiety. David Clark, Ph.D., of Oxford University, theorized that full-blown panic attacks are actually *caused* by people's misinterpreting normal bodily sensations of anxiety as symptoms of heart attack, going crazy, or dying.

The period in the late 1970s and early 1980s also saw the explosion of knowledge about how the brain works. Not a week went by, it seemed, when one neurobiologist or psychoneurologist or another did not announce the discovery of a new brain messenger, those little proteins in the brain called neurotransmitters that carry messages from one brain cell to another and govern our entire conscious and unconscious beings—from anger to chocolate craving, from sexual attraction to fear of heights.

These discoveries had two major effects on the treatment of anxiety disorders. First, they provided evidence that the disorders had a major biological component. Second, they gave the pharmacologists, the chemists who develop drugs, a vast new field to explore. New medications to either inhibit or potentiate these brain chemicals began to appear on the market.

In the early 1960s, Donald Klein, M.D., of the Columbia College of Physicians and Surgeons, observed that antidepressant medications blocked panic attacks in some patients. But it wasn't until many years later that his work was fully accepted.

Those of us who had been so successful with variations of cognitive-behavioral therapy were highly suspicious of what seemed like the "quick fix" of medicating patients. The advocates of pharmacological therapy were just as skeptical of our approach. At the early meetings of the organization I helped found—first the Phobia Society, later to be known as the Anxiety Disorders Association of America—there were heated and passionate debates between the drug and antidrug forces.

Then, seemingly overnight, the debates became virtual love feasts.

What had happened was the astonishing discovery that not only did both approaches work, but used together they were synergistic—that is, drug therapy plus cognitive-behavioral therapy seemed to work *better* than either approach alone.

Unless a person is in great distress, I still prefer to begin with cognitive-behavioral therapy alone (for reasons I detail in Chapter 11). But I can now tell my patients with great confidence that if we don't see significant improvement in, say, five or six weeks, there are other approaches, and combinations of approaches, we can try. Not all of the disorders respond to all therapies, however, and not all of those who suffer from the same disorder respond the same way to a given therapy. But the good news is that now there are many treatment options available.

As effective as our current treatments are, there are still many barriers to treatment. The first obstacle often lies in the patients themselves. Because anxiety disorders strike their victims as bizarre, patients feel compelled to hide their symptoms from the rest of the world. Their thinking goes: "If it seems irrational to me to go into panic over 'nothing'—over meeting with colleagues, over being in an elevator, over going shopping—or if I have a compulsion to count things, or I'm afraid to drive across a bridge, then think how weird it must be to the rest of the world."

For many, hiding the disorder becomes an all-consuming job, and it is often done so well that not even a family physician spots it.

Education of physicians and of the victims themselves is the key to coming out into the open—quite literally for some patients.

Lack of awareness among primary-care physicians is a second obstacle to treatment, one that is being addressed head on by the National Institute of Mental Health, which is conducting a national educational campaign for health professionals as well as patients.

Frederick K. Goodwin, M.D., director of the NIMH, attributes some of the failure to identify patients with anxiety disorders to a kind of poverty in our language. At a recent conference he put it this way: "Everybody gets panicky. It's like when I was some twenty miles away and had twenty minutes to get down here I panicked. Now that's trivialization, and it's a fault of our language that we use common words like panic and depression and anxiety to indicate normal human feelings, and at the same time we expect that same word to convey a serious mental disorder. We have to correct that. We have to educate the public that panic with a big 'P' is a different issue than the panic that everyone so glibly refers to as part of their normal life."

Thomas Uhde, M.D., of Wayne State University, who ran the anxiety disorders research program at NIMH for many years, believes that a further obstacle to treatment is the tendency of many therapists to cling to a single therapy or a single drug. He points out that the different anxiety disorders are often governed by different neurotransmitter systems, and different drugs and therapies are active in specific systems. Literally scores of neurotransmitters have now been identified, and although there is often overlap among them, each one of these messengers regulates specific physical and mental functions. Even patients with similar symptoms may be suffering from a disorder in different neurotransmitter territories. So, as you will see in the following case studies, approaches must always be tailored to the needs of the patient.

Our greatest successes have occurred in one of the most common of the disorders: panic, with and without phobias; that is the one I will discuss most fully.

Scientists now know that drugs can influence neurotransmitters. They also know that psychological therapies can have the same influence, although they may take longer. The pioneers in cognitive-behavioral therapy have shown that leading their patients by the hand through the situations that induce the most anxious feelings can actually change the chemistry of the brain in powerful, long-lasting, curative ways.

Anxiety disorders are chronic and may recur, especially after some traumatic life event, the death of a spouse or a child, for example. The most successful patients, and the ones who are most likely to recover quickly from any future relapses, are those who work hard during our therapy sessions and later at home, practicing what they are learning. Only in that way can they truly convince themselves that the chemistry in their brains can be modified, and that the disturbing symptoms can abate.

I have driven with my patients, ridden elevators with them, walked them to the corner mailbox, flown in airplanes with them, literally crossed high bridges with them and watched them cross those bridges to freedom from the anxieties and the worries that had crippled their lives.

During a typical course of treatment, I meet individually with an anxiety-disorder patient at least once a week, but more frequently if necessary. (I initially meet three times a week with those suffering from obsessive-compulsive disorder.) In addition, most patients also participate in a twelve-week group therapy program. In both the group and the individual sessions, the patient "practices" confronting the feelings and situations that he or she has been avoiding, while I introduce many of the techniques that are described in Parts Two and Three of this book.

Near the beginning of the program each patient sets goals and uses a diary or log to measure progress. Although the ultimate goal is being able to lead a normal, unrestricted life, patients also learn that this does not mean being anxiety-free forever; that would be unrealistic for even the "calmest" among us!

Patients who complete treatment learn that although the symptoms of their anxiety disorder may present themselves from time to time, they no longer need to be ruled by the symptoms. Even after the treatment program is finished, ongoing practice is critical to keep from falling back into old patterns. So as a therapist, my goal is not only to help the patient practice in various situations, but also to encourage habits of practicing that will continue after therapy has ended.

In the following chapters you will meet seven individuals whose stories illustrate in more detail the major treatment approaches available today. In each case, the techniques of cognitive-behavioral therapy—often combined with medication—led to significant recovery. As you will see, the patients' commitment to hard work and their determination to get better were also essential to their eventual success. The obstacles they faced are also typical.

Along with their thick medical histories, many of my early patients brought with them a small and usually tattered paperback. It was almost always one of several books written by Claire Weekes, M.D., an Australian pioneer in the treatment of phobias and panic disorder. Although some of Weekes's titles—*Hope and Help for Your Nerves, Peace From Nervous Suffering*—used the language of an earlier generation, her advice was amazingly on target, and her tone was warm and encouraging. Those who happened on her books carried them around almost like a security blanket.

About ten years ago, just before she died, Dr. Weekes came to speak at one of our conferences, and she stayed at my house. By that time she had become something of a heroine to anxiety-disorder therapists in the United States and Canada, and her books had been on the bestseller list in England. Sadly, as she told me, she was barely known in her own country, and was still regarded with skepticism by the mainstream medical profession there. I have borrowed her theme of hope and help for my subtitle. I'd like to think that my own work reflects her compassionate philosophy, together with some of the science and clinical experience that have since confirmed its worth.

9

Grace: Facing the Fears

IMAGINE THE EXPRESSION on the face of someone who ventures forth from her house for the first time in ten, twenty, or even thirty years. Her triumph is tinged with regret: how much she has missed in all that time! And the fear of venturing forth is still there; perhaps it always will be. But there can be no mistaking the joy in her expression as she walks along the sidewalk, looking at the trees, grass, and sky, staring at the unfamiliar sight of strangers who pass by. To be present at such a moment is a privilege I can only compare to being present at a birth.

Grace was one of the agoraphobia patients I treated shortly after I moved to Washington, D.C., in 1978 and began working with Bob DuPont. Grace was so housebound that she might never have found help, had it not been for the alertness of a social worker. Our first contact came indirectly, through a telephone call from Peggy McMahon, a staff member at a legal services group for the elderly.

Peggy quickly explained the reason for her call. She had read about the work Bob and I were doing with phobia patients in an article published in *The Washington Post*. The article described a woman with agoraphobia and discussed her experiences before and after treatment.

Peggy was reminded of this article when she received a call from Grace, a sixty-year-old woman who was responding to an ad Peggy had placed in a local newspaper looking for someone to help stuff envelopes. Grace told Peggy that she needed to earn some money and was eager to help, but that she would need someone to bring the envelopes over to her house. She lived about seven blocks from Peggy's office. When Peggy asked Grace why she couldn't come in, she was evasive. She said she just couldn't come. "Do you need a ride? Would it help if someone picked you up and drove you here?" Peggy asked. Grace said no. There was nothing wrong, she said. Her health was fine, and she knew where the office was—but all the same, she couldn't come in. Peggy said she would get back to her in a few days.

As Peggy thought about that conversation, she became more and more curious about Grace. It was almost as if she had some disability that she didn't want to admit. With *The Washington Post* story fresh in her mind Peggy wondered if perhaps the reason Grace couldn't come into the office was that she couldn't leave her house!

Following her hunch, and armed with a copy of the newspaper article, Peggy went to Grace's apartment. No one answered the first ring, or the second.

Finally, Peggy knocked loudly. She heard a distant voice—"I'm coming. I'm coming." But it was a long time before the door opened—and then only a crack.

During that first visit, Peggy never did get into the house. But she did hand the article to Grace, who read it eagerly.

Grace's response to the article left no doubt in Peggy's mind: "*Oh, my god—that's me! That's me!* Do you think the people who helped that lady could help me?"

That was why Peggy had called me. Would I be able to help Grace?

Certainly I would try, I said, and took down Grace's telephone number.

■　■　■

The voice that answered the phone was quavering and questioning. But as we talked, I could sense Grace listening closely, hanging on my every word. Then the fear came through.

"I have to go now," she said suddenly. But she didn't hang up.

She was afraid of having a panic attack while on the telephone—terrified of losing control and embarrassing herself. Yet she hung on, as she later told me, "for dear life."

Yes, she had read the article and talked to Peggy. People in the article described feelings the same as those she had—feelings that no one had ever understood or talked to her about before. This could be her only hope; her fear of losing this chance to get help proved stronger than her fear of talking to me.

But the attraction of wanting to get better was at war with the repulsion, the fear of what she would have to do. Would I make her go out and do things she was afraid to do? Would I force her into situations that terrified her? She made it very difficult for me to see her. When I finally succeeded in making an appointment with her, she called back to say she didn't know if she wanted to meet with me now. She had a headache. She didn't feel good. Maybe she'd call back some other time, she promised.

In those conversations, I would just let her say what she had to say and reassure her that all I wanted to do was come and meet with her. I told her she wouldn't have to do anything she didn't want to. In fact, she didn't have to let me in the apartment. I said I would just come to the door; she could look through the peephole, and if she decided she didn't want me there, I would leave.

I knew that every inch forward was important. *Any* movement would be progress, even if it was just to let me come to her house and stand outside her door.

The morning of our first appointment, Grace again called and tried to cancel—but agreed to "check me out" by letting me stand outside her apartment.

Once she had agreed to that, she became very protective of me: It wasn't a safe neighborhood; she told me exactly where to park and to make sure to lock my door. There was no bell, but she assured me she would be watching for me from the window.

I found her building and parked in front, but there was no sign of Grace. At the front door that led to the entryway, I peered through a window into the lobby. No one was there. I knocked loudly.

After a while, the door opened a crack, and Grace peered out.

She stared so intently that I felt as if she were literally looking *through* me. The eyes were like those of wounded animal or a terrified child that doesn't know whether to trust or not. Her hair was disheveled. She was wearing an out-of-date pants-suit combination that looked as if it had been ordered from a 1950s catalog. But her skin was perfect: pale, untouched by the sun, the translucent complexion of a woman who had not been out of her house for thirty years.

In Grace's piercing blue eyes there was both stark terror and a plea for help.

The terror-struck eyes were those of a woman who *wanted* to trust—but how could she put her life in the hands of this stranger standing outside her door? She was watching me, watching every move I made, wondering whether she should let me in—literally and figuratively.

She did let me in, first into the building and finally into her apartment, where she immediately retreated to a large, worn couch on the far side of the living room. There she curled up, hugging the arm of the couch, cowering. She didn't seem to know where to look. She had no idea how to relate to me.

Then she began talking. Her talk was incessant, unremitting, as she tried to recall every detail of events that preceded her becoming a prisoner of her own home for over thirty years.

It began in 1948, with a trip to the hairdresser.

"I was getting ready to go to a fancy party," Grace recalled, "sitting under the hair dryer in a beauty parlor.

"Suddenly, out of the blue, my heart started pounding. Then

this weird kind of sick feeling came over me—overwhelmed me. I had this bizarre urge to pull the rollers out of my head and scream at the top of my lungs. I didn't know what was happening to me. I felt like my mind and body were betraying me. I wanted to run, but I was too scared, too embarrassed.

"Then I couldn't stand it any more. I ran out from under the hair dryer with curlers in my hair. I slapped down five dollars on the counter and ran home, crying the whole way. I didn't know what was wrong with me. I just sobbed and sobbed and sobbed.

"I never went back to the beauty parlor. I didn't go to the party that night.

"A few days later, I was still bewildered, but feeling better. I was in the grocery store talking to my neighbor, and a feeling started to come over me. 'Oh my god . . .' It felt frighteningly familiar. 'Oh my god, it's happening again. I've got to get out of here.'

"I left my packages and ran home.

"Then it happened at work. It happened with friends. It happened when I was on the street.

"I didn't know how to explain it to anybody, so I didn't. I just started making excuses. I went to my doctor and told him I thought I had a terrible disease. He said no, I was fine. But I didn't believe him. I went to four or five other doctors. They also told me I was fine.

"Then I went to a psychiatrist. He told me it was 'just nerves'— I should stay home and rest." Grace laughed. "I stayed home, all right—for thirty-some years. . . ."

Before Grace became housebound she had been living the life of a 1940s career woman in the nation's capital. "The belle of the ball" she called herself. She had an excellent position as an executive secretary in a government agency. With her friends, Grace was the life of the party. She was the one who could easily be talked into standing up in the middle of a party and belting out a torch song.

But after the panic attacks began, "I was so angry at myself. I just stayed in my house, barely keeping myself on this side of a very thin line between sane and crazy. I feared that if I stepped over that line, I would lose my mind. I knew very little about things happening outside. Decades passed. I vaguely recall President Kennedy getting shot. I knew the Vietnam war was going on, but I didn't pay much attention. I *couldn't* pay attention. I couldn't concentrate because all of my energy was used up focusing on my anxiety and my fears."

During the years she was housebound, Grace had gone through periods when she couldn't talk on the phone. Sometimes she couldn't even go into her kitchen to get food for herself. Sometimes she was afraid to take a bath. What if she was in the shower, had one of her terrifying attacks, and couldn't get out quickly enough? She would be trapped!

After a while, she said, she didn't even keep track of the days, or weeks, or years. She just stopped paying attention to the passage of time. She barely turned on her television. When she did it was to watch TV evangelists, to whom she prayed out loud, "PLEASE, somebody help me!" She sometimes drank, and at one point she considered suicide.

"One time there was a fire in my building. When the alarm went off, all the tenants ran out on the street. But I stayed in. I remember arguing with myself: 'Grace, if you don't go out, you might die!' But the fear of having one of those attacks seemed worse than dying. I felt paralyzed. Fortunately, the fire was put out quickly, and I wasn't hurt. But the realization hit me: 'My god, what has become of me? What has become of my life?' "

For a number of years, Grace had a friend, Trixie, who shared her apartment. They also had room for Trixie's invalid father, and Grace took care of him until the day he died. With someone else in the apartment all the time, and with Trixie to do the shopping and outside errands, a kind of balance was struck. Grace never had to go out as long as Trixie lived with her. And with Trixie contributing to the household budget, Grace could just get by on a small amount of income she received from her father's estate. In caring for Trixie's father Grace felt she was making her own contribution as well.

A year before I met Grace, everything had changed. Trixie had died of cancer in Grace's arms. After that, Grace was alone, and when the income from her father's estate dried up, she was also penniless. At that point she phoned the legal services organization and talked to Peggy McMahon.

Although desperately wanting help, Grace was intent on convincing me that her situation was hopeless. Repeatedly she told me that she couldn't imagine how I could possibly help her. "You *can't* understand," she said. "You can't possibly know what it's like."

"I think I do, Grace," I said.

As I began describing my panic attacks to her, the terror in her face dissipated. She began to listen with a kind of fascination, then began asking questions. The questions poured out almost without pause as she probed to understand what had happened to me, and what was perhaps happening to her. "But you look so normal," she kept repeating. "How can you get out and do things? When that happens to you, what do you do? Tell me again. Did you ever feel like you would just suddenly go crazy?"

"Yes, Grace, I did," I said. "I felt like that feeling would never go away. And after it passed, I would begin thinking, 'What if it happens again and this time I really lose it?' "

"That's it! That's *it*! *When is it going to happen again?*"

I felt an instant bond with Grace. Despite the severity of her case—and hers was by far the most extreme I had ever seen or even heard of—when I looked into her eyes, I saw something that told me I could help her. On the surface her behavior was somewhat bizarre. But clearly she was not psychotic, not out of touch with reality—nor, I believed, had she ever been, although she lived in constant terror of crossing the line. She *wanted* to get better, and that was all I needed to know.

I carefully explained to her how we would work together.

"You're going to *make* me do things," she kept protesting.

"Grace," I said, "I'm not going to force you to do anything. I'm here to help you—not to make you do anything you don't want to do. I'm not going to try to control you or push you. We're going to go very slowly."

"Okay, where do we start?" she asked.

"How about just walking out the door?"

"You know I can't do that."

"Okay," I said, "how about putting one foot outside the door?"

"That's so silly," she laughed. "I can put one foot out."

"Well, let's start that way. Because if you can put one foot out, you can put two out."

She put one foot out. Then she took another step and she was outside the door, both feet together. Quickly, she stepped back. "Okay, I did it."

"Okay," I said. "Let's do it again and stay there. And while you're doing that, I want you to count backward from one hundred by threes as fast as you can."

"Oh, that's so silly," she exulted. "I can do that." She hesitated, then added, "But I don't want to step out."

"Well, let's do this together. I'll step out. Then you come out, both feet, and let's count."

In a little while we both stood outside the door counting aloud: "Ninety-seven, ninety-four, ninety one, eighty-eight, eighty-five . . ."

Looking at each other as we counted, we both burst out laughing. Then a terrified look came over her face.

"Keep going," I said. "Eighty-two, seventy-nine, seventy-six, seventy-three . . ." The fear passed.

We stepped back inside. Grace looked triumphant. "That wasn't so bad!"

"Let's do it again," I said quickly. "And this time, let's take *two* steps." She nodded.

We repeated the exercise a number of times, always counting down by threes from one hundred. Since that seemed to help, we stayed with it. Gradually we made progress away from the door and down the front steps. Fifteen minutes after we started the session we were standing several feet away from the front door of the apartment house.

I said, "My car's right in front of your apartment. Grace, do you think you'd like to walk across, tap my car, and come back to the house?"

"No way," she said quickly. "I'm not going to do that!"

"You don't have to if you don't want to. And if you don't want to do it this session, we can wait until next time. But it's not going to be any easier the next time. And if we can do it now, you'll know you *did* it. No matter how frightening it is, nothing's going to hurt you. I'm here with you now: I wouldn't let anything happen to you."

Grace had trusted me as far as a few steps outside her door. But going out to my car and returning again was another kind of challenge.

"You really *had* these feelings?" she demanded, her penetrating blue eyes looking through me. "You really felt this?"

"Yes," I said. "I know how scary it is. And I know the feelings aren't dangerous—they're frightening, but not dangerous. And, they always pass."

She considered my words. Then, all of a sudden, without warning, she darted down the walkway at breakneck speed, ran across the sidewalk, tapped the car, and came running back.

"I did it! I did it! Okay?"

"Okay." I let her catch her breath. "Now I want you to do it again. I want you to walk out to the car, slowly this time, and count to ten before you come back."

"Oh, no," her face fell. "Jerilyn, don't make me do it—don't make me do it!"

"Grace," I said, "do you want to get better?"

"Yes."

"Okay. I want you to go out there and try to *stay there* until you count to ten."

It was important that she stay there long enough to see that the frightening feelings would pass.

Step by step, she made her way to the car and stood there with her hand on the roof, eyes lowered, counting to herself, her lips moving. Suddenly, she looked up proudly, and then looked around and smiled.

"How did it go?" I asked when she stepped back inside the house.

"That was—that was *okay*," she replied, catching her breath. "Actually, it wasn't as bad as the first time."

"Want to do it again?"

"Sure," she said, then grinned. "But it's really no big deal."

"It is a very big deal, Grace," I said. "You just won your first gold medal."

Peggy McMahon had offered to help Grace "practice" between sessions. So I left Grace with an assignment. "When you see Peggy," I said, "practice the things we did today. Walk from your building to the curb. Let Peggy be there with you at first. Then let her wait in the doorway while you go back and forth on your own, over and over again, until you can comfortably remain at the curb for several minutes. When you feel anxious, know that it's part of your recovery. Take a rubber band with you. Snap it between your fingers and say, 'I've felt this way before, and the feelings passed— and they will pass again.' "

I left the first session totally exhausted—and elated.

The next week wasn't any less challenging. As soon as I came in, Grace said, "I almost canceled this time. I didn't want you to come. But at the same time, I did. I guess it's like taking bad medicine to get better. Darn it, this is tough. But I'm going to do it. . . ."

Several times she referred to our previous conversation, when I had told her that I'd had panic attacks. She asked me many personal questions, and I answered. That seemed to reassure her. She was beginning to trust me.

As had happened the first time, Grace wanted to stay in the house and talk. It was very difficult for me as a therapist—and personally—to say to her that we couldn't talk about the things she wanted to. But I had to. If I was to help Grace, we had to keep moving.

"Grace, I'm here to help you," I told her. "All the things you have to tell me about your life are very important, and they need to be dealt with. But right now, we have something else to do. We need to get you out. We can talk, but while we're doing that, let's go for a walk."

For Grace, talking was a distraction and manipulation. I had to be very clear that my role was to help her get out of the house. Other things could be dealt with at a later time. But nonetheless I was very torn.

We set the corner mailbox as a goal. She didn't think she could possibly go that far. During the week between our first and second meetings, she had worked with Peggy, and she could now stand in front of the house. But the mailbox was half a block away.

"Grace," I said, "I want you to describe what you see."

"Why? What for?"

"Do you see any flowers?"

"Yes, I see flowers."

"What color are they?"

"Oh, this is so silly."

I explained to her that she had a choice. She could focus on the fear inside her, or she could focus on what was in front of her: the flowers, the cars, and the people on the street. She began describing what she saw to me. I saw a smile creeping across her face. "How long will it take me to go to the mailbox?" she asked.

"Let's time it," I said. "I'm going to walk to the mailbox and back, and you time me." I left her, walked to the mailbox, and returned to her side. "How long did that take?"

"About one minute."

"Grace, no matter how bad it feels, can you stand to be uncomfortable for one minute—knowing it will bring you that much closer to your recovery?"

"I guess I can stand it," she said. "But what if I pass out? What if I go crazy?"

"Have you gone crazy or passed out before?"

"No," she said sheepishly. Then she asked, "You've done this with other people?"

"Grace, I've worked with many, many people with all kinds of phobias. And most of them feel just like you—like they're about to lose control of their mind and body. But guess how many actually have?"

"How many?"

"None."

"None?" She stared at me. "*None?*" she repeated in disbelief.

"None—zero. People don't lose control. Even though you may feel you are losing control, it's just a feeling. Did you ever lose control during the thirty years you were in the house?"

"No, but I came so close—"

I told Grace that there was a very big difference between coming close and actually losing control. "It's like having chest pains," I explained. "Those pains could be the sign of indigestion or a heart attack. The symptoms may be similar and the fears may be similar, but indigestion and a heart attack are entirely different. It's the same with what you're feeling. I know you *feel* like you're going to lose control of yourself. That's a terrifying thought. But it is *just a thought* and is not at all related to any psychosis or physical illness. That thought, or the feelings associated with it, is no more dangerous to your mind or any part of your body than indigestion is to your heart."

Grace was staring at me, hanging on to every word. She was scrutinizing me as closely as I had ever been examined. From her point of view, her life literally depended on her evaluation of me. Could she trust what I was saying—or *not*?

"Grace, if a lion were charging you right now, your fear would be an appropriate reaction to what's happening. But instead, you're feeling that fear when there's no danger. I'm here with you. There's nothing threatening you. It's your body's alarm system going off at the wrong time, responding as if you're in danger. What you're really afraid of is the fear itself. You're afraid that this feeling will just overwhelm you, and you'll give in to the fear. But in fact it's *just* fear. You don't trust yourself yet; so what I'm helping you to do is to trust me—trust that I won't let anything happen to you."

Did she believe me? Her eyes were unblinking. I had to make her feel safe with me, even if she still held the belief that something terrible might happen to her.

"I drive in cars with people who have the same feelings you do," I told her. "I have no problem at all being driven by someone who's telling me that she's having a panic attack. Because I know it's just a feeling. She's not going to do anything dangerous."

Grace looked from me to the mailbox. Then, as she had done the previous week, she suddenly took a deep breath, raced to the mailbox, slammed against it, and raced back again. It had taken me nearly one minute to cover that distance. Grace did it in an instant.

Breathless, she looked at me, made a wry face and said, "I know, Jerilyn. 'Go back!' " And she laughed.

As we extended our journeys down the street, we did a number of things to help Grace keep her mind off the fear.

Sometimes when we got ready to walk, she would say, "No, don't leave me—don't go."

"Okay, I'm going to take two steps, then you take two steps. Do you want to hold my hand?"

Sometimes she wanted to hold my hand, and other times she didn't—it made her feel trapped. I would leave that up to her.

I gave her a rubber band to put around one wrist. Whenever she felt uneasy, she would snap the rubber band. The snapping sound and the sensation on her hand kept her mind off her fear.

As she began to focus on what was happening on the street, her eyes widened in amazement. Grace had never seen a WALK/DON'T WALK sign. And she had never seen a jogger. "I can't believe it!" Grace stared as a woman ran past, wearing a T-shirt and running shorts. "Did you see that woman in shorts? That's disgusting!"

"That's a jogger, Grace."

"When did they start dressing like that?"

"Grace, that's the way women dress today when they go running."

She shook her head. "Disgusting!" Then she laughed. "I'm not a prude. But no woman would dare dress like that in my day."

A week later we set a goal of walking around the block. She had practiced with Peggy again during the previous week; they had made numerous trips to the mailbox together. So we started with a trip to the mailbox.

I reminded her about the technique of counting backward. I also got her to pay attention to her breathing. A few sessions later I taught Grace "diaphragmatic breathing" (described in detail in Chapter 19), but for now it was important for her not to hold her breath, and not to breathe in shallow gulps.

"Just allow yourself to breathe normally," I told her. "Imagine that there is a silver ball in your chest that goes go up and down as you breathe. Watch it carefully, letting it move to a gentle rhythm."

This helped her pace her breathing and also gave her something to visualize, to help her take her focus off the fear.

When I noticed her muscles tensing, I suggested a simple relaxation exercise. "Imagine your whole body going limp, like a rag doll. You can't be tense and relaxed at the same time. You have a choice. Choose to be relaxed. Picture Raggedy Ann. How does Raggedy Ann look? Let your shoulders go loose—shake out your muscles, move your head and neck around."

As we started out, we agreed that I would walk a few steps behind her. "Any time you want to know whether I'm here, just turn around and look."

She often did, as we proceeded along the block.

At one point, she stopped and seemed to cower.

"What is it?"

"That man over there," she said. "He's staring at me because he thinks I look weird."

"Well, stare back."

She took my suggestion. Turning to face the man, she gaped at him with an open-eyed stare. Uncomfortable, the man turned and walked away. Grace looked at me in delight.

■ ■ ■

Two special events stand out in my recollection of Grace's therapy, both representing her growing trust in herself and belief in her powers of recovery. The first was her trip to the record store; the second was Christmas lunch. Grace loved music, and she often listened to the same records over and over again. She especially loved old-time blues and jazz. She had a phonograph in her house, and during the years she spent indoors she often put on Fats Waller records and danced.

One week a friend brought Grace an Ann Murray record with the song "You Needed Me." Grace loved the song. She thought it described our relationship, how I felt about her as well as the way she felt about me. She knew how much satisfaction I got from working with her, that in many ways I needed her as much as she needed me.

Several weeks into therapy, when we were out driving, Grace said she wanted to buy the record for me. She would give me the money if I would go into the store.

"Grace," I said, "the real present would be *you* going into the store. I'll give you the money. I don't want you paying for a gift for me. The present will be if *you* can go in the store and get it for me."

As we drove up to the front of the store, Grace said, "You won't drive off now—will you?"

I'm sure her fears would have sounded strange to any other ears. Why would I, her therapist, abandon her?

But I also understood how she felt. People with agoraphobia often have a morbid fear of abandonment. The feeling is akin to that of a three-year-old lagging behind her mother in a supermarket who looks around and suddenly realizes her mother is nowhere to be found. The three-year-old doesn't realize that her mother is certain to come back, that if she just stays in the same place, there's nothing to fear. The child just feels deserted, lost, abandoned—and panic-stricken.

"Grace, I've never tricked you. I would never do that: It would damage everything we've accomplished. Think of all the things we've done together because you've trusted me: I would *never* betray that trust."

She thought a moment, glancing out the window at the store-front.

"Wouldn't you leave, just once, to show me that I can do it on my own?"

"No," I said. "I'm not going to trick you. You're in charge here: You're in control. Actually, you're in control of my being in control of you. You can tell me what to do, and I will not push you further than you want. But I'm in control in that if you ever need me, if you feel like something is going to happen to you, I will take care of you. Do you *want* to go in that store?"

"Yes, I do. I want to get better."

Abruptly, she flung open the door and hopped out. She darted into the store. Within three minutes she was back in the car, face flushed, the record in her hand.

We hugged each other and cried.

As the Christmas season approached, Grace's world was truly beginning to expand. She could go short distances from her house or travel in my car. She could go into several stores. But she still had not gone into a restaurant.

On Christmas morning, I realized that apart from plans to have dinner with friends that evening, I was free for the day. I knew Grace would be alone.

I called her.

"Grace, it's Christmas Day, and I want to invite you out for lunch. Would you like to go to a restaurant?"

She was torn. To have her therapist call and invite her out to lunch was like a teacher calling a student on a weekend and inviting her to a picnic. It was a special invitation, and she didn't want to refuse. On the other hand, she was terrified: She had not been inside a restaurant in more than thirty years.

"Why do you want to go to a restaurant with me? Why do you want to do that? Shouldn't you want to be with your family?" she asked a number of times.

"Grace," I said, "I want to spend Christmas Day with you."

"I can't go to a restaurant. My hair's a mess. And I have nothing to wear."

"Well, we'll pick a place that's very casual."

"I *can't* go in a restaurant," she said finally, when she had exhausted all other excuses.

"Grace, let's remember how we work. I'll come over, and I'll pick you up, and we'll just stand outside the restaurant. We don't have to go in. We can just look at it."

One restaurant in Grace's neighborhood, a simple but colorful luncheonette, was a long-enduring establishment with a few tables and a lunch counter. Grace remembered that restaurant from the 1940s. She mentioned it to me, then quickly added, "But it's too fancy."

"It might have been, thirty or forty years ago, but it's very casual today. Wear whatever you have, and I'll wear jeans."

When I came to pick her up, I was wearing jeans and a T-shirt. She was wearing her fifties-style pedal pushers. We walked several blocks to the restaurant and stood outside the door, looking in.

"I can't go in," said Grace. "I can't." Then she looked at me. "You gave up Christmas Day to be with me. I can't do this to you."

I was willing to make her feel a little bit guilty—but guilt alone wouldn't tempt her to take the next step.

"Grace," I said, "for me it's a wonderful Christmas just being with you and knowing that we've gotten this far. If we do nothing more than stand here and look at the menu, that's okay. And if we go in and sit down, and you decide you want to leave, that's okay, too."

"What if I order the food and it comes, and then I have to leave?"

"We'll ask the waiter to wrap it up. We'll bring it back home with us."

I was helping Grace to establish Outs. Earlier, as we were walking over to the restaurant, I had explained to Grace that an Out is anything that gets you in. (When and how to establish Outs is described in more detail in Chapter 15.) If knowing you can leave in the middle of a meal enables you to go into the restaurant in the first place, it's perfectly okay to give yourself that option. *Knowing* you can leave is *not the same* as leaving. But what it does do is give you "permission," in your own mind, to enter into a situation you may otherwise avoid.

"I'll bet the restaurant's full," Grace continued. "What if there are a lot of people and they all look at me?"

"What if they do?" I asked. She groaned. "If you feel too uncomfortable, we can leave," I went on. "We can sit near the door if you like. Here, let's do some reality testing. Let's just look in and see how many people are there."

We looked in the window. Two men were sitting at a small table, engaged in earnest conversation. Otherwise the restaurant was empty.

Grace turned to me. "Right—just two people. Maybe I could try. What do you think?"

Before I could reply, Grace made her move—in a manner that was now familiar to me. Without warning, she suddenly broke away and rushed inside. The two men looked up, startled, as Grace rushed to the table next to them and pulled up a chair. I joined her a moment later. She buried her face in the menu.

"Look at these prices. I can't believe it!" she exclaimed. "Four ninety-five for a tuna-fish sandwich! That's robbery! I used to pay twenty-five cents."

We gave the waiter our order. When the food arrived, Grace began eating her tuna-fish sandwich. Every once in a while she would become aware of where she was and begin to feel anxious. Again I reminded her that her feelings were normal, and even though they were frightening, they weren't dangerous. Again I asked her to watch her breathing and describe things around her, to help bring her anxiety level down. She managed to finish every bit of her lunch.

When she was done, we were both so exhilarated we could hardly contain ourselves.

Grace went to two more restaurants with Peggy that week. Like everything else she was doing, it got progressively easier.

The seven blocks between the legal services office and Grace's house was a route we practiced during several sessions. One of Grace's goals was to get to Peggy's office by herself to do part-time clerical work. One day, she left an excited message on my answering machine in which she said, "Not only did I get to Peggy's office this morning, but I stayed for two hours—and I'm going back tomorrow!"

Five months after I began working with Grace she was able to get around her neighborhood by herself, shop for her own clothes and groceries, eat in any of several local restaurants, and enjoy an occasional visit to the corner movie theater with Peggy. Her envelope stuffing turned into a more responsible, salaried position, something she was extremely proud of. Although we kept in touch by telephone, our formal therapy ended at this point. Every few weeks we'd get together for a "booster" session, but Grace now had all the tools she needed to keep moving forward. And that she did!

A year after we ended therapy, Grace entered a second-career program for senior citizens at a local university, which gave her the opportunity to get a degree in paralegal studies. She frequently stayed up all night studying for exams. She was a straight-A student.

Grace had told most of the others in her class about her agoraphobia. Now that she was recovering, she felt she had a mission to help other people who were in the position where she had once been. Someday, others in her class would be likely to have clients who were agoraphobic or had panic attacks. Grace asked me to send her some literature to distribute to her classmates that would inform them about agoraphobia and about what might be done to help someone with the disorder.

Shortly before her graduation she called to tell me excitedly that she was valedictorian of her class. And she had a special request: Would I come to speak to the class before they graduate?

I was delighted at the news and the invitation. As Grace relayed the details, I found myself wondering whether she had changed very much physically. Though we continued to keep in touch by phone, we hadn't seen each other for almost two years. It seemed like a long time since I had watched her take those tentative first steps from her apartment.

I arrived at the classroom before her, and as the minutes ticked by, I began to wonder whether something was wrong. Why hadn't she showed up? The head of the program came in and began his introductory remarks.

As he spoke I glanced around the room. Grace still wasn't there. She had not yet arrived when I stood up to begin my talk.

In fact, I hardly recognized the woman who quietly walked through the door in the back of the room a few moments later. She was dressed in a stylish purple suit. Her hair was perfectly coiffed. As she took her seat, she flashed me that impish, delighted smile that I knew so well.

I was totally unprepared for the first sight of her. As soon as I set eyes on that well-dressed, professional-looking woman so in command of herself, an image flashed through my mind of the old Grace, cowering in fear in the corner of her sofa. What I saw now was a complete transformation.

I tried to go on—then stopped. There was an enormous lump in my throat . . . tears in my eyes . . . I regained my composure and finished my speech, but I could not take my eyes off the new Grace.

Two weeks later it was Grace's turn, as valedictorian to take her place at the podium in a large auditorium in front of several hundred people, while an ABC News team pointed cameras at her face.

"Six years ago," she began, "I couldn't have conceived in my wildest dreams that I'd be standing here before you, let alone making a speech. You see, I was housebound for thirty years, a victim of agoraphobia. . . ."

Today, when Grace speaks of the woman who was confined to her house for thirty years, it is often in the third person. She says the former Grace is a stranger. Many of those years that she spent indoors remain a blur to her. What she remembers all too well, however, are the dreaded panic attacks.

One of the things she learned as she began to experience new situations and face new challenges was that *a panic attack is always a panic attack*. It doesn't change significantly, no matter where it happens, who is around, or what's happening at the time. It is always scary, but, as Grace learned, it always passed and never hurt her.

As she made her way out into the world, Grace began to become desensitized to these attacks. She learned that when they came, she didn't need to fight them. The fear of having a panic attack no longer stopped her from doing whatever she wanted to do.

Yes, Grace continued to have attacks from time to time, though they became less and less frequent. But she now knew that as frightening as they felt at the moment, what she dreaded most would not happen to her.

During a phone conversation one afternoon Grace said, "The old Grace is dead—she's gone."

I explained to her that it was important for her not to simply dismiss thirty years of her life. She needed to focus on who she is today, but also to have compassion for the part of her that was in pain for so many years. What had happened to her wasn't her fault and she needed to understand that.

When she did talk about the time and the opportunities she had lost, it was with the appropriate sadness. In 1948, when she closed the door behind her for the last time, she was in the midst of a successful career, with lots of friends, living a wonderful life.

Grace saw the years that followed as a series of missed opportunities. She talked about not being able to go to her father's funeral. She had loved her father dearly, but when he died, she couldn't leave the house to attend the service. She felt guilty—and angry. "What's wrong with me?" she cried again and again.

Had she known what was wrong with her in 1948, had she been diagnosed and treated, she would not have had to endure thirty years of isolation. But in 1948, little was known about the disorder that emotionally crippled her. In the years since then we have learned more about the causes and treatment of agoraphobia than we had learned in the preceding five hundred years.

While writing this chapter I tried calling Grace several times to ask for her help in recalling some of the details of our therapy sessions. Much to my frustration and delight I could never find her at home. When I finally heard her voice on the phone, I teasingly asked her, "Where have you been? I haven't been able to reach you all week." She laughed, ran down a list of activities that made me exhausted just hearing about them and smugly said, "What do you expect me to do, stay home all day?"

10

Richard: Setting Goals and
Using the Six Points

MANY YEARS AFTER he obtained his law degree, Richard wrote
about what it was like to be "the phantom of the law school."

"While other students attended class and became caught up in
law school activities, I went only to those classes in which the
professors were not given to calling upon students for protracted
recitations. If the professor said class attendance was not manda-
tory, I was gone. In other classes where seats were not assigned, I
slipped into a seat in the back of the room, preferably behind
someone tall, eyes always averted, looking down into my books. I
was withdrawn, hanging back from the people I had known as an
undergraduate, for fear of contaminating them with my fear. Mys-
teriously materializing only for exams, I was on my way to becoming the invisible student."

It wasn't that he didn't know the answers or couldn't do the
work. Richard avoided classes and professors because he was terrified of speaking in class. In his own words, he would rather have
faced "a pool of live, hungry sharks" than be called upon to give an
answer.

Richard managed to do well on his exams, and most professors
were willing to overlook the fact that he never appeared in class.

But one requirement was unavoidable: Richard had to appear in moot court, in which students had to prepare and present appellate briefs and arguments. The least visible role was co-counsel, and Richard managed to get that assignment, which meant that he only had to appear for an oral argument once, in the evening, and not in front of the whole class.

The days before that event were filled with terror. His nights were sleepless. The only way Richard could figure out how to make it through the speech was to arm himself with a small deck of note cards, each containing only a brief sentence. Feeling as if the whole world was about to collapse on top of him, he had to stand up in front of the professors who acted as moot court "judges." Before he spoke, Richard opened his collar button and loosened his necktie. When his turn came, he ran quickly through the deck of cards, speaking fast. He answered a few questions from "the bench" and then quickly sat down.

When it was over, one of the professors harshly criticized Richard for loosening his collar—an action that constituted disrespect for the court.

Richard couldn't have cared less. He was done! His part in moot court was over, and he had survived. From that day until he finished law school, Richard never spoke again in front of his professors or in front of a class. It was a record of silence that has probably never been broken.

After graduating, Richard was faced with the necessity of finding a job that would not require him to do any public speaking. The thought of having to appear in court or in arbitration, or even having to speak at a meeting among colleagues, left him paralyzed with fear. Although he received offers from law firms, he turned them all down, feeling it would be impossible for him to function as an attorney. In the end, he took a job as an editor for a legal publishing company in Washington, D.C.

Even though Richard achieved a substantial level of success in his job, he was continuously plagued with thoughts of how much his fear of public speaking held him back professionally and personally. When he finally came to see me ten years after graduating from law school, it was no wonder he was depressed. With his self-esteem at a low ebb, and his law career looking like history, Richard was beginning to wonder how he could survive at all in the world.

Ironically, Richard gave no obvious signs of having a psychological disorder. Indeed, he appeared completely well adjusted. After all, he had a law degree, a good job, and a wife and young children. His problem with public speaking obviously caused him distress, but the uninformed might wonder, how serious could his problem really be? He seemed so normal. And a rapid heartbeat, sweating, trembling, and nervousness before giving a speech are certainly sensations most people can relate to.

One might naively ask, "Why not just take a public-speaking course and 'get over it'?"

"Why not just jump out of an airplane without a parachute?" would be Richard's response.

It was unmistakably clear that Richard was not simply suffering from preperformance jitters. Functional in other respects, Richard had panic attacks *only* when he was called upon to speak in front of a group, and as long as he avoided these situations he could almost guarantee that he would be free from further attacks. And yet, because avoidance was such a critical part of his day-to-day life, the disorder had affected him almost as profoundly as Grace's agoraphobia had affected her. He was like a man with functional arms and legs who has been denied their use for many years. For someone in his position and with his education, to find himself voiceless, speechless, and terrified in front of an audience was a severe handicap.

With each year that passed after law school, Richard felt that his fear was if anything getting worse. Although no public speaking was required in his current job, just meeting with his superiors was difficult. As an editor, he rarely had to come out from under his paperwork, but he always feared that god-awful moment when he might have to introduce himself. Even worse, he might be asked to appear before an editorial board, address a sales meeting, or give a report.

At one point Richard's supervisor asked him to make an instructional tape on a legal topic he had researched for the firm. Richard immediately broke into a cold sweat, but he did not want to tell his boss about his fears. Besides, he was proud of his expertise in this area of the law.

He told himself that he was going to do it. He conscientiously tried practicing by himself, rehearsing out loud.

But when the time actually came, he panicked. Although he did manage to complete the first part of the tape, upon playback he heard a hesitant, quaking voice that left him humiliated. His boss sensitively suggested that it might be best to have someone else complete the project from Richard's script. Richard felt demoralized and defeated.

Before Richard came to see me he had been in a traditional psychotherapy group for a year, but he left in frustration, feeling even more alone than ever. Talking about his family and childhood didn't solve the problem.

He had also tried hypnotherapy. Hypnosis relaxed him, but it had little impact on his ability to feel more comfortable in public situations. Then his hypnotherapist handed Richard a magazine article that focused on the work I was doing to help people overcome phobias. "Maybe this is something you should try," the therapist suggested.

In the very first session I asked Richard to think about some long- and short-term goals. I explained that it was important to establish specific goals early on, allowing them to be redefined as the therapy progresses, so that he would always have concrete steps to take and milestones to work toward. To help him focus on this more clearly, I asked him to begin by thinking about his ultimate goal. I framed my question in deliberately magical terms so that he would not feel as if I was about to throw him into a situation he couldn't handle: "If somebody waved a magic wand and you woke up tomorrow and the fear disappeared, what would you like to see yourself doing?"

Without hesitation Richard replied, "Practice law and do the things that lawyers do, like speak in public." Then he quickly added, "Whoops, I'd better not say that to you. You'll end up wanting me to do something like join Toastmasters." (Toastmasters is an international self-help organization that teaches people how to give effective presentations.)

We both laughed, and I assured him that I wouldn't make him do anything he didn't want to do or wasn't ready to do. Clearly, he did want to be able to give public presentations. Admitting *this* was an important step.

"There's a big difference between not wanting to do something because you really don't want to do it and not wanting to do something because it's too anxiety-provoking," I said. "It's better to set a goal that feels overly ambitious and let *me* worry about how to get you there. For now, we'll just both store your long-term goal in the back of our heads. Okay?"

"Okay," Richard mumbled in a tone that said, "It would probably be easier for you to get me to climb Mount Everest."

Our first challenge was to find a starting point, a short-term goal, and I knew that attacking Richard's problem would need a lot of creativity. Toward the end of our first session, I asked him to read a paragraph aloud to me. He said, "No, I can't do that. I'd be too embarrassed."

"Okay, how about reading one sentence?" I asked.

"One sentence?" He grinned at the silliness of my challenge and said, "Sure, I can do one sentence, but what difference will it make?"

I was certainly accustomed to that response from a patient. I knew I had my starting point. "Well, let's just see. Let's see how it goes."

He opened a magazine that was on the table next to him, read one sentence, and looked up. "Okay, I did it."

"Now read the next sentence."

By the end of the session Richard had read several paragraphs. When he was finished, he looked joyfully bored.

"That was quite an accomplishment," I said.

He shrugged. "You're safe. You're a therapist. It's no big deal. I'm thirty-five years old, and I can read in front of my therapist!"

"But ten minutes ago, you didn't even think you could do that!"

"True."

He was beginning to get my "one-step-at-a-time" approach.

"How would you feel if I brought another person, a stranger, into our sessions?" I asked.

"No way!" We talked about what he feared: that he would begin blushing and shaking. He was sure that his nervousness would be perfectly obvious to anyone who was watching him. "Reading to someone I don't know—that feels as hard as if you asked me to go into a lion's cage," Richard said. "You might say, 'Don't worry, that lion hasn't bitten anyone today!' But that doesn't make any difference. I still feel the same way. I would be mortified if someone saw how embarrassed and scared I was."

Suddenly the proverbial light bulb went on in my head. I wondered what it would be like for Richard to read to someone who *couldn't* see him? Would that be the next step for him? I had an idea about how to make that happen.

But I didn't tell him my idea at that point. Instead, I described in a general way some of the techniques that he might begin to use in anxiety-producing situations. I showed him how to use diaphragmatic breathing to help control his anxiety, and I suggested some ways of interrupting his negative thought patterns. (These techniques are described fully in Chapters 18 and 19.) During the second session I told him I would introduce another basic tool called the "Six Points of Contextual Therapy."

I had first learned the Six Points from New York psychiatrist Dr. Manuel Zane, who was one of the true pioneers in understanding and treating anxiety disorders. A practicing psychoanalyst, Dr. Zane broke away from the traditions of his colleagues, stepping outside the boundaries of his office and into the real worlds of his patients. He treated people with phobias by exposing them to real-life anxiety-producing places and situations and teaching them that by staying, rather than leaving, anxiety levels come down.

Dr. Zane developed the Six Points to give his patients minute-to-minute support in these anxiety-producing situations. The Six Points provide techniques for coping with a panic attack while it is happening. Just as important, they offer a way to defuse anticipatory anxiety, the fear of the panic that can be as crippling as the panic itself.

The Six Points help the person to focus on what is happening at the moment, rather than on imaginary dangers of the future. And they change the entire focus of the experience: from avoiding fear to confronting it.

Like most people with a phobia, Richard had managed to avoid or escape from situations that he feared would bring on a panic attack. As a result, he thought those feelings went away *because* he left the situation: "Thank God I got out of there—just in the nick of time!" But if he stayed in anxiety-producing situations and applied the Six Points, he would see for himself that the anxiety would naturally diminish. And every time that happened, it would reinforce his confidence that the Six Points would work for him. He would be able to say to himself, "Bad as it might be, I've been here before and I survived."

As we began his second session, I handed Richard a card that had the Six Points printed in bold, raised lettering:

POINT #1: Expect, allow, and accept that fear will rise.

POINT #2: When fear comes, stop, wait, and let it be.

POINT #3: Focus on and do manageable things in the present.

POINT #4: Label your level of fear from 0 to 10. Watch it go up and down.

POINT #5: Function with fear. Appreciate your achievement.

POINT #6: Expect, allow, and accept that fear will reappear.

The first point, I explained to Richard, instructs you to *acknowledge* that certain situations will make you feel anxious and fearful. Point #1 suggests that rather than fight these feelings when they arise, you can actually *permit* them to be there. You do not have to be free of fear in order to function successfully!

Point #2 is " '*When the fear comes, stop, wait, and let it be.*' That's exactly what I want you to do," I told Richard. "Now, you believe that escaping the frightening situation is the only way to make the fear and feelings of panic pass, because that's what you've always done. In the past, that 'worked'—if you want to look at it that way. But escaping those situations has also kept you from getting on with your life. And it's kept you from knowing that in fact when you remain in the situation rather than leave, the feelings also pass. They will *always* pass because physiologically, the peak of a panic attack last only a few seconds, even though the anticipatory anxiety can last for minutes, hours, days, or weeks. But you don't trust that yet, because you've never stayed long enough to experience it for yourself. The second point tells you to let the fear happen to you and pass through your system. Just stay with it until it passes."

"Are you kidding? That sounds like *torture!*"

"Well, what do you think is the worst thing that will happen to you if you try it?"

"I'd lose control and make a fool of myself."

"How many people do you think have lost control during a panic attack?"

Richard smiled. He already knew the answer. Zero—none!

"You know that intellectually, but you don't really believe it yet because you never stayed with the feelings long enough to see that indeed they pass. So as soon as they start to come, you assume the worst is going to happen, and you bolt."

"But what if I panic—and can't talk?" he protested.

"Well, what *would* happen? It's very unlikely, but what if you were giving a speech and you found you actually couldn't talk?"

"Everyone would be staring at me."

"So what? What would that mean?"

"I wouldn't know what to do."

"What *would* you do?"

"I guess I might have to sit down."

"So if you sit down, what does that mean?"

"People would laugh at me."

"Why would they laugh?"

"Because I couldn't give the speech."

"Okay, well, if you were in the audience and saw someone who was about to give a speech, and then that person sat down, what would you think?" I asked.

"I'd think he had some problem."

"Right—and what would you think about that person?"

"I wouldn't know what to think. Maybe that he wasn't feeling well."

"You'd be pretty compassionate, wouldn't you?"

"Yes."

"But you're not allowing yourself to be worthy of that same compassion from others," I pointed out. "The more concerned you are with not allowing those feelings to be there, and trying to hide them, the harsher you are to yourself. The more anxious you are, the more you feel you have at stake. You probably fear how much you could lose if you run into a problem. And when you feel that way, you are less likely to take a chance. One of the things we'll work on is understanding that the worst thing that could happen would be that you'd be embarrassed. Could you stand being embarrassed if that were the worst consequence of facing your fear?"

"I wouldn't like it. But I know it wouldn't kill me. It sure would be uncomfortable, though."

"So the worst that will happen is that you'll be uncomfortable. But think how uncomfortable you are *now* when you turn down opportunities. Do you think you can stand it?"

"I'd be willing to try."

"Okay, and if those feelings do come, Point Number Three will help you deal with them. Point Number Three is based on the fact that you always have a choice. You may not have a choice about whether or not you feel the fear, but you do have a choice in how you respond to it. You can think about the fear and focus on it, which will make it even bigger. Or you can focus on something else—refocus your attention away from the fear—by actually doing something very concrete, such as touching something, counting backward from one hundred by threes, or snapping a rubber band on your wrist. Or look up at the wallpaper and count the stripes on it. Count the number of people in the room, or the numbers on your watch.

"This is Point Number Three, focusing on and doing *a manageable task in the present*: finding something to keep your mind in the 'here and now' rather than thinking about the 'what-if's,' the imaginary dangers of the future.

"During a panic attack, you feel that the terror will keep building, getting progressively worse, eventually ending in some disaster. In fact, though, even if you reach a full-blown panic attack, after a few seconds the anxiety will always come down. If you use your senses—touching things, feeling the texture and temperature, smelling something like cologne or a flower—and focus on what's really going on about you, you'll notice that your anxiety *will* come down.

"In fact, in everyday life, your anxiety level is constantly changing. The fourth point helps you see this: *'Label your level of fear from zero to ten. Watch it go up and down.'* When you feel anxiety, I'll ask you to assign it a number from zero to ten—zero being no phobic fear or anxiety, and ten the ultimate, the panic attack.

"What you probably have thought up to now is that your increasing anxiety levels 'just happen'—that you have no control over them." I reminded Richard of his feelings about an upcoming meeting that his boss requested he attend to briefly discuss a project he is working on. "Thinking about being in the room with your coworkers and being called upon to speak, Richard, what level are you at?"

"Eight or nine," he said. "Just thinking about it makes me really anxious."

"What are you afraid of?"

"Well, I'm afraid I'll suddenly panic while I'm speaking. I'll want to run out, I'll make a fool of myself—"

"Richard," I interrupted him, "tell me about some of the people who will be present at the meeting. What do they look like?"

He described an older gentleman, noting how well dressed he

always was, a woman with a foreign accent who had long red hair, and a young man who was so tall that he had to bend over to avoid hitting his head against the chandelier in the middle of the room. He began talking about what an interesting and diverse group of people attended these meetings. One man had lived in eight different countries. . . .

I let him talk about that man for a while, and then said, "What is your anxiety level now?"

"About three," he said, and smiled.

He realized that when he focused on something concrete, visualizing the people he would be meeting with and being very specific in describing what he saw and was thinking about, his anxiety level went down. In this case, I had interrupted his escalating fears. But as we worked together, he would be learning to do that for himself. So even when he had a thought that brought his anxiety level up, he would learn there were things *he* could do to bring his level down.

"We're not going to try to make the fear go away," I went on, "but rather show you that you can function even when the fear is present. That's what Point Five is about. Your goal is not to *never* feel fear or anxiety again, but to function in spite of the anxiety. You're on the right track when you can say, 'I feel anxious, and that's okay'—and you feel good about what you're doing.

"If your anxiety shoots up while you're introducing yourself at a meeting, you'd be tempted to think, 'I was a failure, because I was really anxious.' Instead, the fifth point says *focus on the accomplishment*. Try saying, 'Yes, I felt anxious—and in spite of that, I did it.' Concentrate on the achievement rather than the feeling.

"The sixth point is '*Expect, allow, and accept that the fear will reappear.*' Your natural instinct is to say, 'Okay, I did it once and got away with it, and it'll never happen again.' If you think that way, you set yourself up for disappointment. Expecting and allowing that the fear may appear again you can say, 'Well, this is how my mind and body react sometimes,' instead of being surprised and saying, 'Oh, my god, I've lost all my gains and I'm back to the beginning—I'm a failure!' It's an opportunity to practice, and it's a normal part of recovery."

During our practice sessions, Richard and I checked his anxiety level often. We did this for two reasons. Over and over again, Richard could see how his thoughts and actions influenced his feelings. It was also important for him to share what was going on inside him. Surprising as it may seem, although I've worked with hundreds of patients, and I've had panic attacks myself, it's not always apparent even to me when a person's anxiety level is rising. In fact, it's usually almost impossible to tell when someone is having a panic attack, even when they feel as though they're dying! People like Richard work so hard at keeping their feelings inside that they may be looking at me with a smile on their face and, all the time, they're trying to control feelings of panic that are building and building.

If someone says, "I'm at a Level Eight," for example, I can assume that they're thinking about having a panic attack and all the terrible things that might happen—"the imaginary dangers of the future."

I told Richard, "It's helpful to think in terms of percentages. If you're at a Level Seven, for example, your mind is probably about seventy percent involved in some imaginary, 'what-if' thinking: 'What if I blush? What if my legs shake? What if I look like a fool? What if I panic?' And you're probably only about thirty percent involved in what's going on right now, because you're preoccupied with your fearful thoughts.

"But if something in the present were to interrupt your thoughts—if I ask you questions about your daughter, for instance—notice what happens to your level. It goes down. When your level is about a four, you're only about forty percent involved in the imaginary dangers of the future and sixty percent involved in the here and now.

"As your anxiety level begins to rise—although everything in your mind and body is telling you to think about your fear, rehearse the feelings, and try to stay in control—the key is to trust that by focusing on something concrete in the present, your level will come down automatically. As you do that more and more, you will begin to develop confidence that the change will happen."

"But sometimes I just go from zero to ten," Richard said. "There aren't any levels in between."

"You *think* you go right up to a ten, but anxiety really never goes straight up to that level. As we work together, you'll see that your mind and body get a lot of hints about how your fear and anxiety are building up, even though you may not even be aware of them right now. You can use those hints to stop the spiraling of the fear before the level gets really high.

"For example, you mentioned to me that before you get really anxious, your hands get clammy. So even though you may not be feeling anxiety or panic at that moment, you know that when your hands begin to get clammy, something is going on. At that very point, start focusing on things in the present, asking yourself, 'Where am I now? What am I doing? What colors do I see? What sounds do I hear?' Begin to do that before the anxiety begins to spiral and takes on a life of its own.

"Even if you do reach a ten and have a panic attack, know that it will come right down again. The chance of reaching a second ten is very small. Physiologically, once the body hits a panic attack, it begins to calm itself down. Afterward you might feel exhausted. You might even want to cry or laugh, but the attack is over.

"If you can *ride through* the panic rather than fighting it, you'll find it's almost like being in the water and riding a wave. If you go halfway up with the wave and then suddenly start fighting, what happens? The wave can come crashing right down on you. But what if you just float over the wave and go to the other side?"

I asked Richard to visualize that experience: "Imagine you're right in the middle of that wave. Picture the water lifting you up to the crest where you have the choice of swimming frantically in an attempt to get to the other side or simply letting go and allowing nature to take its course. Even though it may be scary to give up fighting against the water, visualize simply putting your hands out in front of you and letting the wave pass as you gently float to the other side."

To help Richard prepare for his upcoming meeting, I asked him to imagine himself arriving in the room, looking around, telling me who was there, what colors he saw, what sounds he could hear. Then I asked him to imagine himself looking around the table where everyone was seated and noticing very specific things, like the color of his boss's tie, the expression on the face of the person he would sit next to, and the hairstyle of his secretary.

"If, during this time, you begin to feel your anxiety rising, ask yourself what level you're at. If it's above a five, you're probably allowing your thoughts to run off into 'what-if' thinking. Just bring yourself back into the present again by focusing as much as you can on things around you.

"Remember," I said, "just as you use your imagination to bring up frightening thoughts, you can redirect it to create pleasant images."

Two weeks later, in a therapy session that immediately followed the dreaded staff meeting, Richard recounted the success of the morning. He said that indeed as he walked into the room, knowing he was going to have to give a short presentation, his anxiety level shot up. Although he felt very uncomfortable, with all his willpower he forced himself to focus on things around him. He described how he counted the people sitting around the table, noticed the stripes on the wallpaper, snapped the rubber band on his wrist, and made a conscious effort to involve himself in "premeeting" chatter with his colleagues.

When he asked himself again what his level was, much to his surprise he realized it had come down—real-life proof that these "tricks" really work.

By the time the meeting started and he was called upon to give his presentation, Richard actually "forgot" to be anxious! He had become so involved in what was going on around him that he simply gave his report as if it were a continuation of his earlier discussions with the others in the room. Richard was beginning to see that he did not have to be the victim of his anxiety.

Remember that first session, when Richard practiced reading aloud to me? Although at first he was anxious, he gradually got used to it. But when I suggested he read to a small group of people I was working with, he felt he wasn't quite ready. As a therapist, my challenge was to find the next step: a short-term goal that would keep him moving ahead. I also kept in mind that tackling things that have real-life meaning, rather than just practicing for the sake of practicing, is important to help move patients forward. Motivation is certainly heightened when there's the reward of personal satisfaction at the other end.

Taking advantage of Richard's sensitivity and his helpfulness to others, in our session following his successful presentation at work I told him the idea I'd had at our first meeting.

A week later Richard and I were sitting in a room with five other people at a training session for volunteers at the Lighthouse for the Blind.

The woman who ran the training session suggested that each volunteer briefly tell something about himself or herself.

We had spent some time before the meeting figuring out how Richard would be most comfortable signaling me when his anxiety level went up, and how I could help him. As the man on Richard's left introduced himself, Richard's anxiety was rising, and he let me know this by unobtrusively raising seven fingers. In previous practice with the Six Points, he had found that his anxiety decreased when he touched and could feel the solidness of some object in front of him, like a table or chair. Now, knowing that touch helped him, I rubbed my own hand along the edge of the table to remind him. He smiled and did the same, then nodded, acknowledging that indeed his level had come down.

When it was his turn to speak, he continued to rub his hand on the edge of the table while he gave his name and a few facts about himself.

The other volunteers probably didn't think twice about what they said that day, but for Richard it was like the first step on his long climb up Mount Everest.

At the end of the session, Richard volunteered to read to a blind person on a regular basis. He was assigned to an elderly woman, Mrs. Sawicki, who was hard of hearing as well as partially blind. Mrs. Sawicki lived alone in a large apartment building reserved for the elderly.

Richard gave her a call and said he and I would come by next Tuesday at three o'clock. For some reason, Mrs. Sawicki didn't want us to come to her apartment, but she agreed to meet us in the lobby of her building and have Richard read to her in a "quiet corner."

I'll never forget the day Richard and I met with this woman. Standing near the elevator, Richard kept glancing around the bustling lobby for the "quiet corner." From his expression I was pretty sure I knew what he was thinking: Not only would he be reading aloud to a stranger, but he would be doing it with an audience.

Finally the elevator door opened, and a thin, white-haired woman appeared, carrying a large stack of mail under her arm.

"Mrs. Sawicki?"

"Yes."

She escorted us to what she called her "favorite spot" and handed Richard her stack of mail, complete with mass-mailer brochures for miracle cures and quack remedies of all varieties.

"Read it, please," she said.

Richard began softly reading to her: "Dear Mrs. Sawicki, if you are one of the millions of people who suffer from constipation—"

"Louder, son!" she snapped.

Richard looked a bit pale, but he read through the mail. He later admitted that he was so distracted by the activities in the lobby, the nature of the reading material, and having Mrs. Sawicki constantly shout at him to read louder, that he nearly forgot about his anxiety.

But whenever he thought about his feelings and noticed his anxiety level shooting up, he signaled me. I would then take some exaggerated breaths to remind him to breathe deeply and evenly. Or I would point to the rubber band on his wrist, reminding him to gently snap it to bring his thoughts back to the present.

About halfway through the session, as we had previously agreed, Richard nodded to me that he was ready to go solo. I walked over to another part of the lobby. Later, as we left, he told me he had set up a time to visit Mrs. Sawicki during the week. This was the first of some small but very significant steps for Richard.

In the weeks that followed, he continued to practice by visiting Mrs. Sawicki on his own and reporting back to me. One night I came home to find an elated message on my machine. "You're right, and those Six Points do work. As difficult as this is sometimes, staying focused on the present does keep my level down. And as an extra bonus, I'm now an expert in miracle cures . . . for everything!"

Reading to Mrs. Sawicki gave Richard something he hadn't gotten from his job or any other kind of work for a long time: He felt a sense of satisfaction and self-worth. In a short period of time, his increased self-esteem began to show its face. Meeting with him now, I could almost feel him coming alive.

At this point I also introduced Richard to the small group of people I was working with who had panic attacks in similar situations. Gradually he began reading to the others in the group and giving short speeches.

About eight weeks after we had begun working together, I reminded Richard of something he had mentioned during our first goal-setting discussion. I asked him whether he was ready to think about going to a Toastmasters meeting. From the expression on his face, I knew that if I had asked him to run for President of the United States he could not have felt more challenged!

I assured him that he wouldn't have to talk at the first meeting. I would go with him, posing as a colleague so he wouldn't have to explain my presence, and say we were both interested in joining the group.

One week later there we were, standing outside the imposing, marble-pillared building where Toastmasters meetings were held.

Attending that first meeting, Richard later told me, was even more of an ordeal than the night six weeks later when he delivered his first speech. Although, as I had assured him, he wasn't required to speak, new participants were invited to stand up and say what they hoped to accomplish by joining Toastmasters. No one *had* to do this; it was an option for first-time attendees. Richard looked at me as if to ask, "Do you think I'm ready?"

There was no doubt in my mind: There's never any danger of somebody *not* being ready to do something. If you *want* to do something, I had told Richard, you *are* ready.

I nodded—and before I even realized what was happening, Richard was standing up and giving his name. When he sat down, there were beads of sweat on his forehead, but the smile on his face told me all we both needed to know.

Afterward, of course, Richard's excitement at having survived the first meeting was dimmed by projecting ahead to the day he would have to give his "icebreaker," the five-minute speech that all new Toastmasters members are expected to give shortly after joining. For several weeks, Richard and I prepared for his speech. He practiced so many times in front of me that I knew his entire speech by heart.

Since I had been attending Toastmasters just as long as Richard, I was expected to give my own "icebreaker" on the same night. But I didn't pay much attention to preparation. I don't have a fear of public speaking, and I wasn't trying to become a full-time member of the club.

D-day arrived!

Richard wanted to go first to get it over with. He told me he hadn't slept at all the night before. Each time he projected his thoughts to being up there behind the lectern, he tried to remember what we had talked about. He saw himself feeling part of his pen, touching the lectern, counting the people sitting around him, noticing stripes in the wallpaper—but in spite of all the preparation he did, he said later, he felt as if he were going to the electric chair.

I can remember watching Richard walk up to the lectern and feeling, on the one hand a sense of pride, knowing that he would do fine, and on the other hand, feeling as if his anxiety were my own. I suppose it's much as a parent feels watching a child take his first step.

I couldn't imagine anyone's first speech going better! Richard spoke clearly, with expression, and looked at people in the audience. From where I was sitting, it was a perfect speech. Though I knew the secret, heart-pounding, internal struggle, I would bet a million dollars that there wasn't another person in the room who had the slightest sense of what he was going through. In fact, I think people would have been shocked if they had been told what Richard was really feeling.

My own observation was reinforced when it came time for the written evaluations. All of them were raves. Longtime members couldn't believe it was Richard's first speech. They couldn't believe how calm he seemed.

When it was my turn, I got up and talked, improvising all the way—not aware that I was doing *everything* wrong. In spite of the evaluators being kind and saying some nice things about my talk, they gently let me know that I had spoken too fast and had too many "uhs" and run-on sentences. They also criticized me because I started speaking before I got to the lectern.

Although Richard had been convinced that people were just being kind to encourage him, the comments about *my* presentation made him realize that this was an honest group. And although he was convinced that every bit of his anxiety showed, it was hard to argue with the written comments he held in his hands.

Richard slept well that night for the first time in weeks.

Successes followed. Richard was able to go by himself to Toastmasters (although I certainly could have used the practice). Months later, long after Richard's formal treatment with me was finished, my much-used answering machine boasted that Richard had been elected head of the local chapter of Toastmasters and was competing in regional speeches. He expanded his responsibilities at his publishing company and was promoted to vice president.

Soon after, he began participating in local political activity, and eventually served on several public commissions.

Six years after completing treatment, Richard called to tell me he had a new job as the chief counsel for a large trade association. At the same time he was beginning a small, private law practice. "The phantom of the law school" had become the lawyer and public servant he had always wanted to be.

11

Ellen: Medications and Panic Disorder

LIKE MANY OF the people with whom I have worked, Ellen was surprised—and resistant—when I suggested she see a psychiatrist to be evaluated for medication. This was eight weeks after she had begun treatment with me for her panic disorder.

Ellen, a thirty-six-year-old graphics designer, reminded me of what she had told me at our initial meeting, that she had already had two negative experiences with medication. One of the medications, prescribed by her internist, made her so drowsy that she felt constantly fatigued and mentally unable to focus. The second medication caused her heart to race out of control and her blood pressure to soar. She also experienced horrible nightmares and, after four "miserable" weeks, discontinued the medication.

When asked how long it had been since medication had been prescribed for her problem, she replied, "About ten years."

It's understandable why someone who sought medication for panic disorder ten years ago could have been disappointed and frustrated and would have given up, as Ellen did. Ten years ago panic disorder was just beginning to be recognized as a discrete psychiatric disorder; the psychological and biological research that has proliferated over the past decade was still in its infancy.

Consequently, although many of the medications doctors were then prescribing to treat symptoms of panic disorder were FDA-approved for general anxiety or depression, they had not been researched or had their efficacy in the treatment of panic disorder specifically been proved. Since the mid-1980s, however, massive research has been conducted by pharmaceutical companies, medical universities, hospitals, and the NIMH to find medications that are effective for panic disorder, as well as for the other anxiety disorders. Although there is currently no pill that will make all the symptoms of an anxiety disorder magically disappear, or that is without potential side effects, giant strides have been made. I was able to assure Ellen that there are many new, safe, and effective medications on the market.

As we talked further, we began to explore her other concerns about taking medication—concerns that many patients share.

For one thing, she felt that taking medication meant that she had failed in therapy—that she hadn't tried hard enough or that she was somehow weak or defective. She was also worried about what would happen when she stopped taking the pill.

"If I'm on a medication that makes me less anxious, or blocks or reduces the intensity of my panic attacks, what will happen if I stop taking it? Will the attacks come back? And will I go back to square one?"

This question is complex and goes to the very core of treatment issues.

Research shows that although panic disorder is highly responsive to a variety of treatments, it is a chronic condition that leaves its victims vulnerable to relapses. Many people *do* recover completely from their distressing symptoms but, to be realistic, anyone with an anxiety disorder must learn to live with the possibility that the symptoms may recur. If a patient has learned to accept the feelings of panic—trusting that as frightening as the symptoms are, they are not dangerous—and to control his or her reactions, relapses are less likely to be as frightening or debilitating.

The most effective way for patients to prove to themselves that a panic attack is not harmful is to experience the frightening sensations repeatedly in a secure environment. But if medication is blocking the sensations, this can present a real treatment challenge. For this reason, even if a patient might get some symptom relief from medication, I prefer to begin treatment while the patient is medication-free. In a few cases, however, the person is in such severe distress that it would be impossible even to begin a cognitive-behavioral treatment program. In this situation, medication can be a necessary and important first step.

On the other hand, once someone has learned the basic cognitive-behavioral skills, as Ellen had already done during the first several weeks of her therapy, adding medication can be a helpful adjunct to treatment. Later on, when the person is ready to taper off the medication, he or she will have developed the confidence to handle whatever symptoms may arise.

When Ellen first came for treatment, she felt as if her life had been put on hold for more than ten years. She managed to function at work and with friends, but otherwise she had created a very narrow world for herself. Whenever she had to travel, or even *thought* about traveling somewhere outside her "comfort zone"—about a ten-mile radius—she became paralyzed with fear. It didn't matter whether she or someone else was driving or she was using public transportation, she simply was terrified of being away from home and having a panic attack. She hadn't taken a vacation or visited her parents at her childhood home in Chicago for over ten years.

Ellen also suffered from spontaneous panic attacks that frequently awakened her at night, or ruined a day at work or evening out with friends; she would feel exhausted for hours afterward. The "constant buzz of anxiety" that she felt in the back of her head never seemed to go away.

Glad to be talking to someone who seemed to understand what she was going through, she was eager to begin the new support group I told her would be starting, as well as individual cognitive-behavioral therapy. She was also relieved when I told her I didn't believe it was necessary for her to be on medication—at least not at this point.

At the first group meeting, Ellen was surprised to find out how many people in the group *were* taking medication. I pointed out they had been on medication prior to beginning therapy and wanted to learn some cognitive-behavioral skills before coming off their medications. Patients who are being weaned from medication seem to have an easier time and less chance of relapse if they are simultaneously participating in therapy.

Several patients taking medication spoke about how much easier it was for them when they didn't have to deal with their anxiety all the time. This confused Ellen, first, because of her own negative experience with medication, and second, because she found herself asking, "How will these people learn how to handle panic attacks if they're no longer having any because of the drugs?" She observed that many of the group members were *feeling* better, but she asked whether they were *getting* better, a question debated in academic circles as well. She still preferred not to take any medication.

As the weeks passed, however, it was clear that Ellen wasn't practicing as much as she wanted or needed to. Her energy was drained by her ever-present general anxiety and by the panic attacks that disturbed her sleep—energy that she needed to voluntarily put herself into anxiety-provoking situations. She kept her weekly therapy appointments, read all the materials handed out to her during the group sessions, and *knew* what it was she had to do in order to get better, but by Week 8 she announced to the group that she was feeling stuck and frustrated and beginning to get depressed. Everyone else seemed to be moving closer toward reaching their treatment goals, but Ellen felt she was up against a brick wall. During the discussion that followed, several of the group members who were using medication tried to persuade her to give it a try, but Ellen held firm; she did not want to take "drugs."

It was after that particular group meeting that I asked Ellen to come into my office and suggested that she be evaluated for medication.

After we talked for a while, Ellen came to realize she wasn't a treatment failure; she simply needed additional help at this particular point in time. During her therapy sessions, she had placed herself in a number of situations where she'd experienced full-blown panic attacks. She had successfully used the techniques she'd learned to remain in the situation, and she had seen her anxiety level come down. But she wasn't practicing on her own, and she hadn't made the effort to find a support person.

Ellen woke up every morning with intense anxiety. Anticipatory anxiety and spontaneous panic attacks continued to overwhelm her. And she hadn't yet attempted her six-week goal: to accompany her friends on a weekend trip to the beach. They went each Friday without her and she felt doubly terrible: once for missing the fun and once for not being willing to put herself in a situation that might bring on a panic attack—the very thing she knew she needed to do to get better.

I told Ellen I believed her chronic anxiety was hindering her progress and that the medication might take enough of "the edge" off for her to begin taking bigger steps in therapy. With much hesitation, Ellen agreed to make an appointment with the psychiatrist whom I recommended.

The psychiatrist reviewed Ellen's earlier experiences with medication and discussed her current concerns. He also checked to make sure that she did not have a history of alcohol or other substance abuse. Then he prescribed a starting dose of Xanax.

Xanax (generic name: alprazolam) belongs to a broader class of antianxiety medications called benzodiazepines. Currently, it is the only medication approved by the FDA specifically for panic disorder. As Ellen's psychiatrist explained, it begins to work right away, and any side effects often decrease over time. The psychiatrist asked Ellen to call to report any side effects, and he cautioned her not to drink alcohol while taking Xanax, since the combination could make her very drowsy and cause cognitive impairment. He made another appointment for a week later to evaluate the dosage.

Luckily, Xanax worked well for Ellen. Apart from feeling sleepy sometimes until her dose was appropriately adjusted, she had no side effects, and she noticed an immediate difference in how she felt and the way in how she reacted to difficult situations. "I haven't had a panic attack for several days, and I have not been waking up each morning filled with anxiety," she told the group at the next meeting. "And I don't have anxiety doing many of the little things that I used to avoid, like waiting in traffic or standing in a long line."

Several weeks later, one of the group members observed that Ellen seemed to be talking less about what she was *afraid* of doing, and more about some of the positive things that lay ahead. She even committed herself to a firm date to go to the beach—"no matter *how* I feel!"

Good changes were taking place. But now Ellen began worrying that the medication might be almost "too magical." And she had yet another concern that kept her from confronting some of her bigger goals.

"Okay, I'm taking medication," she said, "which I view as a last resort. What if I have a panic attack while I'm on medication? What if one time the medication doesn't work?"

Before I could respond, Joe, one of the group members, jumped in. "You've had panic attacks without medication and you survived," he pointed out. "What do you think will happen if you have a panic attack on medication? It can't be much worse!"

"You're right, Joe," Ellen replied, laughing. "The worst that could happen is that I will feel absolutely awful—and *feeling* awful never killed anybody!" This matter-of-fact attitude was new for Ellen. It signaled to me that she was beginning to take her fears much more in stride.

That same day, however, Ellen requested a private meeting with me to air another concern. By now she had been taking Xanax for several weeks and although she was taking a relatively small dose, she had noticed that her anxiety level started to rise if she missed a single dose. "It would be hard to stop taking this medication," she said. "I can see my dependency on it and I hate that. I'm afraid I'm becoming hooked."

This was a realistic concern. I had told Ellen, as had her

psychiatrist, that Xanax and other antianxiety medications could cause withdrawal symptoms when discontinued after they've been used for several months. Withdrawal problems can include hyper-arousal, sleep problems, and increased anxiety. Problems are more likely to occur in someone taking higher doses than Ellen was, or in someone who has had a previous drug or alcohol addiction. (This is one of several reasons Xanax should generally be avoided by any-one with a history of drug or alcohol abuse.) But even at low doses, and without a history of abuse, for some patients there is potential for withdrawal symptoms.

I explained that once Ellen was ready to discontinue the medi-cation, the psychiatrist would reduce the dosage very gradually so as to minimize the discomfort of withdrawal. "You may have some psychological dependency because the medication has been help-ful to you," I told her, "but that's not at all the same as the worry you have about addiction. You won't need larger and larger doses to get the therapeutic result. And the medication doesn't make you high. You won't crave it when you stop taking it."

This conversation allayed Ellen's fears somewhat, and she con-cluded that the benefits of the medication outweighed its negative aspects at this point. She was moving forward and confronting situations she had previously felt were impossible, and at the mo-ment that was her highest priority.

During the final session of our twelve-week group, Ellen said that although she now felt more comfortable taking medication, she was glad she'd waited until she had acquired some cognitive-behavioral techniques.

"I think if I had started on medication immediately, I wouldn't have trusted the techniques. But now I know that when I am ready to do without medication, I will have enough tools in hand to keep going. Even if I do have a panic attack, I know I will be able to be in control rather than allowing it to control me."

Ellen also said that she found the group support so helpful that she was going to enroll in another twelve-week session. She would use it to prepare for her major goal: the trip to Chicago.

Six weeks later she brought in a picture of herself sitting around the Thanksgiving table with her family and gave everyone in the group a T-shirt that read WELCOME TO CHICAGO!

As of this writing, several medications currently approved for treatment of anxiety and/or depression are being considered for FDA approval specifically to treat panic disorder, PTSD, OCD, or GAD. And the list of potential new medications is rapidly expanding.

However, even if an "ideal" medication is found and approved by the FDA, mental health professionals will still have to deal with the issues that affect and concern patients like Ellen.

All medications must be carefully monitored throughout the course of treatment. If they are not, serious problems can occur. Xanax can cause severe withdrawal symptoms if it is discontinued abruptly. Patients must be weaned from Xanax very gradually— often over a period of weeks or even months—in order to minimize this effect. Many patients are also prescribed an antidepressant or other medication to smooth the transition.

The physician should work very closely with a patient who has been prescribed any antianxiety medication, and the patient needs to fully understand the importance of complying with the doctor's directions. At no time should someone using any tranquilizing medication on a regular basis decide, "I'm feeling better, so I'll just stop taking the pill."

For longer-term maintenance, Ellen's psychiatrist prescribed Prozac (generic name: fluoxetine hydrochloride). Prozac is an antidepressant belonging to a group of drugs called serotonin-specific reuptake inhibitors (SSRIs). Many physicians have found Prozac and other antidepressants such as imipramine (brand name: Tofranil) helpful in the treatment of panic disorder and other anxiety disorders. Xanax and other benzodiazepines work quickly, providing immediate relief to people with severe anxiety and panic attacks, but they should not be used indefinitely. Antidepressants, such as Prozac, that inhibit panic attacks take several weeks to become effective. But they do not create dependency and so can be used for longer periods of time. And patients don't have to worry about potential withdrawal symptoms. For this reason, a physician may begin a patient on a benzodiazepine and wean him or her off it as soon as the other medication has taken effect.

Ellen helped herself greatly by being so forthright about her concerns. Many patients are afraid of a medication's physical affects or of being unable to control their reactions once they swallow it. Others are concerned the pill will become a crutch or represent a sign of weakness. Some are uncomfortable with or afraid of the side effects, especially if they've had a negative experience with medication before. Many worry about becoming addicted. But they may hesitate to raise these issues with their physicians.

Indirectly, these concerns often contribute to another problem: undermedication. Patients who are reluctant to take medication may take less than their prescribed dose. As a result, they do not receive the therapeutic benefit and continue to experience significant anxiety. In addition, they're likely to conclude that the medication simply doesn't work.

Physicians who are experienced in the treatment of panic disorder typically go to great lengths to educate patients in the proper use of medications and are available to answer concerns as they arise—no matter how trivial they may seem. This can make the difference in whether a trial of medication creates problems or helps to solve them. Patients need to be as fully informed as possible so that any side effects do not come as a surprise or actually make them feel worse about themselves.

At this point in time, we know that both cognitive-behavioral therapy and medication are effective treatments for panic disorder, but we can't always predict which treatment or combination of treatments will work best for individual patients. Therefore, it is important for both the mental health professional and the patient to keep an open mind when developing a treatment plan.

Physicians who treat panic disorder primarily with medication should inform patients about the importance of seeking cognitive-behavioral therapy as well, especially the need for gradually confronting the fears. Available information suggests that the majority of patients treated with medication alone are likely to relapse once the medication is discontinued. If patients face financial constraints or lack of access to a cognitive-behavioral therapist, a trusted family member or friend can be recruited to provide at least some support.

Conversely, cognitive-behavioral therapists should be more open to adding medication when and if it is indicated.

Flexibility is often the key ingredient in effective panic disorder therapy. For example, of the eight patients in Ellen's first group, three began the cognitive-behavioral treatment while already taking medication. Two of these patients found the medication to be moderately helpful. They still had anticipatory anxiety and were avoiding many situations, but they weren't having panic attacks. The third, David, seemed to me to be very much undermedicated.

David was still having frequent panic attacks and continuous free-floating anxiety. He said he wasn't taking the full dose of medication prescribed by his physician because of unpleasant side effects: insomnia, constipation, and dry mouth. I urged him to call his physician for a reevaluation. Changing medications resolved the problem fairly quickly, and David began to do much better.

The four other members of Ellen's group weren't on medication, and I didn't see any reason why they should be; they were all making excellent progress. They repeatedly entered into and remained in anxiety-producing situations, often challenging themselves beyond their expected limits.

In general, the ones who were on medication *felt* better than the ones who weren't because the medication allowed them to experience relief from their symptoms. However, this in itself created a problem. Since the medication blocked the panic attacks, those taking it didn't have a chance during exposure therapy sessions to fully put into practice the cognitive-behavioral techniques they were learning. They were delighted they were able to do things they hadn't done in a while, but they periodically asked, "What's the point in going out with my therapist to practice, when I'm not having a panic attack?"

This can become a bitter dilemma for patients and therapists. In order to become desensitized to panic attacks, it's necessary to confront them repeatedly and see for oneself that they can be successfully handled. So if someone never gets to use the various anxiety-reducing techniques while having a panic attack, he is unlikely to trust that they work.

In Ellen's first support group, the four patients not on medication were struggling at the beginning. But they actually made more significant progress than those who were taking it, despite the fact that their early practice sessions were difficult and painful. As the weeks passed, they began to report how much less fearful they were of having a panic attack since they now knew nothing dangerous would happen to them if they did. And they trusted this because they had experienced it first hand.

The question of whether or not to use medication and, if so, at what point to begin and end it, is a very personal one and must be dealt with on an individual basis. And it often takes a certain amount of trial and error to find the right treatment mix, which can be frustrating both to the therapist and to the patient. But having choices optimizes each person's chance for a full recovery.

Ellen's decision to add medication later on in her treatment turned out to be the right one for her. A few weeks after her triumphant trip to Chicago, she reported that she had booked a flight to the Caribbean with a friend for a long-overdue vacation. She indicated she wanted to stay on both medications until she returned home. Then she would begin the process of discontinuing the Xanax. "I know that my trip won't always be easy, and neither will cutting back the medication," she told me. "But I'm ready!"

12

Brian and Jennifer: Diagnosing and Treating Children

ANXIETY DISORDERS ARE among the most prevalent categories of psychiatric disorders in children and adolescents. Yet, until about a decade ago, a pediatrician or mental health professional would not have considered an anxiety disorder diagnosis for a youngster—even if the presenting symptoms were similar to those experienced by an adult diagnosed with an anxiety disorder.

Most child-rearing books give tips for handling common childhood fears—from large dogs to "monsters" under the bed—and reassure parents that they will soon be outgrown. "Separation anxiety" is also regarded as a natural developmental stage. It is normal for nine-month-old babies to scream if their parents leave them with strangers, and parents and teachers are well prepared for tears at the kindergarten door. Only if a child persists in showing terror at going to school is there a hint of trouble. In these cases, it is often suggested that the mother herself is "overinvolved" or "reluctant to separate" from the child.

Today, the data suggest otherwise. There is no child equivalent of the adult NIMH Epidemiological Catchment Area study. But a number of large, well-documented studies have recently demonstrated that anxiety disorders in childhood and adolescents are common, afflicting between 5 and 10 percent of general pediatric patients. They often occur simultaneously, in combinations of two or more of the following: panic attacks, social phobia, simple phobia, separation anxiety, and what researchers call "school avoidance," a genuine phobia about going to school. There is also a good deal of overlap in children with anxiety disorders and so-called disruptive behavior disorders, which include attention deficit hyperactivity disorder (ADHD) and oppositional defiant disorder (ODD). Anxiety disorders are about half as common in children as are disruptive behavior disorders and between 25 and 40 percent of youngsters with ADHD or ODD also suffer from an anxiety disorder.

Many patients first diagnosed with panic disorder in adulthood recall symptoms during childhood. Yet it wasn't until the early 1990s that researchers began publishing information about the number of American youngsters who suffer from panic disorder. One study showed that about 0.6 percent of high school students had panic disorder. Fewer than half of the students in that study had received treatment of any kind.

Having one panic attack does not mean that a child is going to have panic disorder. But there is a higher risk of developing panic disorder if the panic attacks begin in childhood.

Consider Brian.

Getting Brian to school had become a daily battle. The twelve-year-old boy and his mother sat in the car in front of the school for an hour every morning while she tried everything she could think of—cajolery, threats, pleas, orders—to push him out of the car and into the school.

Until he started the sixth grade that fall, Brian had been a star pupil—happy, athletic, popular, bright. Then one unseasonably hot September day during a soccer match he suddenly felt faint and ran off the field. Schoolmates and teachers clustered around him, but in a few minutes he felt okay. Embarrassed and perhaps a little strange, but okay.

His parents took him to the family doctor immediately. They

had read too many news stories about school athletes dropping dead during practice to take his symptoms lightly. After a thorough physical, Brian was told that he was in fine condition and could freely participate in sports. "Just drink more water and don't overdo it on hot days," his doctor instructed.

But Brian didn't want to go back to soccer practice. His parents thought they understood that he was afraid he would faint in front of his teammates and the thought was embarrassing. "Give him a few days," they said to each other. Two weeks later, Brian's dad decided it was time for a talk. If Brian didn't start going to practice, he'd miss the entire season. But the talk was to no avail.

Then suddenly, out of the blue, Brian announced he did not want to go back to school, and the morning battles began. If his parents' arguments and threats did get him there, he usually found some way to persuade the school nurse to send him home. He stopped participating in class and withdrew from friends during recess.

His worried parents met with his teachers, the principal, and the school psychologist. Numerous explanations, from malingering to attention deficit disorder to trouble at home, were suggested, but none seemed to fit the reality of Brian's situation. Nor did this fit the definition of school phobia; Brian's troubles had started on the soccer field.

It was an aunt who finally spotted Brian's panic disorder. She had been treated for panic disorder herself, and she knew that it tended to run in families. In fact, researchers have found that the children of parents with one or another of the anxiety disorders are seven times as likely as other children to have an anxiety disorder themselves. Childhood anxiety disorders have also been linked to family histories of other mood disorders, including depression.

On his aunt's recommendation, Brian's parents found a psychiatrist knowledgeable about the disorder. He saw Brian for a few sessions and then referred him to my treatment center. He also prescribed a medication to treat the initial, acute symptoms of Brian's panic attacks. Although Brian would discontinue all medication relatively quickly, calming his central nervous system medically helped to get him and his family past their sense of immediate crisis.

At my treatment center, Brian began working with Judy, a staff therapist who specializes in treating children.

Once Judy gained Brian's confidence—she had to convince him that she wasn't just another adult bent on getting him back into school—she asked him what it was about school that frightened him so. And she received the classic response that anyone who has ever experienced a panic attack will instantly recognize:

"I don't exactly know," Brian answered. "I just get this horrible feeling I can't really explain, but I feel like I'm trapped, *and if I don't get out right away something awful is going to happen!*"

Judy was able to explain what is known about panic disorder to Brian and assure him it was neither life-threatening nor anything to be ashamed of or even embarrassed about. She faced an additional task as well, one she is becoming accustomed to. She needed to educate Brian's parents, teacher, and principal about the nature of his anxiety disorder. She also wanted to talk to his classmates.

Judy asked for Brian's permission to meet with his class. "It's important to help them understand," she explained. "Otherwise, they won't have any idea what you're going through or what they can do to help you."

Brian gave his okay as long as he didn't have to be there while everyone talked about him.

After discussing panic disorder with the principal and teacher, both of whom knew about the problem in adults but had never confronted it in one of their pupils, Judy had a session with Brian's classmates.

She tried to get them to relate what Brian was experiencing to someone famous and respected who was known to them. Many of the boys had heard of John Madden, the sports commentator, and a few of them knew that he regularly traveled on trains or in his own private bus because he didn't like to fly.

Judy also asked the students about friends and relatives. Did anyone have a parent or an aunt or uncle who was afraid to drive or ride an elevator?

Several hands shot up. One student told about a grandmother who always stayed at home and never wanted to go beyond her front door. Another said that whenever her father drove, he always stopped the car before crossing a long bridge and changed places with her mother. After they crossed the bridge, he would get back into the driver's seat.

Judy described for the class what it was like for Brian to sit behind a desk: "Imagine what it would be like to be sitting here and feel as if a freight train were headed right for you at full speed. Imagine how awful it would be if you thought you could die any minute."

"What can we do for Brian?" one girl asked during the discussion that followed.

"Just ask if you can do anything to help. Sometimes you can. Sometimes you can't. It's important to let Brian know that even though you don't totally understand what he's feeling, that you respect that it is *real* for him. And don't be surprised if one minute he's okay and the next minute he wants to run out the door. You can help a lot just by not making it a big deal."

Judy's main focus, however, was on giving Brian the information and techniques he needed to manage his disorder.

"We don't know exactly what causes panic attacks or why some people and not others get them," she told him. "But we do know that no one ever died or lost control from a panic attack. You might *feel* that way when it's happening, but the scary feelings always pass. I'm going to teach you some 'tricks' that will help you see for yourself that nothing bad is going to happen. At first, I'll be nearby to help you. But even when I'm not here, you can get help from your parents, your teachers, or your friends. And most important, you'll learn how to help yourself."

Judy taught Brian the same techniques we use with adults. Most children, in fact, learn them more easily and enjoy applying them. Brian quickly memorized the Six Points and caught on to labeling his levels. He knew when his heart was pounding and his palms were sweating, he was at Level 7 or 8. And he began to see that he could do things to make his level come down.

Most important of all, Brian had to know that he always had an Out.

139

A computer was set up in an alcove outside the classroom. Anytime Brian needed to, he could excuse himself, leave the class, and work at the computer. This helped in two ways. It meant he always had a safe, familiar place to retreat to if he was too uncomfortable, and it gave him something specific to concentrate on until the frightening feelings passed.

As we know, panic attacks can create powerfully reinforced negative behaviors. Adults often try to interrupt or change these behaviors in youngsters by telling them what they *should* or *should not* do, only to find the child or adolescent even more resistant. By creating an environment that gave Brian control over his exposure activities, permission to move at his own pace, and a set of strategies and an ally he could count on, Judy opened the door for equally powerful but *positive* behaviors to develop.

During the first four days after Brian was back in school, Judy spent the first hour of each morning in the library near his classroom. Brian knew he could go see her if he needed help. After the hour passed, Judy would walk back by Brian's classroom and watch for his hand signal that it was okay for her to leave. Knowing she was willing to stay if he needed her allowed Brian to relax and gave his anxiety level time to diminish. Surprising even himself, each morning Brian would give Judy the "high five" sign when he saw her. By the fifth day, he was willing to go to school without having Judy there.

It was hard work for Brian, harder than any assignment he had ever had. When he felt his heart beat faster and his palms starting to sweat, he forced himself to concentrate on some of the exercises Judy had taught him.

"Count all the letter H's that you see on the page," she told him. If he could just focus—just concentrate—on that single exercise, counting the H's one by one, his mind was distracted from the fear. His level came down from a 7 or 8 to a 3 or 4. It gave him a sense of mastery over his panic. He no longer feared being overwhelmed.

Judy learned that even before the incident on the soccer field, Brian had been avoiding movies. After one bad experience, when he had to leave halfway through, he simply stopped going. Neither his parents nor his friends noticed anything strange about his excuses, or even how long it had been since he had gone. But now Brian himself recognized that his movie problem was part of his disorder. So he and Judy went to the movies.

As they approached the theater, Judy reminded Brian of the techniques he'd learned to use in the classroom. Those techniques would work just as well inside the movie theater. "Let's go sit in the back row. If you want to leave, all you have to do is tell me."

They bought their tickets and went inside. But a few minutes after the movie started, Judy felt a tug on her sleeve. "I want to leave," Brian whispered urgently. "Let's go."

"Brian, we can leave whenever you want to," she whispered. "But remember what we talked about? Rub your hand on the side of the arm of the chair. What does it feel like?"

"It's smooth," he said, after a few seconds.

"All right. Now rub your hand on the seat. What does it feel like?"

"Rough," he reported.

After a few minutes, Brian was involved in watching the screen again. Though he asked to leave several more times, Judy took each request as an opportunity to help him practice the techniques he'd learned. And each time he tried them, the level of his anxiety came down.

"That was awesome!" Brian's eyes shone as they left the theater. For the first time in more than a year, he had seen a whole movie from beginning to end.

After six weeks, Brian was spending most of his school day in the classroom again. He frequently used the computer in the alcove, and he occasionally had to go see the nurse. Judy continued to see Brian in sessions outside school.

Brian also resumed sports. He had an understanding with the coach that he could leave a game anytime he wanted to. (Judy had persuaded the coach to treat Brian's signal like an injury.) The Out was always available.

There were still some days when he didn't want to go to school. Judy and his parents reached an agreement with Brian: He had to go to school in the morning, but if he wanted to leave after half a day, he was allowed. But he couldn't do that more than twice a week.

Once Brian knew he wasn't trapped, it actually became easier to stay.

Brian was fiercely proud of his accomplishments. "I still get those feelings," he told Judy, "but I don't have to leave."

He had been concerned about what his classmates would think of him when they found out about his panic attacks—but he discovered that he didn't have anything to worry about. "Sometimes they ask me whether everything's all right," he told Judy. "But the rest of the time, they forget about it. So I guess I'm just like everyone else."

■   ■   ■

People who were introduced to Jennifer at an Anxiety Disorders Association of America national conference met a poised, self-confident young woman who had just entered graduate school with the goal of becoming a therapist. They were very moved during the educational session when she and her mother described the problems that dominated her growing-up years and, in some ways, still shape her life today.

Jennifer was eight years old when she came home one day and told her mother she had had a dizzy spell in school. It was to be the beginning of a years-long nightmare. Jennifer's mother called the pediatrician, who suggested she wait to see if the dizziness recurred.

The next day Jennifer again experienced the spells, during which she felt everything was swimming around her. She was sent home by the school nurse. Maybe the problem was a learning disability or school phobia, suggested the pediatrician when he could find no trace of physical illness.

Jennifer, however, loved school, did well in her classes, and had many friends. She was determined to attend every day, but the dizzy spells continued to plague her.

One day she simply froze on the way home. She was crossing a street with her mother, a street she crossed every day. Halfway across was a yellow line. That day the yellow line became a force field of fear for Jennifer. She *knew* if she took another step something unimaginably terrible would happen. She clung to her mother, her head spinning, then burst into tears and ran back to the curb. She was trembling uncontrollably and sobbing with fear and embarrassment.

Then began the tests: blood tests, eye tests, hearing tests, eye tests, urine tests, and then a CAT scan. The tests showed nothing, but the spells of lightheadedness persisted, and now seemed transformed into full-blown panic attacks with a phobia of crossing a street. However, it would be years before the diagnosis of panic disorder was made. In the meantime, her phobia of crossing the street developed in almost classical form.

At first it was only the big street near her house that she couldn't cross. Gradually her world began to shrink, and soon she could cross no street at all.

Her walk home from the neighborhood elementary school became a surreal nightmare for her and her family. If she was late her mother knew she might find her at a street corner, curled on a lawn by the side of the intersection clutching the grass, and unable to move.

After three years of frustration, anger, and sadness for Jennifer and her parents, she finally was referred to a compassionate psychiatrist who was well known for his respect for his young patients. He looked at all the test results and then set them aside.

Drawing his chair up close to Jennifer, he gave his full attention to the little girl before him and asked her to tell him exactly how she felt during one of her spells.

She painted a graphic picture.

After a few more visits he felt sure Jennifer had panic disorder with agoraphobia.

Now to find the right treatment.

This all happened fifteen years ago, when few psychiatrists or psychologists—and even fewer general practitioners—were familiar with panic disorder.

Treatments were hit or miss, often depending on a pet theory developed by an individual therapist. There were only a few studies and even fewer clinical reports to draw upon. Jennifer was taken to hypnotists, nutritionists, and psychotherapists. She also continued to see the psychiatrist who had made the diagnosis.

Some of these professionals may have helped Jennifer to cope and to develop as a person, but she still had disabling attacks. Although they no longer occurred every day, she never knew when her world would shatter into wave after wave of terror. And in fact—although I didn't meet Jennifer until she was in college and never personally treated her—I believe her panic disorder was one of the most severe I have ever encountered.

What is remarkable is that she never gave up, and neither did her family. They were united in their determination that Jennifer should lead a normal life. Jennifer pushed herself to go to school, and her mother constantly intervened with her teachers. At the beginning of each school year, her parents also made a formal visit to explain her situation and ask for cooperation.

For the most part this approach worked. But Jennifer will never forget one teacher's thoughtless cruelty.

Her sixth-grade class was on a field trip and Jennifer had a panic attack in the parking lot. She was clinging to a chain-link fence, rigid, nearly paralyzed with the familiar, palpable panic. "You'll miss the bus," the teacher said crossly, trying to pull her away from the fence. A fellow student rushed over to help, but the teacher snapped, "Don't help her, she has to learn to help herself." The teacher walked away, leaving Jennifer sobbing and helpless.

Friends and another teacher finally got her onto the bus, but she recalls the experience as one of the most painful of all the painful memories over the years.

Things were not easy at home, either. As supportive as Jennifer's parents were, her mother Margot admits that she sometimes cracked under the day-to-day strain. "The clinging drove me nuts," she says. "One minute Jen would be doing fine, and the next she'd be grabbing me and holding on for dear life. There were times when I couldn't stand her to touch me anymore, I felt so suffocated. I'd yell at her to leave me alone, then I'd run somewhere and cry. I felt incredibly helpless and incredibly guilty. How can a mother not want to help her child?"

As the years brought more information about panic disorder and about the therapies, behavioral and chemical, that could help it, Jennifer gradually improved. One of the first medications found to be helpful for panic disorder was a class of drugs called tricyclic antidepressants. One of these drugs suppressed Jennifer's most distressing symptoms, and, together with therapy, helped her get through high school.

Jennifer also developed a remarkable ability to take charge of her life and to ask for the help she needed. She was determined to go away to college, and she added an unusual factor to her college decision-making: how possible the campus would be for her to navigate by herself. Before the first term opened, she and her parents mapped out routes from her dormitory to classroom buildings and to the locations of typical social events. Then they practiced them together over and over until she was confident enough to walk alone.

Jennifer also was very honest with her professors and fellow students about her disability. Her lack of embarrassment and matter-of-fact approach made it easy for them to accept, and she was always able to recruit someone to accompany her when necessary. It was her desire to educate others that first brought her to our organization.

These days, things are becoming less difficult for Jennifer, and her attending the ADAA meeting was a very special triumph.

When I called Jennifer at college to ask her to speak at our annual meeting, she accepted with delight, but she knew this would entail confronting a major hurdle.

Although her mother would be joining her at the conference in Chicago, they would be coming from separate cities, and Jennifer had never flown alone before. She wasn't particularly afraid of flying, but she was terrified at the thought of negotiating her way through a large airport with its wide-open corridors. Jennifer's mother Margot knew that Chicago's O'Hare Airport would be particularly difficult—the dizzying lights, long and narrow moving walkways and tremendous crowds would be overly stimulating to Jennifer. Ironically, the sense of excitement and drama that modern designers often try to achieve when creating public spaces can be a nightmarish maze of sensory overload to someone with panic disorder. Many patients notice that fluorescent lights, loud noises and bright colors can trigger a panic attack. What may be fun and exciting to many people can be overwhelming for someone like Jennifer.

With this in mind, Margot reserved a flight that would place her at O'Hare forty minutes before Jennifer's flight arrived, leaving enough time for her to walk over and meet Jennifer at her gate, which was at the opposite end of the airport.

Minutes prior to their scheduled landing, the pilot of Margot's plane announced they were in a holding pattern and would have to circle the airport for a while. Margot became frantic at the thought of Jennifer getting off the plane and not finding her waiting. She could barely contain herself when her plane finally landed forty-five minutes late. She charged off—almost missing Jennifer, who was standing at her mother's gate with an ear-to-ear grin across her face.

Jennifer began her conference speech by saying, "I no longer think about what I can't do, but instead think, how can I do it? I put one foot forward and keep walking."

I glanced over at Margot and saw the proud look of a mother who knew that she could finally let go of her daughter's hand.

13

Sylvia: The Impact on the Family

"YOU CAN'T BE a good mother and a good wife and be scared all of the time. A responsible mother is supposed to be there for her children."

To Sylvia, who was forty-eight when I first met her, being a good mother when her children were young included picking them up after school if the weather was bad, accompanying them on class trips or driving them to their friends' homes, and showing them how to face their fears.

Likewise, a devoted wife was supposed to be accessible to share in her husband's life. In Sylvia's marriage this meant accompanying her husband on business trips, attending office parties and other functions where spouses were invited, and being able to drive into town to meet her husband after work from time to time.

But what if a wife and a mother can't do these things? What if she becomes paralyzed with terror during a thunderstorm and can't pick the children up? What if she panics at the mere thought of taking the elevator to her husband's office or of driving on a highway during a class outing? What if she's so afraid her children will mimic her fearfulness that she makes excuse after excuse for her inability to do these things—but never tells her children the real reason?

■　■　■

Although illnesses, physical or psychological, happen to individuals, one person's disorder can exact a toll on everyone around him or her. If one member of a family becomes ill, the routine of the whole household can be disrupted. If the illness is short-lived, the family can return to its normal activities quickly and without lasting impact. But a chronic illness or one that is disabling is likely to have long-term effects on everyone involved in the day-to-day life of the person who is ill.

An anxiety disorder can be equally disruptive as many physical ailments, or even more so. Normal family or work activities may become difficult or impossible. Economic loss may occur within the family if the anxiety disorder limits a working member's ability to function on the job.

In addition, while there are certainly many instances where a parent disappoints a child or a spouse disappoints a mate, there are usually good reasons—or at least rational explanations—for such occurrences. But when an anxiety disorder is involved, such behavior becomes the rule rather than an occasional occurrence. Many people who suffer from an anxiety disorder spend a good deal of time making up excuses and/or manipulating people and situations to avoid facing the dreaded fears. It is often difficult or impossible for family members to see any rationale for the avoidance behavior. And because anxiety disorders absorb so much energy, those who suffer from them may also neglect other emotional issues in their closest relationships.

Sylvia was about halfway through her therapy for panic disorder and was participating in a support group. She felt triumphant about the progress she was making, but when I suggested to the group that they invite spouses to the next meeting, she jumped at the opportunity. "Frank says he's thrilled with what I'm doing," she said, "but sometimes I wonder. He makes little comments—like 'I hardly recognize my wife these days' or 'You don't seem to need me to drive you places anymore, so maybe I'll just stay home and you can go by yourself'—that really get under my skin. He says he's proud of me, but I'm not sure how he really feels about my doing things without him. Maybe I'm overreacting. I want to see how other couples are handling things."

A self-described "traditional male," Frank was a very successful business executive, the president of a large international consulting firm. He had always been very protective of Sylvia. Her discomfort distressed him greatly, and he attentively helped her avoid anxiety-producing situations. When they were first married and looking for an apartment in New York City, for example, he had instructed the real estate agent not to even show them any apartments above the third or fourth floor of a building. They found a third-floor apartment and Sylvia walked up and down the stairs several times a day, even after she had their first baby. Later, although Frank very much wanted her to accompany him on the business trips which took him all over the world, he knew that Sylvia was fearful of taking long airplane flights, so he never pressured her to join him. But all the time he was away he would feel anxious and guilty, partly because he felt badly that she was missing out on so much, and also because he was afraid that she might need him while he was gone and he wouldn't be there to help her.

Conversely, though, Frank also often felt angry and frustrated with Sylvia and with the situations created by her condition—emotions he hadn't shared with her. Not until he came to our group meeting, that is.

"It certainly was difficult to be in some interesting or romantic part of the world and find myself the only married man without his wife at every function," Frank admitted when I encouraged him to talk honestly about how Sylvia's condition had affected him. "Sometimes the hosts would even offer to 'arrange some entertainment' for me," he told the group. "I knew what that meant, and it made me feel humiliated and repelled—I really do love Sylvia. But there was a part of me that thought she'd be to blame if I did have a fling.

"On the other hand, I knew that if I pushed her to come on the trip with me—even if I simply suggested it—she would get so anxious that it would affect every other aspect of our lives. It seemed easier to simply resign myself to the fact that I had a wife who couldn't travel."

Sylvia looked up with sadness in her eyes. "Frank," she said, "there was a time, early in our marriage, when you would go off on one of your business trips and I was terrified that you would be tempted to cheat on me. But I felt I had no right to say anything to you. That night you left for Hawaii, I cried myself to sleep. It made me sick to realize that I was willing to risk losing you rather than to risk having an anxiety attack on the plane.

"And I knew in my heart that you resented my limitations," Sylvia continued. "I knew you hated always having to make excuses for me with your colleagues or our friends. And you were always so patient with me. You never pressured me to do things that might frighten me or make me uncomfortable.

"But sometimes now I can't help wondering," she said hesitantly, "whether I might have overcome some of my phobias sooner if you *hadn't* been so protective of me."

Where to push and where to hold back is always a tough dilemma for family members who want to be helpful.

Frank and Sylvia agreed to work toward finding a good middle ground. Frank would no longer *not* ask Sylvia to do things that he thought might make her anxious, and Sylvia agreed to at least attempt activities Frank suggested that she previously would have avoided. This is not as easy as it sounds. What if Sylvia wanted to say no for reasons other than her phobias, and how could she—or Frank, for that matter—be sure of the difference? They would need a new set of ground rules to negotiate those situations.

Recently, another patient, one of whose phobias was riding over bridges, told the people in her group that she rarely goes to restaurants she likes. "Whenever my husband suggests that we eat at a restaurant where we would have to cross a bridge, I have no trouble speaking up and insisting that we go someplace else.

"But then," she continued, "I feel guilty and readily agree to go to *any* other place he suggests—even if it's a place that I hate! The truth is," she went on, as the group members nodded their heads in recognition, "I rarely do anything just for myself because I'm always more concerned with pleasing my husband than pleasing myself. I feel so badly about the demands I make on him because of my phobia that I don't feel as if I have a right to ask him to accommodate my more trivial needs or interests."

During one of our private therapy sessions in which we were focusing on Sylvia's elevator phobia, I suggested that she attempt a solo ride without me. After we spent a few minutes doing some diaphragmatic breathing to calm her, Sylvia reluctantly agreed to ride in the elevator from the first to the second floor by herself—but only after I solemnly promised to run up the stairs to be waiting as the elevator doors opened. "Just in case I've passed out," she said, half joking and half seriously.

Sylvia *did* ride the elevator by herself that day—for the first time in over twenty-five years! When she stepped out, I hugged her quickly. She looked dazed, as though she was in a state of shock. "I've got to call Frank," were the first words out of her mouth.

Frank had always been available to take Sylvia's calls at his office, and this time was no exception. When she returned from the telephone with tears running down her cheeks, she told me that, although her call had pulled Frank out of a board of directors' meeting, he had insisted on hearing every small detail of her triumph.

Later that week Frank told the members of Sylvia's support group, "I remember Sylvia's phone call to me at my office when she went into labor with our first daughter, and, believe me, for her, riding up one floor in an elevator was almost as monumental an accomplishment as giving birth to our child!"

If Sylvia's children, two girls now college age, had been aware of her fears, as Frank was, at least they would have understood her strange absences from their lives. But they didn't know. They saw *other* mothers going places and doing things with their friends, and they knew their mother was different for some reason, but they didn't know why.

Sylvia avoided accompanying her daughters on class trips. They didn't know it was because she might have been obliged to drive on the highway.

She refused to go with her children on the train or subway. They couldn't know it was because she was certain she would have a panic attack and not be able to take care of them.

Whenever there was a rainstorm, or even the threat of one, her children learned to expect a message from the principal's office saying, "Your mother won't be picking you up today; you are to get a ride with Mrs. X." But they didn't know their mother was terrified of thunder.

Only after Sylvia began treatment did they learn what their mother had endured through their childhood. This revelation took place one night while both girls were home from college for vacation, and Sylvia and Frank invited them to join our weekly meeting. In a choked voice, Sylvia recalled all those years when she felt she had disappointed her children. As she described her frustration and guilt over not being able to pick them up at school in bad weather, she turned to her elder daughter and asked, "Do you remember?"

With tears in her eyes, her daughter replied, "Mom, of *course* I remember. *Why* didn't you ever tell us? Whenever there was a storm, we used to dread getting that note from the principal. We thought you didn't care about us or that other things you had to do were more important. We knew we wouldn't be left standing out in the rain, but we hated always having to ride with someone else's mom. It would have been far less hurtful for us to know you were scared. Even at that age, we could have understood that better than just wondering why you didn't come."

"I *couldn't* tell you," Sylvia said. "I was afraid if I did, you might somehow become infected by my fears. Or that you'd be ashamed of me. I was so embarrassed. I *wanted* to be the right kind of mom for you both, and I didn't want my problems to interfere with your living a normal life."

But of course they had.

Frank and Sylvia's younger daughter, particularly, has had difficulty trusting people. She believes that people close to her want to "protect" her from bad news and therefore withhold negative information. So she has lived with the nagging fear that something is wrong that she does not know about. Her inability to trust took its toll on the relationship with her boyfriend and impacted her relationships with her other friends as well.

Turning to Frank, the elder daughter sharply asked, "Why didn't *you* ever tell us about Mom's problem?"

"Well, now that we're talking openly about it," Frank quietly began, "this will sound foolish, but at the time, Mom was very ashamed of her behavior and I didn't want to embarrass her in front of you girls."

As it went on, the group session opened up many old wounds which the family agreed to use as stepping stones to begin a process of healing. They arranged to have a few private family therapy sessions while the girls were still in town.

Frank continued to attend the support group as he and Sylvia explored their new relationship.

"I know I risk sounding chauvinistic in saying this," he jokingly confessed the night after Sylvia had driven him to a restaurant on the other side of town, "but after all these years I feel kind of weird getting all dressed up to go out and having my wife drive!"

The women in the group hissed good-naturedly, but then they became serious as they looked at the circumstances that were at the heart of Frank's concern.

As someone recovers from an anxiety disorder, it's not uncommon for family members or friends suddenly to stop feeling "needed" or to feel their long-established roles are being disrupted.

The husband accustomed to coming home from work each night and finding his agoraphobic wife waiting for him may feel very uneasy when he comes home to an empty house. Even though he may realize that it's far healthier for his wife and their relationship for her to be able to do things on her own, her independence may be threatening to his identity.

Nor is it surprising when the wife of someone whose flying phobia had kept him from going on business trips now finds it difficult to deal with the fact that her husband is frequently away from the family.

Even though supportive spouses look forward to the day their loved one is free of his or her phobia, life with the "new" person that emerges undoubtedly means making some adjustments for both parties.

No one in Sylvia's group will forget the meeting when another member, Dolores, arrived with her husband, Stanley, both of them still fuming from a confrontation the night before.

Dolores was making tremendous strides in overcoming her agoraphobia, which had been so severe that she had not ventured out of the house without her husband in fifteen years. But the previous evening, Stanley had arrived home from work and discovered that Dolores was nowhere to be found. Nor was there any note indicating where she had gone or when she expected to return. By ten P.M., after calling all of the neighbors to see if they had seen or heard from her and exhausting all other possibilities to find out where she might be, Stanley finally called the police.

When Dolores walked into the house at ten forty-five with her arms loaded with packages, grinning from ear to ear—barely able to wait to share her victory with Stanley—she was greeted by a frantic husband and two policemen.

"Where were you? Why didn't you call? I was terrified that something had happened to you!" Stanley shouted, his face crimson red with anger and embarrassment.

Dolores told the group that late the previous afternoon, she had mustered up the courage to go to a shopping mall alone. Expecting only to be able to go in and out of the mall, much to her surprise and in spite of some occasional waves of anxiety, she found herself actually enjoying the experience—focusing on the stores and the people rather than her anticipated fears. Feeling "on a roll," Dolores walked into every single store in the mall and then, for the first time in many years, ate dinner in a restaurant by herself! Lost in her sense of elation and accomplishment, she was unaware of how much time had passed and at no time did it even occur to her that Stanley might be concerned about her whereabouts.

Stanley had calmed down somewhat as she explained, but he had been still too worn out from his own anxiety to say anything more than "Let's talk about it tomorrow."

Dolores had gone to bed that night deeply disappointed that he hadn't once commented on her success. And she was still furious that he had called the police. "You were treating me like a child," she protested in the group. "How can I get better if you don't trust me to go out on my own?"

Even as Dolores told her story, however, her anger subsided. During the discussion that followed, she acknowledged that Stanley always called when he was going to be late, and how alarmed she would be if he simply failed to show up. With the group's help they began to explore other changes that were likely to take place in their relationship as Dolores recovered.

That evening Dolores apologized to Stanley. "It's ironic that one of the things that has always made it so difficult for me to go places without you has been my fear of abandonment," she said. "But last night *I abandoned you.*"

Sylvia's long-term therapy goal was to accompany Frank on a trip to Israel for their twenty-fifth wedding anniversary. However, her fear was not exactly of flying; in fact, she had been able to take short flights with Frank. But she avoided flights that took over three hours. Why? Because her claustrophobia made it impossible for her to step into one of the tiny lavatories on a plane!

"Going into an airplane restroom," Sylvia told me, "is as frightening to me as the thought of getting into a coffin. It literally feels as though I were being buried alive."

But she was determined to try. In order to make the practice session as real as possible, I made arrangements for us to board a grounded DC-9 airplane at the airport.

"You go first," she said to me anxiously, as we stood outside the tiny bathroom at the end of the narrow aisle. I smiled at her reassuringly, walked in, closed the door, waited a few seconds, opened the door, and came out again.

"Now let's try it together," I said when I emerged.

That brought a burst of nervous laughter from Sylvia, as well as from the attendant who had accompanied us onto the plane.

"How can we?" Sylvia said. "We won't *fit*!"

But we did manage to fit. And so we practiced . . . and practiced . . . and practiced. First, both of us went in; then Sylvia went in alone, leaving the door open. Finally, after many laughs and a few tears, she took a deep breath, stepped into the restroom, and closed the door behind her.

A split second later, the door flew open and Sylvia burst out into the aisle!

"I did it! I did it!" she screamed.

By the time we left the plane nearly an hour later, an exhausted but exuberant Sylvia had stayed in the lavatory alone for a full three minutes. She now felt confident she would be able to make the twelve-hour flight to Israel.

She and Frank planned their trip with great excitement, but it wasn't until I received a postcard a week after they had arrived in Israel that I was to learn how Sylvia had fared with her challenge. I laughed aloud in my mailroom as I read: "Jerilyn, I had a good flight over. And I *went—by myself*!—twice!"

14

Darlene: Fighting the System

THE CALLER HAD a low, soft voice with a slight Southern accent. She said she was twenty-six years old and lived alone; her husband had left her. "I was watching that program," she said, "and I think I have what that woman has. I thought I was going crazy." And then she began to cry.

We talked for a long time.

She told me her name was Darlene and that her life had been "going along fine" until the day that she and her husband, Kevin, stopped at a drive-through restaurant for something to eat on the way to the movies. As she began to eat her food, she suddenly felt as though she couldn't breathe or swallow. Everything seemed to fade away, and she broke out in a cold sweat.

"I'm going to choke to death," she remembered thinking.

As Darlene began coughing and gasping for air, Kevin quickly pulled over to the side of the road. He patted her back as she tried to force the food up from her throat, but there didn't seem to be anything there. She stopped gagging, but immediately became hysterical. She kept trying to swallow but couldn't. As though from someplace far away, Darlene remembered hearing Kevin say something about calling an ambulance and her own voice replying no, she didn't want to go to the hospital.

The rest of that evening was fuzzy to Darlene, although she recalled going home and lying in her bed, exhausted, scared, and confused from her experience. She was relieved at being able to swallow again and for the fact that whatever had happened to her had passed. But she was left wondering exactly *what* it was that had happened, *why* it had happened, and whether or not it would happen *again*.

The choking sensation and panic about not being able to swallow were the first manifestations of the anxiety disorder that gradually, over the next two years, left Darlene housebound, penniless, and alone—the state she was in when she telephoned me that afternoon.

"Do you think you could help me?" she asked, and added in a broken whisper, "and does it cost anything?"

My heart sank. "Do you have any health insurance?" I asked.

"No," she said. Nor did she have a steady source of income. After Kevin left, which had been over a year earlier, she had started babysitting for children in her building to pay the bills, but lately business had been very slow. She had difficulty collecting her meager alimony payments from Kevin, and her parents—who blamed her for the breakup of her marriage and accused her of developing her problem to get attention—were unwilling to give her more than an occasional small amount of money. She was barely able to pay her rent and buy food. She had sold most of her possessions.

Could I help her?

I listened to more of her story. She had become so afraid of eating that her weight had dropped from 168 to 103 pounds in less than six months. One doctor told her she had anorexia nervosa; another said she was having a nervous breakdown and prescribed Valium. But taking a pill involved swallowing, so she never filled the prescription.

Haunted by her fear of choking, even when she didn't have food in her mouth, she became reluctant to go anyplace by herself. When she no longer felt safe leaving her house, even with Kevin, he had used force to get her to leave—sometimes dragging her by her hair through the door. The explosive arguments that Darlene and Kevin had because of her "unwillingness" to leave the house ended with his walking out for good.

Darlene's only source of comfort was the one luxury item in her house she hadn't sold: her television. And that was how she saw me and learned that people in her situation could get help.

How could I *not* help her?

It was a longer distance to Darlene's apartment than I had anticipated.

I had agreed to meet with her for a few sessions without charge, just to get her started toward recovery. I hoped I could teach her enough coping skills so she would be able to leave her house and work a steady job. Some financial security would enable her to receive the kind of ongoing treatment that she needed.

When I first walked into the apartment, which was as grim and barren as she had described it, Darlene handed me a stack of medical reports. As I suspected after talking to her on the phone, there was no indication of any physical abnormality or illness that could account for her symptoms.

Tears rolled down Darlene's face as she described going from one doctor to the next, scraping up every penny to pay her bills. But no one had been able to give her any explanation for her symptoms. Nor was she able to get any relief from them. The television show she had seen and a magazine article she had subsequently read provided enough pertinent information for a self-diagnosis. By the time I left her apartment an hour later, I had confirmed in my own mind what Darlene had figured out for herself: She was suffering from panic disorder with agoraphobia.

I began working with Darlene as I had with Grace: one step at a time. We engaged Darlene's friend Paula to act as her "support person" and help her practice the things she learned during our therapy sessions. Darlene was very motivated to get better and made tremendous progress from the beginning, but there were many obstacles in her way. Because she had neglected her physical health, she was badly in need of minor foot surgery and dental care, and was often in a great deal of discomfort and pain. And although he had been abusive, she missed Kevin terribly and repeatedly berated herself for their breakup. Her ability to be self-supporting, even to fulfill her most basic needs, was in jeopardy.

It surprised me to learn that Darlene was not receiving any Social Security benefits. I asked her why; had she not applied?

She explained that before she became housebound, she had worked as a security guard for a federal agency. After her condition had forced Darlene to stop working, her Social Security disability claim was rejected because she had been unable to provide a correct medical diagnosis. I urged her to refile, after which she did begin receiving a small monthly payment.

Because of Darlene's gratitude for the television show that had led to her treatment, one of her fantasies was that she would like to join with me in educating others about anxiety disorders when she was well enough. I tucked that away in the back in my mind.

The thought didn't stay tucked away for long, however, because three months after I first met Darlene I received a call from the producer of a local television talk show. Would I be willing to come on the show and discuss agoraphobia, and could I bring someone with me who would be willing to openly talk about his or her personal experience with the disorder?

At this point, with my occasional visits to her home and Paula's steady, hands-on support and encouragement, Darlene was able to walk around her neighborhood and go into a few local stores. She had applied for a job as a security guard in a nearby building. She had even ventured into a restaurant with Paula and managed to finish an entire bowl of soup. But she had not yet ridden in a car or walked beyond a half-mile radius from her home. The television station in downtown Washington, D.C., was thirty minutes away.

"Go on television with you? Wow—I'd love to do that!" she said when I called. But then her voice cracked. "Jerilyn, you know I can't go downtown."

But Darlene did go downtown. And she did go on television. And she touched the hearts of many people—several of whom, like Darlene, found out for the first time that they had a treatable illness.

A week later Darlene shared with me a letter she had written to a friend.

"I was a bird whose wing had been wounded," she wrote. "My wing is healing now and I'm getting ready to take off. Soon I'll be soaring through life."

Indeed Darlene did begin to soar. Over the next two years she called me regularly to report on her progress. She maintained steady work as a security guard, became actively involved in a local church group, and was able to drive out of her neighborhood with Paula. And she and Kevin began talking about a reconciliation.

In the short amount of time we had spent together, Darlene had accomplished more than I had anticipated. But then I didn't hear from her for several months, and I became concerned and telephoned. A recording said the phone had been disconnected; there was no forwarding number.

I sent a telegram: "Darlene—is everything okay? Please call. Jerilyn." She called.

There was a catch in her throat, and then sobbing. She was staying home in her apartment again. She had lost her job. Kevin was gone. Paula had moved back to Kansas City to care for her sick mother. Darlene's phone had been disconnected because she couldn't pay her bill. She was using her next-door neighbor's phone.

It was just like before, she said—only worse, because this time she blamed herself. She had had two panic attacks at work; then she began taking days off for fear of having another. Calling her irresponsible, her employer told her to leave. She asked Kevin to help her practice after Paula left, but he had no patience. Instead, he bullied her, and he had become abusive again. As frightened as she was to be alone, she mustered up the courage to kick him out three weeks after he moved back in.

When I asked why she hadn't called me, she replied she hadn't wanted to bother me; I'd already done so much for her. Again she was isolated and penniless; she couldn't possibly pay for treatment.

Darlene was furious at herself. How could this have happened? In such a short time she had found a new life—and in an even shorter time, it had slipped through her fingers.

At that time, Darlene was paying $325 a month for her apartment, and her income was $387 per month from Social Security and $68 in food stamps. But desperate though she was, Darlene had not been idle. Not wanting to call me, but knowing that she needed the kind of therapy I had begun with her, she had put together a list of all the mental health facilities in her area that she thought might help her. She knew that without health insurance her options would be limited, but it turned out that things were even bleaker than Darlene had anticipated. In call after call, as soon as she indicated she couldn't pay for treatment, the response was the same: "Sorry, but we can't help you. Did you try calling the Community Mental Health Center?"

Yes, Darlene had called the Community Mental Health Center (CMHC). Community mental health centers, or agencies as some are called, are the providers of last resort for persons who cannot afford to pay for treatment and do not have any personal health insurance. Funded by the federal government under the 1963 Community Mental Health Center Construction Act, they were originally designed to make mental health care equally available to all patients, regardless of diagnostic classification.

In 1981, however, the Reagan Administration sharply reduced federal funding and turned the financing and oversight of CMHCs over to the states. At the same time, there was widespread "deinstitutionalization," in which patients in large state mental hospitals were, in effect, turned out in the streets. Responsibility for this population was largely transferred to the CMHCs. Not surprisingly, state administrations told the CMHCs to focus on those with conditions such as schizophrenia and manic-depressive illness. Priority was specified for those patients who had suffered a psychotic episode or been hospitalized for a psychiatric illness during the previous year.

Today, anxiety-disorder patients total less than 10 percent of the CMHCs' clients, though their percentage is higher in the population requiring mental-health care.

As Darlene quickly discovered, treating people with anxiety disorders was a low priority for the CMHC in her community. Frustrated with talking to people who were unwilling or unable to help her, she succeeded in having her call put through to the director of the CMHC. She told the director that if she could just find someone to help her for a few sessions, she was sure that she would be able to get out again and go back to work.

The director was sympathetic. There was only one problem: She had never met anyone with agoraphobia and didn't know a thing about it. But she suggested that if Darlene wanted to set up an appointment and come in to the clinic, she would make sure that someone would be available to help her. This was *after* Darlene had told the director that she was not even able to walk from her apartment to the corner mailbox.

When she hung up the phone, Darlene felt as if she had reached the end. She desperately needed treatment—she even knew what kind of treatment—but she had nowhere else to turn.

Listening to Darlene, I, too, felt helpless. I had moved my office and was too far away to begin therapy on a regular basis. At this point she needed other assistance, as well: financial help to pay her bills and for proper nutrition; ongoing therapy; and medical attention for her progressively worsening foot and dental problems.

I felt strongly that Darlene also needed medication for her anxiety disorder, although she had previously refused to consider it. A physician who was sensitive to her concerns might be able to convince her that medication would not "mess up her mind"—a fear initially shared by many patients.

I listed every program I could think of that might offer free treatment, including anxiety-disorder clinical trials, treatment programs at the National Institute of Mental Health, and various local academic institutions and hospitals.

Darlene called a few days later to say she had pursued every lead I had given her, and they had all come to a dead end.

The term *chronically mentally ill* was defined before anxiety disorders were recognized as a separate group of ailments. As a result, few resources are set aside for anxiety-disorder patients, even though most anxiety disorders *are* chronic. Many recover fully, but like those prone to high blood pressure or migraine headaches, people who have had an anxiety disorder remain vulnerable to relapses. Nevertheless, if a particular type of treatment has worked previously, it will work again. Yet under the current system, anxiety disorders—the most treatable of mental illnesses—go largely untreated. Another painful irony is that anxiety-disorder patients, denied access to CMHCs because they are not sick enough, are frequently denied health insurance coverage because they are said to have a "chronic" preexisting condition!

People with anxiety disorders are falling through the cracks in our public mental-health-care programs.

Darlene had already proved that she could become functional with appropriate treatment in spite of the severity of her condition and her other psychological and physical problems. But because her condition was not technically defined as "chronic," and because she had not been hospitalized, she was discriminated against *on the basis of her illness*. In effect, the community mental health centers have been forced to implement a form of mental-health-care rationing that undercuts the original rationale for the CMHC network.

Many of the letters that come to the Anxiety Disorders Association of America are from people like Darlene who desperately need treatment and can't afford it. A thirty-two-year-old agoraphobic woman with a ten-year-old child writes, "In the last year I have been completely housebound. I cannot shop for food or clothes for my son. I am living on welfare right now, which is $249 a month with $50 a month child support. My rent is $285 a month. I'm writing you to find out where I can turn to get some help. I cannot find anyone to counsel me at my home. . . ."

Attached to her letter is an official case sheet from the Department of Health and Human Services. It states: "The medical evidence shows that you are subject to anxiety or panic attacks which make you afraid to go out." Then it continues: "We have determined that your condition is not severe enough to keep you from working. . . . If your condition gets worse and keeps you from working, write, call or visit any Social Security office about filing another application."

Or consider the closing lines of a letter written to me by a father of three, whose inability to find affordable treatment has kept him unemployed and housebound for several years: "The system as it stands today *pays* people to be *disabled* by their disorder, but not to be treated for it. I, for one, would much prefer to be able to go back to work and become a taxpayer than to be a tax burden."

In Darlene's case, we had a stroke of good luck. Not long after she reported reaching a dead end, I received a call from a graduate social work student who wanted to do some practice training under my supervision. Working with Darlene was an ideal opportunity for a trainee. I was able to arrange for the student to meet with her once a week, and Darlene began to get some of the treatment she needed. It certainly wouldn't solve all of her problems, but it would enable her to get back on her feet. And since this was a training experience for the student intern, there would be no fee.

But I continue to worry about Darlene. Should she need additional treatment later on, she will be cast on her own resources once again. And I worry about the countless other Darlenes who could get better, who could live full and productive lives and are denied the means to do so.

PART THREE

Recovery from Panic
Disorder and Phobia:
A Self-Help Program

15

Setting Goals and Using the
Daily Task Sheet

I NOW WANT to share with you the information that I give to
my phobic and panic disorder patients while they are in my twelve-
week group therapy program. You can use this treatment and self-
help manual as an adjunct to your individual therapy, incorporate it
into a self-help group you belong to or might wish to start, or follow
it on your own. Keep in mind, however that this manual is *not a
substitute* for treatment. The majority of people who enter my
group program are simultaneously receiving either one-on-one
cognitive-behavioral therapy, medication, or a combination of both,
on the basis of individual assessment and need. Therefore, while
you can expect to make significant strides in overcoming your
anxiety disorder by following the suggestions in the forthcoming
chapters, this information is *most effective* when used in combination with professional treatment.

The Anxiety Disorders Association of America (ADAA) can
provide you with the names of mental health professionals in your
city who specialize in the treatment of anxiety disorders. The
organization can also provide you with a list of local self-help
groups (see the address of ADAA in the back of this book).

I strongly recommend, if you have *not* had a complete physical in the past two years, that you do so prior to beginning any treatment or self-help program. Since many of the symptoms of phobic and panic disorders mimic those of other physical illnesses, it is important to make sure that your problem is correctly diagnosed.

It is impossible to describe a self-help or a treatment program that will work for everyone, so feel free to select and use the pieces of my program that best address your individual needs. Many of the exercises I suggest can be done with a trusted friend or family member, or on your own. Some of these exercises and coping techniques come from my own personal experience of overcoming a phobia. Others I have learned directly from my colleagues or developed by incorporating data from scientific studies into my practice. Many of the most creative ideas have come from my patients themselves.

I urge you to try as many of these suggestions as you can. If one thing doesn't work, try something else, or a combination of things. It is best to be flexible and to have a variety of ways to approach your problem. You will quickly discover what works best for you.

GOAL SETTING

When patients first enter my group they are often concerned that they will "catch" each other's symptoms. I assure them that if that was the case *I* would be worse than housebound—I'd be "bed-bound" by now! While they may *think* about each other's symptoms after hearing them, symptoms are *not* contagious.

Another concern people have is that they will sit around week after week and hear people complain about how much their anxiety disorder is disrupting their life. We all know that having a phobic or panic disorder can wreak havoc on every aspect of one's life, but focusing on the negative is neither constructive nor productive. So instead, at the first session, rather than have everyone talk about their symptoms and disabilities, I ask the group members to introduce themselves to each other by telling *what they will work toward achieving* in the next twelve weeks. We identify ourselves by where we are going rather than by where we have been.

I ask you now to think about your own goals. Decide on a short-term (six-week) goal and a long-term (twelve-week) goal. Make your goals as concrete and specific as possible. Your six-week goal should answer the question "What task or activity could I do that would demonstrate to me that I was making significant progress in overcoming my anxiety disorder?" Or "If I could——I would consider myself well on my way to recovery."

Your twelve-week goal should answer the question "What task or activity could I do that would demonstrate to me that my anxiety disorder is no longer interfering in my life?" Or "If I could——I would consider myself recovered."

When setting your goals, it is very important to focus on the *activity* you wish to accomplish rather than on your feelings. If your fear of being in public places has prevented you from going grocery shopping, for example, it will be tempting to say, "My twelve-week goal is to walk into a store and not have any anxiety." But true growth comes when you are able to function *in spite of* anxiety and even panic. Therefore, a productive goal would be, "In twelve weeks I would like to do the weekly grocery shopping for my family."

As we're setting goals in our first session, many of my patients hesitate to set the goals they would really like to achieve, either because they can't possibly imagine doing the things they have been unable to do for so long or because they are afraid they will feel forced to do something they may not be ready for.

Eleanor, a woman who had a phobia of driving on any road at all, reluctantly set her twelve-week goal as "Driving on the super-highway to my son and daughter-in-law's home by myself." She later admitted that when she set down that goal she thought she must be out of her mind, since she didn't really believe she could reach it at all, let alone in twelve weeks. But that was what she *wanted* to do and I encouraged her to go for it.

With the goal of visiting her son and his wife tucked way back in her mind, Eleanor worked very hard, practicing every day, taking one step at a time. Week after week she faced new challenges: driving around her neighborhood, expanding to outlying areas, and gradually working her way onto the highway. During the *tenth* session, she proudly reported to the group that the previous after-noon she had driven, by herself, on the superhighway, to her son's house! After their applause and hugs quieted down, Eleanor told the group that although part of her didn't believe she could possibly achieve her goal that first night of the group, having something so seemingly monumental to work toward motivated her to take the smaller steps necessary to get there. And she "arrived" far sooner than she ever imagined she would.

As Eleanor learned, it is *always* better to set goals that feel overly ambitious rather than ones that are safe and comfortable. This may seem frightening or overwhelming to you, but keep in mind that once you learn how to cope with the unpleasant sensa-tions of anxiety and panic you will be able to do *whatever* you want to do.

Think of it this way: If you woke up tomorrow with a guarantee that you would never have another panic attack, what would you like to do? Go ahead and write that down on the form below for your twelve-week goal; don't worry about how "impossible" it seems. Your twelve-week goal should be anything that anyone leading a normal life would be able to do almost "without thinking about it."

For your six-week goal you can select something that is either a step along the way toward reaching your bigger goal, or some-thing completely different that would still indicate to you that you were very much closer to recovery. For example, if you are cur-rently unable to travel away from home at all, your twelve-week "ambitious" goal might be to take an *airplane* trip by yourself to visit a friend or relative. Your six-week goal might be to spend one evening away from home with your spouse or another "safe" person.

After you've established your goals write them down here.

My six-week goal is _____

My twelve-week goal is _____

You're now ready to begin using your Daily Task Sheets.

KEEPING A DAILY TASK SHEET

When I first introduce the idea of keeping a daily log of practice activities, some of my patients balk at how inconvenient and tedious they anticipate this will be. However, as they complete the sheets, they very quickly discover that what they learn about themselves and their disorder, and the rewards of seeing concrete evidence of their progress, is a very valuable part of the recovery process.

The progress you make is not always immediately obvious. Often progress not only seems slow, but is quite subtle. The Daily Task Sheet helps you track this subtle progress. I recall one woman who came to me for treatment because she was no longer able to work and was very close to being housebound. Nine weeks into the program, she was able to spend many hours every day outside her house. But she was upset because she was unable to drive alone. When she looked back at her Daily Task Sheets, she realized that she now left the house frequently; she could take public transportation by herself; and she had resumed a full-time job. Despite her disappointment that she still could not drive, the Daily Task Sheet told a different story: She had made tremendous progress. When she saw what she used to avoid and was now able to do—all written in her own hand—she was able to acknowledge her accomplishment.

You can make copies of the Daily Task Sheet on page 175 or adapt the form for your own use. There is a sample of a completed Daily Task Sheet on pages 176–77. Be sure to date each sheet, and to keep your completed sheets together in a folder or notebook.

In the pages that follow, I will discuss each item on the Task Sheet in turn.

Your Weekly Goal

Begin each week by setting a specific Weekly Goal, a task or an activity that you would like to accomplish by the end of the week. As you did when setting your six- and twelve-week goals, make your weekly goal *specific* and *concrete*. Examples of Weekly Goals include:

1. Attend and remain through a class or lecture.
2. Get a haircut.
3. Ride the subway alone to the department store.
4. Give a dinner party.
5. Use the elevator to visit a friend who lives on the fifteenth floor.

Your Positive Statement

Find SOMETHING positive to say about yourself and write it down each week. It can be a direct personal affirmation, such as "I am a loving person," "I am capable of being all I want to be," or "I have a terrific sense of humor!" Or it can be a positive statement about your ability and/or determination to tackle your problem, such as "I made significant progress in confronting my phobia last week," "I no longer need to be afraid of having a panic attack," or "I am able to learn from my difficult days."

To get the most out of your Daily Task Sheet, fill in the first row of entries for each day *prior to* beginning a practice session. Complete the second row immediately *after* you've finished.

Your Daily Task

Choose Daily Tasks that will help bring you closer to reaching your weekly goal. Again, daily tasks should be *specific* and *concrete*. Examples of Daily Tasks to help reach the above-mentioned weekly goals might include:

1. Select and sign up for a lecture or class.
2. Visit the hair salon with a friend who is getting a haircut.
3. Ride the subway for one stop with my spouse.
4. Make a list of the people I will invite to my dinner party.
5. Ride the elevator for one floor in the department store.

DAILY TASK SHEET

Week of: _____

Goal: _____

_____

Positive statement: _____

_____

DAY:

Before Practice	Task			Time of Day	With Whom	HPL	Out

After Practice	HAL	How Long	Physical Symptoms	Thoughts	Helpful Techniques	Satisfaction

DAY:

Before Practice	Task			Time of Day	With Whom	HPL	Out

After Practice	HAL	How Long	Physical Symptoms	Thoughts	Helpful Techniques	Satisfaction

DAILY TASK SHEET

Week of: __Oct. 3__

Goal: __Drive to White Flint Mall (about 5 miles) with Carol__

Positive statement: __Each step I take, no matter how small, brings me__
__closer to recovery.__

<table>
<tr><td rowspan="2">MONDAY</td><td>Before Practice</td><td colspan="2">Task</td><td colspan="2">Time of Day</td><td colspan="2">With Whom</td><td>HPL</td><td>Out</td></tr>
</table>

		Task		Time of Day		With Whom		HPL	Out
MONDAY	Before Practice	Drive to the grocery store (4 blocks away.)		1:00 P.M.		Carol		10	I can pull over anytime I want.

		HAL	How Long	Physical Symptoms	Thoughts	Helpful Techniques	Satisfaction
	After Practice	6	15 mins.	A little light-headed. Heart racing (a lot!) Sweaty palms	I used to do this without even thinking about it. I feel like such a baby.	Telling myself it's okay to feel embarrassed. Focusing on things around me – the trees, the houses, other cars. Watching my breathing.	Yes

		Task		Time of Day		With Whom		HPL	Out
TUESDAY	Before Practice	Pick up my son from school (10 blocks away).		3:00 P.M.		Carol		10	Carol can drive on the way back if I feel too bad.

		HAL	How Long	Physical Symptoms	Thoughts	Helpful Techniques	Satisfaction
	After Practice	5	20 min. (there and back!)	Racing heart Slight headache Tightness in back of neck	This isn't as scary as I thought it would be. What if I panic while my son is in the car?	Picturing my son's face when I pull up to the school. Counting backward from 100 by threes	Yes

176

		Task		Time of Day	With Whom	HPL	Out
WEDNESDAY	Before Practice	Drive to the dry-cleaner's (cross a major intersection)		8:30 A.M.	My husband	10	My husband can take over the wheel if I panic.

		HAL	How Long	Physical Symptoms	Thoughts	Helpful Techniques	Satisfaction
	After Practice	9	20 min.	Trembling Heart pounding Waves of nausea Tightening around my head and neck	I can't stand these feelings. I'm really losing it. What if I panic and have an accident?	Telling myself that the worst that will happen is I'll FEEL BAD. I'm not going to die or lose control. Focusing on things around me. Talking to my husband.	Yes

		Task		Time of Day	With Whom	HPL	Out
THURSDAY	Before Practice	Drive to the bowling alley (use four-lane highway)		2:00 P.M.	Carol and Jane	9	If I have to pull over I can make believe I have a flat tire.

		HAL	How Long	Physical Symptoms	Thoughts	Helpful Techniques	Satisfaction
	After Practice	2	15 min. each way	Sweaty palms Slight heart racing	I can't believe I'm driving my friends someplace! I feel really good.	Snapping the rubber band on my wrist. Talking to my friends — a lot!	Yes

		Task		Time of Day	With Whom	HPL	Out
FRIDAY	Before Practice	Drive to White Flint		10:00 A.M.	Carol	10	I can try again tomorrow if I feel too awful.

		HAL	How Long	Physical Symptoms	Thoughts	Helpful Techniques	Satisfaction
	After Practice	7	40 min.	Dizzy Tension in head and neck Pounding heart	What if I panic and swerve into another lane? What if I pass out?	Diaphragmatic breathing Telling Carol what "level" I'm at and noticing which thoughts make it go up.	Yes

Whenever possible, choose activities that have "real-life" meaning to you, as opposed to ones that are simply "practice for the sake of practicing." This isn't possible all of the time. But the more you can build your practice sessions into your daily routine activities, the sooner you will find yourself doing the everyday things you have been avoiding—without even thinking about them. (See Chapter 17 for more about this.)

Time of Day

Write down the *time of day* you plan to practice. This is important because it will push you to commit to a specific time to begin your practice session, no matter how you feel. This is helpful in learning to deal with anticipatory anxiety and in learning to face your fears at both "good" and "bad" times. Knowing in advance how long you plan to stay in the anxiety-provoking situation will help prevent the tendency to keep going only until you feel you must leave.

With Whom

Will you do this task alone or with a support person? (Write "Alone" or your support person's name.)

Highest Projected Level (HPL)

To compare how you *actually* feel when carrying out your Daily Task with how you *expect* to feel, begin by writing down, prior to each practice session, the highest *projected* level of anxiety you anticipate reaching, using a scale of 0 to 10. Zero means "no anxiety" and 10, "absolute panic." This is a purely subjective rating—there is no right or wrong. Simply note the highest level *you think* you will reach during your practice session. If a family member or friend will be helping you complete your Daily Task, it is important to share this information with that person. Labeling your anticipated anxiety will help your support person have a more concrete understanding of how difficult and courageous it is for you to confront seemingly nonthreatening situations.

Outs

An Out is anything—realistic or imaginary—that helps you get *in* to the feared place or situation by giving you a guaranteed *out*. It's your "escape clause"—even when you don't think you have one. When establishing an Out allow yourself to be creative and imaginative. And, it's okay to be completely irrational! One I personally used was "If I'm in a high building and I really get out of control, I'll ask someone to *knock me out!!*" Of course, I would never do this and, in any case, by the time I finished looking around the room to find someone to "take me out of my misery" the panicky feelings would have subsided. But just knowing that there was *some way out*—no matter how irrational—would allow me to go IN!

Make sure you select Outs—not Crutches.

An Out is anything that gets you in and keeps you in.

A Crutch is something you use to keep yourself out.

To make this clearer, consider these Crutches. Someone who has agoraphobia might depend on someone else to do the shopping. Someone who feels panic when she drives on a highway might limit herself to driving on side streets only. A person who fears elevators might walk up steps to avoid using the elevator. Someone with a fear of flying might get drunk before boarding an airplane. All of these are Crutches because they help the person evade or avoid situations and/or unpleasant sensations, rather than face their fears.

Having an Out, on the other hand, enables you to go forward and confront the situation with a greater amount of ease. Knowing you *can* leave will lessen your urge *to* leave. For instance, if you have a problem in high-rise buildings, the Out might be to note where the exits are on each floor, telling yourself that *if* you need to escape, you can. If you are afraid of having a panic attack in a restaurant, give yourself permission to leave *if* you need to, even if

179

you are in the middle of a meal. If driving on the highway is something you have avoided, tell yourself that *if* you want to pull off the road, that's okay. I'm not suggesting you use these Outs, but knowing that they are available and that you won't be "trapped" will help you enter anxiety-provoking situations.

It is always helpful to give yourself an Out, even if the Out does not seem appropriate (like my thinking that I would ask someone to knock me out if I got panicky). If telling yourself you can pull over anytime you want gets you *on* the highway, that's certainly better than saying, "I *can't* go on the highway because once I get on I'm stuck" and not driving on the highway at all. (You may be thinking, "But that would be so embarrassing!" But what if you had a flat tire and had to pull over? Would you not do so for fear of being embarrassed?). If standing in a grocery line is difficult, tell yourself that if you absolutely had to, you could leave your shopping cart and exit from the store. Remind yourself that the worst that would happen is that someone else (who would probably never see you or recognize you again) would have to put your groceries away. So what? If you suddenly developed a bad migraine headache and had to abandon your shopping cart and immediately go home, would you be concerned about who saw you leave? If giving yourself the option to leave a store that you would otherwise avoid enables you to go *into* that store, that's a perfectly acceptable and constructive Out.

Invariably, someone who has a flying phobia asks, "If I'm in the air and want to get off the plane, what's my Out?" One of my patients came up with a creative "airplane Out" and, although its as irrational as the one I use in high buildings (remember, fantasy is okay), many people find it helpful. This patient called the FAA and asked how long it takes to land a plane in an emergency. He was told that in the United States a plane is always within twenty minutes of an airport. He then decided that *if* he had a panic attack and *had* to get off the plane, he could tell the flight attendant that he was having a heart attack. The pilot would *have* to land the plane. My patient rationalized that he could "bear" suffering for twenty minutes. Having this Out enabled him to get on the plane and eventually conquer his flying phobia.

Some of my patients protest that the Outs seem foolish or inappropriate. Some of the most creative ones *are*! And, if keeping them in the back of your head enables you to move forward, so what? Compared to living with fear and avoidance, feeling silly is a small risk.

It's a good idea actually to play out your worst fantasies of embarrassing yourself or feeling foolish. Go ahead and take an Out while you are feeling okay and observe what happens.

- Pull off to the side of the highway—carefully, of course—and notice whether anyone is paying attention to you.
- Leave your groceries in the cart and walk out of the store. Look around to see who's watching.
- Walk out of the restaurant in the middle of a meal and then return. Did anybody look at you funny?
- Tell the bus driver you feel sick and want to be let off immediately. Did people think you were weird, or were they concerned that you might be ill?
- Leave your seat in the middle of a performance. Did anybody point their finger at you or think less of you for leaving?

Think of how you would react to seeing someone leave a restaurant in the middle of a meal or walk out of a theater during a performance. You might be puzzled, empathetic, amused, annoyed, or just indifferent, but certainly not as shocked or horrified as you think others would be if it were you.

You probably would not even notice—being, like most people, too concerned about yourself to notice what others are doing. The experience of having taken an Out while practicing will enable you to confront the feared situation more easily the next time, since you will now know that if you must leave, the consequences are not so terrible.

Highest Actual Level (HAL)

After you have completed a task, note the level of anxiety you *actually* reached when you were in the situation. What was your highest *actual* level of anxiety?

Something interesting usually happens when you compare the HPL and the HAL. The anxiety level that you actually reach is *almost always* lower than the one you thought you would reach. It is very important to pay attention to this so that the next time you think about entering a situation where you are afraid you will experience a high level of anxiety, you can recall that *the last time was not as bad as you anticipated*. Even if you do reach a high level, you will begin to notice that your anxiety level will *always* come back down if you *stay* in the situation—no matter how difficult it is to do so.

How Long?

Note *how long* you spent in your practice situation. This doesn't mean how long you felt uncomfortable, but rather the length of the practice session itself. How long did you stay in the store, ride the elevators, or drive on the highway?

Physical Symptoms

Note any distressing physical sensations or symptoms that you experienced while anticipating or confronting your anxiety-provoking situation. Did your chest or throat tighten or your heart beat rapidly? Did your palms feel sweaty? Did you feel dizzy or "spacey" or have an upset stomach?

As you continue to record these symptoms, you are likely to see that they change over time, and from practice to practice. Seeing your symptoms as a response to your anxiety-provoking situation also tends to make them less frightening. You will begin to say to yourself, "My heart is racing because I am anxious," rather than "I wonder whether I'm having a heart attack."

Thoughts

Write down any thoughts that increased or lessened your feelings of anxiety prior to and during your practice session. Notice whether your thoughts involved magical or exaggerated thinking, and if so, how your level of anxiety was affected.

If you found that a particular phrase or saying works to lessen your anxiety, be sure to note it for future use.

Helpful Techniques

Note any helpful techniques that you used to complete your task. Even if you used something that seemed silly or insignificant, write it down—remember that *anything* that helps you enter into and remain in an anxiety-producing situation is a fair gambit. By writing down what was most helpful each time you approach a task, you'll develop a handy list of what works best for you. You'll find many helpful techniques throughout this book, in the stories about the people who worked toward overcoming their anxiety disorder and in all the chapters of the self-help section. Of course, many of the most helpful ideas will come from your own imagination!

Satisfaction

Were you *satisfied* with your efforts to complete your task? Jot down "yes" or "no," remembering to evaluate yourself in terms of what you *did* rather than how you *felt*. You may be tempted to feel satisfied only when you accomplish you task without feeling high levels of anxiety. But remember, the more you are able to remain in uncomfortable situations *despite* the anxiety or panic, the more progress you will make in desensitizing yourself to the uncomfortable feelings.

You deserve to feel good about yourself if you made it to the store even if you *did* pull off the road for a few minutes. The fact that you got back on the road again and completed the task marks a successful practice session—you should feel proud of yourself!

While you're working with your Daily Task Sheets, make a "contract" with a family member or friend to be your support person. Ask you support person to review the task sheet with you at the end of each week. Encourage that person to be tough with you. He or she should insist that the sheets be completed each week. That way, you know there is someone else who cares—someone who will make you think twice about skipping a practice session or missing your homework. Finally, be *sure* this person is aware of the courage it takes for you to complete each task so you can feel free to share your triumphs.

16

Applying the Six Points

IN CHAPTER 10 I discussed the Six Points of Contextual Therapy developed by Dr. Manuel Zane (repeated on page 186). I teach these to all of my phobic and panic-disorder patients, as they are extremely helpful in managing both anticipatory anxiety and the panic attacks themselves. The concepts taught in the Six Points are compatible with most cognitive-behavioral and pharmacological treatment programs. However, if there is something presented here that doesn't apply to you or is different from what you are learning in your own therapy, feel free to adapt them to conform to your individual needs and therapeutic program.

PUTTING THE SIX POINTS TO WORK

When you are in a panic-producing situation (or anticipate entering one), the tendency is to focus on and react to imaginary dangers, most of which are in the future and, of course, do not happen, e.g., "What if I lose control of myself?"; "What if I have a heart attack or pass out?"; "What if I run wildly through the store?"

By understanding and practicing the concepts outlined in the Six Points, you will learn how to focus on and react to the present

185

THE SIX POINTS

1. Expect, allow, and accept that fear will arise.

2. When fear comes, stop, wait, and let it be.

3. Focus on and do manageable things in the present.

4. Label your level of fear from 0 to 10. Watch it go up and down.

5. Function with fear. Appreciate your achievement.

6. Expect, allow, and accept that fear will reappear.

---

reality: "Although I feel frightened, I am not in danger"; "My hands are on the wheel, my foot is on the gas, and I am driving safely"; "I am not having a heart attack. My heart is simply beating fast."

Copy the Six Points and post them at your desk, put them up on the refrigerator door, tape them to the dashboard of your car, keep them in your purse or wallet. Look at these points anytime you feel your anxiety rising. By practicing the Six Points over and over again, you will begin to trust that they really work.

POINT #1: *Expect, allow, and accept that fear will arise.* Because of your biological makeup and/or your past experiences, certain thoughts and situations can automatically trigger your fear reactions. If you have panic disorder without phobias, the fear reaction can surface "out of the blue." In either case, rather than trying to fight the spiraling process of anxiety—which only increases it— recognize what it is and give it permission to be there. This shifts you from hopelessly trying to escape panic toward accepting its inevitable appearance and learning ways to keep the fear from running your life.

POINT #2: *When fear comes, stop, wait, and let it be.* Once fear or anxiety arises, you usually expect the worst to follow and automatically start to think about and prepare to escape from anticipated disasters. This intensifies the frightening feelings and physical sensations. Point #2 teaches you to do just the opposite: to remain in the challenging place or situation and simply let the feelings be. As difficult as this sounds, each time you succeed you further reinforce your confidence in trusting that by waiting, rather than running, the expected dangers will *not* happen and the panicky feelings will subside.

POINT #3: *Focus on and do manageable things in the present.* When you are in the anxiety-producing situation, it is tempting to concentrate on and react to frightening thoughts and imaginary dangers, most of which are anticipated. This focus on what *might* happen, as opposed to what *is* happening, creates a spiral of catastrophic thinking. Point #3 teaches you how to interrupt this process. It guides you toward focusing on concrete, familiar activities in the present, things that you can think about or do that will keep you involved in the here and now and reduce the distressing psychological and physiological sensations. Examples include diaphragmatic breathing (described in Chapter 19), observing reality, talking, writing, singing, counting, and feeling the textures of things around you.

POINT #4: *Label your level of fear from 0 to 10. Watch it go up and down.* To help you discover and better understand what makes your anxiety increase and decrease, you are directed by Point #4 to observe and study changes in your levels of fear. A level of 10 means that the anxiety is perceived as seemingly unbearable (a panic attack), and 0 means that it is absent. From these observations you begin to realize that your anxiety goes up and down and does not just run wild once it appears. You become aware that there are factors in your life, including your own thinking and activities, that affect the changing levels. As you become familiar with what thoughts or activities increase and decrease your anxiety levels, you will begin to develop a sense of mastery over them.

POINT #5: *Function with fear. Appreciate your achievement.* Experiencing extreme anxiety or panic in a place or situation that poses no real threat or danger is *not* a reason to leave. It is, instead, an opportunity to practice; a chance to see that you can function *in spite of* even the most seemingly debilitating feelings of anxiety. Once you truly understand and trust this concept, usually through much hard work and practice, you will no longer be afraid of facing your fears. Your fearful feelings and thoughts will instead become a signal for attending to and accomplishing a realistic, manageable task, rather than avoiding a situation or becoming preoccupied with the uncomfortable feelings. Each time you achieve this, no matter how insignificant the task, you're moving closer to recovery.

POINT #6: *Expect, allow, and accept that fear will reappear.* All learning, including learning to change negative thinking and behavior, is an up-and-down process. Therefore, setbacks must be accepted as part of learning, of getting better. Sometimes progress itself brings more difficult goals that can intensify fear. Point #6 tries to prepare you for such setbacks. As you learn to understand and cope with them, your progress will be strengthened and deepened. Every "failure" is a learning opportunity—a chance to grow stronger.

HOW THE SIX POINTS CAN WORK FOR YOU

The Six Points are designed to help you experience for yourself and thus develop confidence in the fact that although your feelings are real and frightening, they are not dangerous. You are not going to lose control, make a fool of yourself, or have a heart attack.

The most frightening sensations experienced during a panic

attack or when anticipating a panic attack are triggered by the "fear of fear." The Six Points teach you how to interrupt the spiraling process that this "fear of fear" sets off. Think of it this way: In order to begin the spiraling panic process, you must first *think* about being afraid. The primary thought in your mind usually takes the form of *"What if . . . ?" "What if* I pass out?" *"What if* I make a fool of myself?" *"What if* I lose control of the car?" Your mind quickly becomes flooded with additional frightening thoughts—which trigger more frightening and distressing thoughts . . . In other words, the *primary fear thought* leads to more fear, which leads to panic.

It is therefore necessary to interrupt or change the primary fear thought as soon as it occurs. But how?

Point #3 builds on a simple principle designed to help you do this: If you are trying to think of two things at the same time, neither one can have 100 percent of your attention. So when you find yourself beginning to focus on what "might" happen, bring another thought into your mind—one that shifts your focus back to the present. You can do this by carrying out a *simple* and *specific* activity—something that demands just enough concentration to hold your attention but is simple enough that you do not have to think a great deal about it.

The more you concentrate on refocusing your attention away from the fear thoughts and onto activities in the present, the easier it will become for you to remain in the anxiety-producing situation. The longer you remain exposed to the things that frighten you, the sooner you will become used to them.

Here are some simple and specific activities that will help you focus on manageable things in the present:

1. Take out the list of the Six Points and read it. To increase your concentration, count the number of words or letters. Say the words out loud. Say them forward, then say them backward.
2. Count backward from one hundred by threes, sevens, or nines.

3. Count anything you can see—the windows on a building, the buttons on an elevator, letters on a sign, or anything else within view.

4. Ask someone a simple question such as the time, directions to somewhere, or the price of an item.

5. Repeat an encouraging phrase over and over to yourself, such as "These feelings have passed before, and I know they will pass again," or "What doesn't kill me makes me stronger."

6. Describe in detail all the things you see around you. Notice color, size, shape, texture, and position.

7. Repeat the words to a song or poem.

8. Make up a list of people you would like to invite to a real or imaginary party.

9. Watch the second hand (or the changing numbers) on your watch.

10. Focus on your breathing. Picture a ball going up and down in your chest as you breathe regularly and normally.

11. Tell yourself that you cannot be tense and relaxed at the same time; consciously tense up and then relax specific parts of your body.

12. Picture a place where you would really like to be, such as a beach, country home, or ski resort. Then describe the scene in detail to yourself or to someone who is with you.

13. Play simple word games such as spelling words backward, switching initials in first and last names, or counting the number of letters in the words someone is saying to you.

14. Make physical contact with things around you. Shuffle your feet on the floor as if you were putting out a cigarette; switch radio stations by touching all the buttons; rub your hand on the arm of a chair or touch an item of clothing.

15. Imagine yourself as a rag doll and let all your muscles go loose and limp.

Obviously, some of these simple activities are better suited to one type of situation than another. For example, while it would not be helpful to try and repeat the words to a song or poem while you were attempting to give a speech, it would be helpful to rub the edge of the table, noting the texture, color, and feel of the wood. You don't want to look at the second hand of your watch while you are driving, but you can count backward, repeat an encouraging phrase to yourself, or focus on your breathing.

The above list of simple and specific activities just contains suggestions, ideas that my patients have found helpful. Feel free to use them as presented, modify them to meet your own needs, or create your own.

While you are attempting to complete your Daily Task, it is likely that you will experience varying levels of anxiety. The Six Points teach you that this is normal and should be expected. Put all of your efforts into staying with your task. With practice you'll learn to trust that the less attention you give to your frightening thoughts and feelings and the more you remain focused on something in the present, the sooner your anxiety level will come down. Do not try to control or fight anxious feelings. Let them *be* while you continue to concentrate on whatever it is you are doing at the moment.

There is a tendency to rehearse the bad feelings, which are based on past experiences or "future thinking." When you find yourself doing this, *stop!* Immediately focus on where you are and what you are doing. Use one or a combination of the techniques described above or in the Six Points to change any frightening thoughts. Your aim is to let those negative thoughts die of neglect.

How do you know for sure that nothing will happen to you? By staying in the present and observing what is really happening.

Ask yourself, "Am I passed out now?" "Am I out of control?"

"Am I making a fool out of myself?" "Are people really looking at me?"

Make yourself aware of the reality of the situation. Notice that your feet are firmly planted on the ground, that your hands are on the steering wheel, or that you are in fact carrying on a normal conversation. Tell yourself that you have felt these uncomfortable feelings before, and nothing bad has happened to you.

Remember, people with a phobic or panic disorder *do not do* the things they are afraid of doing. You may think you have come very close to losing control in the past—but remember, there is a big difference between what you "think" you may do and what you actually do.

Have you ever lost control? Have you ever done anything dangerous while having a panic attack? Have you ever passed out because of your anxieties? The answer to all these questions, I am confident, is *No*.

And you won't.

And the only way for you to truly believe what you know intellectually is to experience it yourself. Each time you expose yourself voluntarily to an anxiety-provoking situation and/or experience a panic attack, you have the opportunity to reinforce the fact that your feelings are frightening, but not dangerous.

Now that you have set your long- and short-term goals, have learned how to use the Daily Task Sheets, and have an understanding of the Six Points, you're ready to put it all to work.

17

Practicing

AS WE HAVE seen, panic attacks have both physiological and biochemical components. But avoidance is a learned behavior. Since it is learned, it can be unlearned. This cannot happen by just wishing it away—but it can happen through hard work and practice. Just as someone can learn to correct a speech problem, stop biting one's nails, or be a better parent, you can learn to change your avoidance behavior by practicing specific habit-breaking techniques. You can learn to replace negative or destructive behavior patterns with those of a more positive, constructive nature.

Of course, avoidance is not learned or developed by choice. If you have a panic attack every time you enter into a certain place or situation, it is easy to understand why you would soon become conditioned to wanting to avoid that place or situation. Even if you had only one panic attack, it is possible that the mere thought of going back into the place where it occurred would be so terrifying that you would do everything within your power to avoid having another panic attack.

When you first began to avoid things you probably made excuses, even to yourself, such as "I really don't have to drive on the highway to get to the store." Or "The train is more comfortable than the plane."

When others pressured you, you learned to make excuses to them as well, such as "I'd love to go to the theater, but I have a terrible headache." Or "The food in the rooftop restaurant isn't supposed to be very good. How about trying that great new place on the ground floor?"

You may have changed your lifestyle so you could avoid dealing with the stressful situation altogether: moving to the suburbs where you didn't have to confront high buildings, taking a job where you could avoid public speaking, or shopping via mail-order catalogs.

It's possible that by avoiding certain places and situations you have become successful at avoiding having a panic attack (unless, of course, your panic attacks are spontaneous and not related to any specific stimuli). However, this "negative reinforcement" has encouraged you to continue the avoidance behavior. When one develops new behavior patterns, both positive and negative, each step, no matter how small, builds upon the previous steps. Without consciously trying, you *mastered* a new behavior: phobic avoidance. Unfortunately, this negative behavior greatly interferes with your living a full, productive life.

And now you have to unlearn your avoidant behavior. You can do this by starting at whatever point you feel comfortable, then begin by taking one step at a time, no matter how small, into your *discomfort zone*. As you take these steps, you will build upon your accomplishments.

When you first begin, it is difficult to trust the process of recovery. It can be as slow and subtle—and as profound—as the process of creating the avoidance behavior.

To unlearn negative behavior and replace it with positive behavior, you need actual *practice sessions*. Practicing is hard but rewarding work. You may have spent many hours—perhaps even days, months, or years—wishing for the bad feelings to disappear or at least become manageable. But just wishing does not produce change. Hard work and commitment are required to overcome a phobic or panic disorder.

There is certainly nothing pleasurable about repeatedly exposing yourself to discomfort, either physiological or psychological. It takes courage, self-discipline, and persistence. Therefore, in order to maintain the proper attitude for learning to overcome your problem, it is crucial to keep the rewards in mind at all times, the most exciting being your newfound ability to lead a full and normal life without limitations.

PRACTICE EVERY DAY

It's necessary to practice *every single day*, because there is a direct correlation between the number of times you *practice* going into an anxiety-provoking situation and the amount of progress you make.

The more you voluntarily expose yourself to anxiety-producing situations—applying the anxiety-reducing techniques described in this chapter and other sections of this book—the sooner you will be desensitized to them.

It is tempting to find reasons not to practice every day. But each excuse you use for not practicing adds to the difficulty of your next attempt, thus prolonging the recovery process. It is important to structure the practice situation in a way that is both practical and motivational. The more you can set up real-life practice situations, with real rewards, the more likely it is that you will accomplish your goal.

For instance, if you are avoiding buses because you have had panic attacks on them, you need to practice riding buses. But if you tell yourself you have to ride around on a crowded bus for an hour with no destination, you will have little motivation to try again. Instead, choose to shop at a particular store that happens to be right on the bus route and where you would like to shop. Thus, there is a real incentive to practice.

It takes imagination and creativity to set up practice sessions that have a practical as well as therapeutic purpose. Make it a challenge—but a challenge that's fun. Call upon friends and family members (including children) to help give you ideas. Here are some examples of "practical" practice sessions that some of my patients created for themselves:

▪ A woman with an elevator phobia accepted her boss's request that she move her office up to the ninth floor. Although this commitment terrified her, she recognized the importance of having a real reason to use the elevator each day. This was a courageous step. Within a short period of time she was using the elevator routinely.

▪ An agoraphobic woman who was afraid to drive alone accepted an interesting part-time job that was a reasonable distance from her home. Although this drive was difficult at first, her motivation to get to the office overcame her preoccupation with what might happen to her if she had a panic attack en route. Thus, she practiced every day and eventually became comfortable with the trip.

▪ A man with a public-speaking phobia accepted the role of president of his synagogue, knowing he would have to speak before the various committees on a regular basis. It was anxiety-provoking at first but, after a while, his only complaint was that he had waited so long to accept the challenge.

All of these patients did well. They entered the anxiety-producing situations over and over again, using many of the coping strategies described throughout this book. They were highly motivated and they practiced on a continuous basis.

From first-hand experience they learned that their frightening feelings, however unpleasant, were not dangerous. That enabled them to stay in situations long enough to develop the trust that nothing bad would happen to them, no matter how close they felt they came to losing control. They also realized they did not have to be victims of their anxiety and fear, that there were things they could do to lessen their anxiety.

PLAN ON PRACTICING, NOT JUST TESTING

In choosing a practice situation, it is important to make sure you are really *practicing* and not just *testing*. You are practicing when you have selected a specific task and, by breaking down the steps and using the techniques to help you stay in the situation, you are able to work toward completing that task.

You are testing when you say, "I'll keep going until I have a panic attack, and then I'll leave."

This is *not* helpful because

- You are assuming a negative outcome before you even begin.
- You miss out on experiencing the sense of accomplishment that you feel when you complete a task or reach a goal.
- Your focus of attention is more likely to be on "future thinking" than on the present.
- You are telling yourself that you can leave a situation as soon as you feel your level rising. As a result, you don't allow yourself to experience your level *coming down* without your having to leave.
- You "reward" yourself by failing: You stop when you panic. (This is an example of negative conditioning.)

By contrast, practicing is quite different from testing:

- Practicing leads to a sense of mastery and pride. (Testing, at best, leads to a sense of having survived and, at worst, a sense of having failed again.)
- Practicing is something you can control in terms of who, where, and what. Try to select tasks and set goals that are a bit *beyond* where you feel comfortable. That way you continuously push back the restraining wall of the phobia. And once you set your sights on a farther peak, the nearer ones are suddenly more manageable.
- Practicing leads to successes built on successes. (Testing leaves you—always passively—back at square one.)

Your aim in practicing is to complete a task that will bring you a step closer to reaching your weekly and, ultimately, long-term goal.

During each practice session you should be prepared to enter into a previously avoided or stressful situation and, in spite of any bad feelings, remain there until you have accomplished your task and/ or the anxious feelings have subsided. Remember to keep your primary thought focused on simple, manageable activities and challenge any negative thinking. Each time you complete a task—no matter how small it may seem—you are making progress.

REMAIN IN THE SITUATION—EVEN WHEN YOU FEEL YOU MUST LEAVE

If you feel you absolutely *must* leave, try to wait out the panic before you go. Stop. Wait. *Don't* leave just to escape the panic. Let the panicky feelings pass.

The worst will be only a few seconds. Give yourself an Out. Tell yourself that you will wait twenty seconds and then leave. When the twenty seconds pass, renegotiate with yourself. Can you stay for another twenty seconds? Keep repeating this exercise until your anxiety level comes down.

If you are driving, you might say to yourself, "I'll pass one more sign—or five more trees—and then pull over." After you've passed the sign or trees, renegotiate with yourself again and keep going. Notice that when you "wait out" the panic, your anxiety level *always* comes down and you are able to complete your task.

This is not a Crutch, but an acceptable Out. Remember, an Out is anything that gets you *in*—and helps you to stay there. Your aim is to delay your leaving long enough for the panic to diminish. Then you may leave, rest a while, and go back into the situation.

It is very important for you to go back to a place where you felt uncomfortable as soon as you can. The longer you delay returning, the more difficult it becomes. Go back, step by step, any way you can—but *go back!*

Spend as much time as possible in the anxiety-provoking situation.

The more time you spend in the situation, the easier it will become. Your body cannot physically maintain very high levels of anxiety for a long time. The most intense and frightening part of a panic attack rarely lasts longer than ten to twenty seconds.

No matter how anxious you feel, after a while your anxiety level will drop. It will go up and down, but the longer you stay, the more comfortable you will become. Therefore, you want to stay in the situation until you feel reasonably comfortable. *Then* you can allow yourself to leave.

Ideally you should spend several hours in an anxiety-provoking situation. But since this is not always practical, try to practice at least one hour a day. You may have trouble finding the time, but daily practice must be made a priority. You will be pleasantly surprised by how much more time you have for everything else in your life once you stop devoting so much time to worrying about when your next panic attack may occur.

HERE'S HOW TO BEGIN

Begin with something easy and manageable. As you progress to more difficult tasks, always remember, *No step is too small.* Each step leads to the next, no matter how insignificant it may seem at the time.

Begin each practice session by selecting a specific task and writing it down on your Daily Task Sheet. The more specific the task, the better. After you have chosen a task, break down the steps you must take to complete it. If the first step is too difficult, cut it in half. Take a smaller step. And if that's too difficult, cut it in half again.

If your task is to go into the store and buy ten grocery items, begin by just walking into the store, picking up one item, and feeling good about it.

If that is too difficult, walk in and out of the store and feel good about that.

If that is too difficult, walk up to the door of the store and try to stand there for several minutes.

If you feel you cannot do that, get out of your car and walk within ten feet of the store.

Keep breaking down the steps until you find one that you can take. As you reach each step, wait a few seconds, breathe deeply, pat yourself on the back, and move on to the next step.

If necessary, take one step back, rest a few seconds, and then go forward again. If you feel foolish about going only as far as the entrance to the store, or only as far as the parking lot, think of the alternative—which is not to do anything at all. Take a deep breath and *go!*

Keep your tasks and steps simple and specific—like buying a specific item, or picking up an item and holding it. Other specific tasks might include:

- Walking into the store and out
- Standing at the door for twenty seconds
- Taking ten steps at a time toward the store
- Walking until you pass three cracks in the sidewalk

Whatever your tasks are, always make sure you are *practicing* and not just *testing*.

Keep in mind that the more uncomfortable you feel during your practice sessions, the more you are truly practicing and progressing. Think of it as taking the bad-tasting medicine to get better!

As you continue breaking down the steps and moving forward, you want always to aim toward and remain in the *discomfort zone* (which will then become the *progress zone*). You are the only one who can determine where this zone is for you, since your feelings are unique to you. What may be difficult for someone else may be easy for you, and vice versa.

Finding your discomfort zone and practicing in it is the most creative and the most important part of your practice. The longer and more often you can stay in situations you fear will trigger a panic attack, the more progress you will make.

I often repeat to patients the words of the late Claire Weekes, the Australian physician who helped millions of people with agoraphobia: "Peace is on the other side of panic."

Try imagining an inner voice telling you that every time you feel

---

SELF-INVENTORY—PRACTICING

1. Describe a practice session that you felt was successful. What made it successful?

2. Describe a practice session that you did *not* feel was successful. Why was it *not* successful?

3. What are some of the things that keep you from practicing? (Be honest!)

4. Describe an occasion when you chose a specific goal and reached it by taking one step at a time. Describe the steps you took.

5. Choose a specific goal you would like to reach and describe how you might break down your steps to reach it.

---

bad and continue to move forward instead of running away, you are getting stronger and healthier.

How to Get the Most Out of Your Practice Sessions

1. Choose specific tasks and goals, making sure they are both reasonable and challenging.
2. Give yourself time in the anxiety-provoking situation, reminding yourself that your anxiety level *will* come down.
3. Make yourself aware of your Outs, but do not dwell on them.
4. Keep a list of helpful techniques in your pocket.
5. Expect to feel uncomfortable.
6. Avoid leaving a situation while you are feeling panicky.

7. Confront your fears. The more you do so, the sooner your fears will disappear.

8. Measure your success in terms of how far you pushed yourself toward completing your task or achieving your goal. You can also measure your success by whether you managed to stay in the anxiety-producing situation in spite of any bad feelings.

9. Feel good about each step forward, no matter how small.

10. Use your Daily Task Sheet after each practice session to record your experience.

11. Deliberately do things that will raise your anxiety level so you can learn how to cope with the unpleasant feelings.

12. Remember that you are trying to learn a new attitude toward your feelings of panic—as opposed to trying to avoid them. Go out and meet them, deal with them, and accept them.

18

Managing Fearful Thoughts
and Impulses

A PANIC ATTACK only lasts a few seconds, but the anxiety surrounding it can last minutes, hours, or days.

Most likely, your worst panic attack was the very first. You
survived that! But afterward, even the *thought* of experiencing a
panic attack again becomes terrifying. Understandably, you don't
feel like exposing yourself to any situation that might bring on the
dreaded sensations.

You probably have become sensitized to anything that *might*
bring on the feared reaction. Most likely, you notice things that
others are oblivious to, such as which floors your friends live and
work on, the distance between exits on the parkway, or how long it
will take to be served a meal in a restaurant.

You begin to have an anticipatory fear reaction well before
you're actually in the anxiety-provoking situation. As soon as you
know you might have to go into a dreaded situation, you begin to
think of all the terrible things that could happen to you.

Your anticipatory thoughts and feelings take on a life of their
own. They are often powerful enough to keep you from entering
situations that pose no real threat or danger.

It becomes increasingly difficult to convince yourself that you *should* put yourself in a situation that you anticipate will cause you discomfort. Each time you avoid an anxiety-producing situation, however, you become more sensitized to it. Thus, it becomes more difficult for you to approach it the next time.

You also feel discouraged and angry with yourself. And even though a full-blown panic attack is usually brief and infrequent, anticipatory anxiety, related depression, and general anxiety can seem ever-present.

But there are ways to deal with the anticipatory anxiety as well as with the panic itself. Here are some hints to help you stop anticipatory thinking:

1. When you find yourself thinking of what might happen— "future thinking"—use one or more of the techniques discussed in Chapters 15, 16, and 17 to help you *stay in the present*. Remember, you are *not* in the feared situation. So keep your thoughts focused on where you are at the moment and what is going on around you.

2. When you begin to think of all the "what-if's," tell yourself, "So what!" Allow yourself to face the absolute worst. Say, "Okay, the worst that will happen to me is that I will become psychotic, have a heart attack, crash my car, or make a fool of myself." I know this sounds strange, but think about it. As your fears begin to escalate your imagination runs wild. And, remember Point #2 of the Six Points: When fear comes, stop, wait, and let it be. *Let it be. Accepting* rather than *fighting* your thoughts and feelings stops the spiraling of fear. A panic attack will *not* cause any of the above things to happen to you. In more than fifteen years of study and practice in this field I have never heard of anyone becoming psychotic, having a heart attack, or crashing their car as a result of having a panic attack. (As a matter of fact, about ten years ago Bob DuPont and I surveyed a group of people who were anxious about driving and, not surprisingly, we found that they had far *fewer* accidents than a random group we surveyed of people who said they were not anxious about driving.) From time to time when patients would tell me that they made a fool of themselves, in

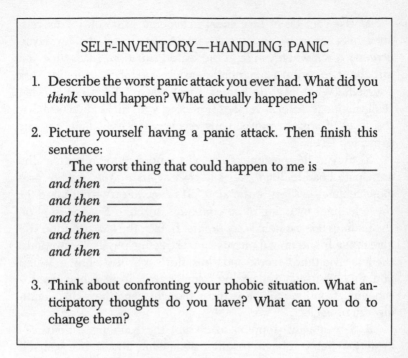

SELF-INVENTORY—HANDLING PANIC

1. Describe the worst panic attack you ever had. What did you *think* would happen? What actually happened?

2. Picture yourself having a panic attack. Then finish this sentence:
   The worst thing that could happen to me is _____
   and then _____
   and then _____
   and then _____
   and then _____
   and then _____

3. Think about confronting your phobic situation. What anticipatory thoughts do you have? What can you do to change them?

almost all cases they would quickly acknowledge that their degree of embarrassment was way out of proportion to whatever actually happened.

Although panic attacks don't result in dangerous consequences, there are certainly many things in life we cannot control—including what thoughts come into our minds. But we *can* control what we *do* with those thoughts. We can fight them and watch them get more frightening. Or we can accept them and, in doing so, diffuse their intensity.

3. Think about an occasion when you thought you could not do something and then surprised yourself because you were able to do it. Think back to how much more difficult it seemed before you actually did it. Remember how it really wasn't that bad (you did survive!). And recall how pleased you felt with yourself afterward.

4. Use your Daily Task Sheet to become aware of the discrepancy between your *anticipated* anxiety level and the level you *actually reach* when you're in the feared situation. Each time you are about to enter a potentially anxiety-producing situation, ask yourself, "What level do I think I will reach?" Then notice what really happens. After several experiences, you will begin to see that the level of anxiety you actually reach is rarely as high as your projected level.

5. Stay in the present. There is a tendency to "rehearse" the anticipated bad feelings over and over again, on the basis of previous feelings or "future thinking." It's as if you try to prepare for these feelings by being more conscious of them. But focusing on the feelings doesn't help you prepare. In fact, the *less* attention you give to the frightening thoughts and distressing physical sensations, the less vivid they become and, thus, the less overwhelming. When you find yourself "rehearsing," let go of those nonproductive thoughts. Continue to ignore those thoughts, and they will eventually die of neglect.

6. Try thought-stopping to disrupt the spiraling anticipatory anxiety. When you begin to anticipate a panic attack, give yourself the command "Stop!" Say it to yourself—or scream it out loud—but make sure you are firm about it. Say it *as soon as* and *every time* you have anxious thoughts about entering a fearful situation or are anticipating a panic attack. Also, put a rubber band on your wrist and snap it whenever a frightening or negative thought occurs. Think of a positive thought to take the place of the negative one. Tell yourself, "Panic attacks are frightening, but not dangerous," or "Each time I face my fears I get stronger," or "These feelings have passed before and they will pass this time as well."

HOW CAN YOU DEAL WITH FRIGHTENING THOUGHTS AND IMPULSES?

Many people have experienced that sudden, overwhelmingly frightening feeling that they are going to lose control of themselves and do something harmful. For a split second, you might feel as though you're going to humiliate yourself or do something extremely harmful to yourself or somebody else.

Standing on a high balcony, you might suddenly feel a compulsion to jump.

While driving, you might feel a sudden urge to head into oncoming traffic.

Sitting in a theater watching a show, you might have an overwhelming urge to scream.

Standing in the kitchen, you happen to glance at a sharp knife—and suddenly you think you might lose control and stab someone with it.

Or you're holding a baby—and suddenly you have an urge to choke it.

These are *common* experiences. While these impulses seem real and are frightening when they occur, they are only thoughts. In some people these thoughts occur only occasionally. In people with obsessive-compulsive disorder such thoughts may become a daily torment.

As a human being you are responsible for your actions, but not for your thoughts and feelings. You have no control over which thoughts and feelings enter your mind. But you *do* have control over what you do with them.

People with an anxiety disorder have terrible fears. They do not do terrible acts.

These frightening thoughts and impulses may seem overwhelming, but remember that you do *not* really want to hurt yourself or someone else—or to make a fool of yourself. And so you *won't*.

Many of these thoughts are similar to dreams—and we all know how creative and bizarre dreams can be. Remind yourself that you have never acted on these or similar thoughts. You never will!

People who do terrible things—who commit violent crimes or engage in life-threatening behaviors—do not do so because they are in the throes of a panic attack and have lost control. They do so either because they have *chosen* to do something terrible or because they have a psychotic illness—a brain disease—and are not aware of or responsible for their actions. Although people with psychotic illnesses may also have an anxiety disorder—just as they could have high blood pressure or migraine headaches—an anxiety disorder itself is *not* a psychotic illness. Even while in the throes of a panic attack, people with phobic and panic disorders do not lose control of themselves.

Of course if you have had frightening impulses of jumping out of windows (a thought I used to terrify myself with), running your car into oncoming traffic, or hurling yourself in front of a train, a natural concern is "Am I suicidal?" Unless you are actually contemplating suicide because you are severely depressed and have given up all hope and interest in life, the answer is no. Most of the unfortunate people who do commit suicide think about it for a long time and plan it out carefully prior to attempting it. It is not something that happens spontaneously during a panic attack.

The more you *try* to lose your frightening thoughts and impulses, the more difficult it is to get rid of them. As you learn to accept them as frightening but not dangerous, they will begin to diminish. As bizarre as this may sound, you can even learn to enjoy them, much as you can learn to enjoy the creative process of your dreams—even your nightmares.

Allow those thoughts and impulses to be there. Do not try to force forgetfulness. Tell yourself, "I've experienced this before, and nothing happened. The scary thoughts and feelings have passed before, and I know they will pass again." Allow yourself to face the "worst."

The "worst" will not happen. You know that intellectually.

To really *believe* it, you must allow yourself to experience it, no matter how scared you are. Try sitting in the middle of the theater when you are afraid of screaming, and imagine yourself actually screaming. Stand on a balcony and imagine yourself jumping.

Now, accept the thoughts, and elaborate on them. Do you really want to do what you're thinking about doing? Of course not. And you won't. You won't drive into oncoming traffic. You won't purposely drop a baby, or hurt someone with a knife, or do anything that is out of control. The less you fight your thoughts, the less vivid

---

SELF-INVENTORY—FRIGHTENING THOUGHTS

1. Write down some of the frightening thoughts and impulses you have had. Do not hesitate to write things that may seem distressful and/or embarrassing. The more willing you are to confront and acknowledge these thoughts, the easier it will become for you to successfully cope with them.

2. Talk with someone you trust about these thoughts and impulses. What did you think this person would say once you "confessed"? What did this person really say?

---

they will become. Recall, as often as necessary, that thoughts are creative and often involuntary. We are not responsible for them, any more than we are responsible for our dreams.

Thoughts are *not* actions. You can control your actions. Once you truly accept those flashing thoughts and impulses, they will lose their nightmarish power and begin to become less important to you and eventually disappear.

Eleven Golden Rules for Coping with Panic

1. Remind yourself that although your feelings and symptoms are very frightening, they are *not* dangerous or harmful.
2. Understand that what you are experiencing is just an exaggeration of your normal bodily reactions to stress.
3. Do *not* fight your feelings, or try to wish them away. The more you are willing to face them, the less intense they will become.
4. Do *not* add to your panic by thinking about what "might" happen. If you find yourself asking, "What if?" tell yourself, "So what!"

5. *Stay in the present*. Notice what is *really* happening to you as opposed to what you think "might" happen.

6. Label your fear level from 0 to 10 and watch it go up and down. Notice that it does not stay at a very high level for more than a few seconds.

7. When you find yourself thinking about the fear, change your primary thought. Focus on and carry out a simple and manageable task.

8. Notice that when you stop adding frightening thoughts to your fear, it begins to fade.

9. When the fear comes, expect and accept it. Wait and give it time to pass without running away from it.

10. Be proud of yourself for your progress thus far, and think about how good you will feel when you succeed this time.

11. Remember that a Level 10 panic attack is, by your own personal definition, "the worst." It is a comforting thought that you have had Level 10s before. They were awful, but temporary, and you did survive. Nothing worse can happen. You have already dealt with "the worst."

CHANGING YOUR BELIEFS ABOUT YOURSELF

It is not difficult to understand why people with phobic and panic disorders often find their self-esteem plummeting. You may begin to think of yourself as defective or inadequate. It may seem difficult to convince yourself that an anxiety disorder is something you can cope with and that having an anxiety disorder does not mean that you are weak or helpless. Your negative thoughts about yourself can become a real barrier to recovery.

It should always be reassuring to remind yourself that an anxiety disorder will not push you beyond the limits of endurance. Although you may say to yourself from time to time, "I can't stand this anymore," the fact is that anyone who has panic attacks cannot

SELF-INVENTORY—SELF-ESTEEM

1. What situations are likely to make you feel discouraged or angry with yourself?

2. When you feel discouraged or angry, what are some of the things you think about?

3. Are you aware of any beliefs and/or assumptions you have that may set you up to feel bad?

4. If yes, What are they?

5. What evidence do you have for them?

6. Can you develop alternative, more balanced beliefs? If so, what are they?

only "stand them" and "survive them," but can also develop techniques to cope with them very well.

When you feel overwhelmed and distraught, try to become aware of what you are thinking and change your "internal sentences." Ask yourself, "What am I believing about myself?" If your answer to that question has a negative tone (e.g., "I don't believe I'll ever feel better), see if you can replace it with a more balanced and realistic statement (e.g., "I know I've felt this bad before, and the feelings went away after a while. I'm sure that will happen again.")

Although "coping" messages may read like "formulas for positive thinking," research has shown that positive messages really do make a difference in the way we feel about ourselves. Some coping messages:

211

"I am strong enough to take this."
"I'll just observe the pain and tell myself that I can stand it."
"Being anxious or depressed only proves I'm human. It does
    not in any way prove I am inadequate or undesirable."

By repeating these and other positive messages to yourself, you give yourself a chance to change your attitudes as well as your behavior.

19

Breathing Control

IMAGINE WHAT LIFE would be like if we had no fear or anxiety. Fear is a protective mechanism that warns us when there is danger and motivates us to take action to protect ourselves, our loved ones, and our property or possessions. It warns us not to touch a hot stove, talk to strangers, or drive carelessly. Anxiety warns us to prepare well for a speech, to pay our bills on time, and to be law-abiding citizens. And it warns us of our need for food, shelter, and clothing.

But sometimes we are alarmed by things we needn't be afraid of: like the bogeyman, someone's not liking us, or even our own thoughts. When the mind registers fear, the body—which by itself cannot differentiate whether the fear is real or imaginary—reacts to protect us. When we experience fear our pupils dilate, giving us clearer vision; our hands and feet get cold as our blood flow is redirected from our limbs toward our central organs; and our heart rate escalates as the increase in adrenaline prepares us to take action. Our attention mechanisms become highly selective and focused, allowing us to respond most effectively to whatever it is that is threatening—even if it only *feels* threatening.

Therefore, I explain to my patients, the physiological sensations experienced during a panic attack are not out-of-control, malfunctioning reactions. They are adaptive, self-protective responses to a perceived threat of danger. It makes sense that if your body is getting a message that it is in danger, it will prepare itself for immediate action. A major challenge as you work toward recovery is learning to recognize the physical sensations that surface in response to your body's receiving the "wrong" message, and correcting the fear/thought process that gives it that misinformation.

RECOGNIZING HYPERVENTILATION

One common physiological reaction to fear, experienced by more than half of the people who have panic attacks, is overbreathing, or hyperventilation. Hyperventilation means that we are breathing too fast or too deeply for the body's needs at a particular time. Some people overbreathe and then react with panic; others begin to overbreathe in response to the panic reaction itself.

If you were actually in a physically dangerous situation and responded by fighting or fleeing, hyperventilation would not occur. Your body would use all the oxygen you took in. But when your breathing outpaces your body's needs, the normal balance between the oxygen you inhale and the carbon dioxide you exhale is disrupted. Because of the complex chemical effects of this imbalance, parts of your body paradoxically end up getting *less* oxygen than they need, even though you may be gulping in air. This, in turn, produces many other physical symptoms.

Symptoms of overbreathing may include dizziness and lightheadedness, blurred vision, confusion, and feelings of unreality. You may also feel numbness or tingling in your arms and legs, cold and clammy hands, and muscle stiffness. These are all physiological sensations—like dilating pupils, redirected blood flows, and increases in adrenaline—that are involved in the body's preparation to take action and escape from possible harm. In and of themselves, however, these sensations or symptoms are *not dangerous*.

214

Although we often think of hyperventilation as a dramatic event, its manifestation can be quite subtle. Hyperventilation may be part of *your* panic reaction if you notice yourself

1. holding your breath or taking quick, shallow breaths when frightened
2. feeling short of breath, as if you are not getting enough air or are suffocating
3. repeatedly yawning or sighing
4. experiencing chest pain, tingling, numbness, and prickling sensations

You may have heard of one remedy for hyperventilation that consists of breathing into a paper bag. This is simply a way of making you rebreathe the carbon dioxide you have exhaled so that the oxygen–carbon dioxide balance is corrected. However, not many people have a paper bag handy or would feel comfortable using one in public! The method I will give you later in this chapter is just as effective—and much simpler to use.

Hyperventilation is now being used in one of the most innovative and effective new treatment approaches for panic disorder, discovered by David Barlow, Ph.D., Director of the Anxiety Disorders Clinic at the State University of New York at Albany. In Dr. Barlow's approach, the therapist teaches patients how to recreate the fearful sensations experienced during a panic attack right in the office. Patients who experience the symptoms of hyperventilation during a panic attack, for example, might be asked to breathe forcefully and deeply for a minute or two to bring on the dizziness and other physiological sensations of overbreathing. They would then be told to close their eyes and breathe slowly until the physical sensations subside. Next they would be asked to think about what symptoms occurred during the exercise and to compare them to those experienced during a panic attack.

I've recently incorporated this exercise into my groups, hyperventilating myself along with the patients to demonstrate that it isn't dangerous. What the patients learn is that even when the physical symptoms that they experience during a panic attack are exaggerated, they are not in any way harmful. Some other techniques Dr. Barlow has used to simulate panic attacks include spinning around in a chair to recreate the sensations of extreme dizziness or staring in a mirror to bring on the feelings of unreality.

When I first present the idea of "forced hyperventilation" to my patients, they respond the same way I suspect that you are responding as you read this: with fear, doubt, and trepidation. But this treatment approach has been carefully studied, replicated, and evaluated by highly respected researchers and clinicians and has proved to be extremely effective in helping people become desensitized to the frightening sensations associated with their panic attacks. I do not, however, recommend that you do these exercises on your own. I am describing them here so that you can discuss them with your therapist and integrate them into your treatment program as you both feel is appropriate.

RETRAINING YOUR BREATHING

If overbreathing or hyperventilation is playing a role in your panic attacks, you can learn to breathe in a way that calms and relaxes you, rather than creates symptoms of anxiety. This breathing is called diaphragmatic breathing: breathing from the diaphragm, or the abdomen, rather than from the chest cavity. It can be extremely helpful in slowing down the body's response when anxiety, nervousness, or distress begins to build.

Once you learn how to breathe diaphragmatically you'll be able to do it easily and effortlessly, but it does take a bit of practice at first. If you were to walk into one of my group therapy sessions when I am teaching diaphragmatic breathing, you'd probably see eight or ten bodies spread out over the floor with books bobbing up and down on their abdomens as they struggle to get the breathing "just right."

I first learned about the benefits of diaphragmatic breathing and the book-on-the-stomach exercise from David Clark, Ph.D., of Oxford University, England, during an informal discussion at an

American Psychiatric Association meeting. I was intrigued as Dr. Clark described what sounded like a simple but profoundly effective process, but was frustrated when I couldn't seem to get everything coordinated. "When you get back to your hotel room later on," Dr. Clark suggested, "lie down on the floor and put a book on your stomach. As you breathe in, let your stomach expand like a balloon and watch the book lift up. As you exhale, let your stomach collapse and watch the book sink down."

He gave me a few more specific instructions and assured me that once I got the hang of it I would be able to do it sitting or standing as well. Fortunately, he was right, and with practice, I could do it quite easily.

Dr. Clark was also right about the calming effect of diaphragmatic breathing. I began demonstrating the technique to my patients and discovered that many of them found it to be one of the most immediate and effective ways of interrupting the spiraling of symptoms that would otherwise lead to a panic attack.

You can practice diaphragmatic breathing on your own, keeping in mind that it may take a while to get your abdominal muscles working the way you want them to. This is because like most people, you probably breathe by expanding your chest cavity, rather than your abdomen, when you inhale.

You must also learn to pay attention to your breathing patterns. The goal is to maintain slow, smooth breathing, with long inhalations and even longer exhalations.

Scheldon Kress, M.D., a specialist in preventive medicine and infectious diseases with the Internal Medicine Associates of Northern Virginia, has developed a set of guidelines for teaching diaphragmatic breathing that my patients have found very helpful. I've modified them slightly in the instructions that follow.

- Begin by loosening your clothes and lying down, on a couch, a bed, or the floor.
- Assume a comfortable and relaxed position and take a few seconds to slow down your breathing.
- Expand your abdomen as you inhale and collapse it as you

exhale, minimizing your upper chest motion. Put a book on your stomach and practice making it go up and down with your breathing (*up* on the inhale and *down* on the exhale).

- Remove the book and continue the breathing. Put your left hand on your upper chest and your right hand on your abdomen. Your left hand should be still, while your right hand should be moving up and down.
- Practice moving your diaphragm down and expanding your abdomen like a balloon as you inhale. As you exhale, slowly release the abdomen to push the air out of the lungs as the diaphragm rises.
- Continue to breathe slowly and smoothly, making your exhale more prolonged than your inhale.
- Breathe in through your nose and out through your mouth, emphasizing the exhalation by making a long "hah" sound with the mouth open and relaxed.

After you've practiced this breathing technique while lying down, sit or stand to practice in an upright position. The process is almost the same as before, with these differences:

- When you are upright, get the rhythm going and assist the exhaling process by pressing on your abdominal wall muscles with your hand each time you exhale.
- Change the exhalation "hah" sound to counting out loud for the duration of the exhalation: "One, two, three . . ." and continue. This also encourages a natural, proper speaking voice. The air is "blown" over the vocal cords as it's exhaled from the lungs. When you exhale, don't try to force out the "last drop" of air. Just allow the breathing to be easy, smooth, and effortless.

This new kind of breathing will require some very conscious effort at first. You may even want to engage the help of a friend or family member who can watch you to make sure that you are breathing abdominally rather than with your chest. I suggest to my patients that they spend about five to ten minutes, twice a day, for about a week practicing the steps outlined above. Then, once they have mastered the technique, diaphragmatic breathing can be done anywhere at any time. When used in panic-producing situations, it can reduce the symptoms of overbreathing that cause the fear reaction and/or reduce the fear reaction that causes the over-breathing.

Many of my patients report that as soon as they recognize a panic-triggering thought or physical sensation, they immediately begin breathing diaphragmatically and are able to stop the sequence of events that lead to a panic attack. One of my patients who had just learned to control his breathing in this way commented to me, "I can't tell whether the diaphragmatic breathing itself calms me down or whether my focused concentration on trying to expand my stomach while I'm inhaling, keep my chest still, and extend my exhalations distracts me from my fearful thoughts!"

"It's probably a combination of both," I responded. Then I pointed out to him the circumstance that was most striking to me. He had asked me this question while he was driving across the Chesapeake Bay Bridge for the first time in five years!

20

Relaxation and Exercise

RELAXATION AND EXERCISE. These sound like the components of a first-rate health regimen, and for most of us, they are.

But for some who suffer from panic disorder, relaxation and exercise are contradictory and poignant reminders of just one more thing that seems to set people with this ailment apart from the rest of the world.

Some panic-disorder patients cannot engage in aerobic exercises without triggering a full-fledged panic attack.

One possible explanation is that exercise causes panic through association: that is, the body's responses to exercise are similar to those produced by panic—rapid heartbeat and shortness of breath, for example. In some people, experiencing these sensations during exercise brings on a panic attack. Whether this is a conscious or unconscious response is a topic of lively controversy, but either way, it can be frightening to the person experiencing it.

Luckily, there are plenty of exercises, such as walking, leisurely bicycle riding, swimming, horseback riding, and ice-skating, that offer health and enjoyment without eliciting the physiological response of a heavy workout of a 10K run.

Even more surprising and paradoxical is the relationship between panic attacks and relaxation. Some patients try relaxation techniques to manage stress, only to find that at the very point of their deepest relaxation, they are suddenly jolted out of it with a pounding heart, sweating palms, dizziness, and waves of terror. And some patients experience panic attacks at the time they should be most relaxed—during sleep. They awaken suddenly with a suffocating sense of impending doom. This can be so distressing that those who experience nighttime panic attacks often fear falling asleep—adding exhaustion the next day to the already heavy burden of the disorder itself.

One might assume that nighttime panic attacks occur during the dream state of sleep, in response to the content of dreams. Interestingly, however, researchers at the National Institute of Mental Health found that attacks actually occur during the nondreaming stage of sleep where one is the most deeply relaxed. Such episodes are still a mystery to researchers.

Nevertheless, many of my patients find it helpful to learn and practice some kind of formal relaxation technique: biofeedback, self-hypnosis, meditation, or progressive muscle relaxation. Whatever technique or combination of techniques you select to help you relax, what's most important is that you practice it regularly—ideally, twice a day for twenty minutes. Any of the above activities will help you to become familiar with how muscles in your body feel when you are under stress and they are tense, how they feel when you are relaxed and how you can consciously relax even those muscles—the ones in your forehead, for example—over which you do not normally exert conscious control.

I introduce relaxation exercises during the group session following the one in which I teach my patients the diaphragmatic breathing techniques described in Chapter 19. I ask them to lie down on the floor and close their eyes as I take them through the progressive relaxation sequence described below. Invariably some patients feel anxious about "giving up control" and/or of having a panic attack. Keeping their eyes open sometimes helps them through the initial anxiety.

221

MAKING A SELF-RELAXATION TAPE

While there are many commercially prepared relaxation tapes available, I suggest to my patients that they record one or several different ones themselves, using the exercise I present here as a sample script. All that's needed is a tape recorder and blank tape. Self-made tapes can be tailored to individual likes, dislikes, and reactions to particular stimuli.

The following exercise involves tensing each muscle group and then releasing or relaxing it. The tension-relaxation mechanism is like a pendulum; the farther you pull it one way, the farther it will go the other. The more tension you produce, the easier it will be to relax.

Creating and controlling your own tension allows you to become very aware of the differences in sensations produced by a state of tension versus a state of relaxation. With practice, you will become proficient at detecting tension even at mild levels. Thus, you will be able to apply the relaxation technique as soon as you are aware of any tension, rather than wait for the tension to build up to uncomfortable levels.

Although eventually you will be able to do this or most other relaxation exercises anywhere, anytime, it's helpful at first to select a quiet, peaceful place where you will not be disturbed. If such a place doesn't appear naturally in your life, create it! Perhaps put a sign on the door to your bedroom or the study indicating that you do not want to be disturbed. It's helpful for you to explain to your family members or anyone else who is around the house, why you need this quiet, alone time.

When making your own tape, be sure to speak slowly, distinctly and softly—allowing plenty of time to tense and relax each muscle group. Allow about 10 seconds to tense the muscles and 20 seconds to relax. You needn't announce each muscle group when you are making the tape—simply move from one group to the next. After a while, you'll find that you can practice this exercise on your own, without listening to the tape.

You're now ready to begin recording the following suggested deep-relaxation instructions:

Get into a comfortable position, close your eyes, take several deep, full breaths, and sit quietly for a few seconds.

HANDS AND LOWER ARMS

Begin by building up the tension in your lower arms and hands. Make fists and pull up on your wrists. Feel the tension through your lower arms, your wrists, your fingers, your knuckles. Squeeze your hand as tightly as you can. Tighter . . . hold . . . hold. . . . Notice the sensations of pulling, of discomfort, of tightness. Hold the tension for 10 seconds.

Now release. Let your hands and lower arms relax limply beside you. Let the palms face down. Focus on the sensations in your hands and arms. Feel the release from the tension. Notice the difference between how your arms and hands feel when they are tense and when they are relaxed.

UPPER ARMS

Now build up the tension in your upper arms. Pull your arms back and in toward your sides. Try to keep the muscles in other parts of your body relaxed. Squeeze your arms, noticing the tension in the back of your arms, your shoulder and your back. Focus on the sensations of tension. Squeeze tighter . . . tighter . . . hold. . . . Hold for 10 seconds.

Now release the arms and let them relax. Notice how heavy they feel when you let go. Focus on the sensations of warmth and relaxation in your arms.

FEET AND LOWER LEGS

Now build up the tension in your feet and lower legs. Squeeze your toes and calf muscles as tightly as you can. Feel the tension as it spreads through your ankles, heels, and soles of your feet. And notice it moving up into your calves and shins. Now tighten the muscle groups even more and hold . . . tighter . . . tighter. . . . Focus all of your attention on your feet and lower legs. Hold for 10 seconds.

Now release the tension. Let your feet, calves and shins relax. Notice the difference in your muscles as they let go. Feel the release from tension and the sense of comfort and heaviness from relaxation.

UPPER LEGS

Now build up the tension in your upper legs. Squeeze the muscles as tightly as you can. Tighten them even more and hold . . . hold . . . hold . . . even tighter. Hold for 10 seconds. Focus all of your attention on your upper legs.

Now release. Let your upper legs relax. Notice your whole leg is beginning to feel very heavy. Let all the tension disappear. Focus on the essence of comfort.

STOMACH

Now build up the tension in your stomach. Pull your stomach in toward your spine. Pull it very tight. Feel the tension. Hold it tight . . . even tighter. Hold it in for 10 seconds, while focusing all your attention on how your stomach feels when you create tension around it.

Now let your stomach go—let it go further and further. Feel the sense of warmth circulating across your stomach. Feel the comfort of relaxation.

CHEST

Now build up the tension around your chest. Take in a deep breath and hold it. Your chest is expanded, and the muscles are stretched around your chest. Feel the tension around your front and your back. Hold your breath. Hold . . . hold . . . hold for 10 seconds.

Now slowly let the air escape and resume normal breathing. Let the air flow in and out, smoothly and easily. Be aware of the difference as your muscles relax.

SHOULDERS

Now move up to your shoulders. Imagine your shoulders are on strings being pulled up toward your ears. Feel the tension around your shoulders as you squeeze them together and lift them up. Squeeze tighter . . . more intensely . . . hold . . . hold. Hold them tightly for 10 seconds. Notice the tension around your neck and back of your head when you hold your shoulders tight.

Now let the shoulders collapse or droop down. Let any tension melt away. Feel the sense of relaxation through your shoulders, upper back, and neck. Focus on the difference of how you feel when you let go of tension in your shoulders.

FACE

Now build up the tension around your face. Frown hard, pulling your eyebrows down and toward the center of your face. Clench your teeth, force the corners of your mouth back into a forced smile, wrinkle your nose and eyes and squish your face into a ball. Focus on the tension. Make a tight, ugly face and notice how your face feels when it is filled with tension. Hold the tension, tightening the muscles . . . tighter . . . tighter. Hold for 10 seconds.

Now abruptly open your mouth and eyes as wide as you can, stick out your tongue, stretch your jaw, raise your eyebrows. Hold that also for 10 seconds and then let go—release all the tension and relax. Let your mouth drop down your eyebrows and forehead relax. Imagine a warm cloth being smoothed over your face. Notice how your face feels when it is relaxed.

Now imagine a warm light traveling through your whole body and stopping wherever you are still holding any tension. Allow the warmth to soften the muscles and let the remaining tension melt away. Feel the tension leave your body as you sink further and further into relaxation. Deeper . . . deeper . . . deeper. Letting go.

Now, as you spend a few minutes in this relaxed state, think about your breathing. Feel the cool air as you breathe in, and the warm air as you breathe out. Your breathing is slow and regular. And every time you breathe out, think to yourself the word relax . . . relax . . . relax . . . feeling comfortable and relaxed. Let about two minutes pass while you are focusing on letting go and relaxing.

Now, count backward from five to one, gradually feeling yourself becoming more alert and awake. Five . . . becoming aware of the room you're in, the furniture. Four . . . beginning to feel more awake. Three . . . moving your arms and legs, waking up your muscles. Two . . . opening your eyes—very slowly. One . . . sitting up and moving around.

When the tape comes to an end, your heart rate and blood pressure might be lower than usual. For that reason, it is a good idea not to stand up very quickly after relaxing.

Initially, some anxiety may be present if you are very sensitive to the sensations that are produced by relaxation. However, this doesn't mean that you should *not* do relaxation. In fact, the best response is to repeat the procedure until you can do it without anxiety.

It is important to concentrate on the sensations in each part of your body during the exercise. Other thoughts will certainly come into your mind, but try to let them pass through. Don't focus on them, and don't criticize yourself for having them. Just gently pull your attention back to your body.

I ask my patients to practice the full procedure twice a day for one week. At the end of the week, ask yourself whether you are able to do it without anxiety. If not, continue to practice for another week or so until you are comfortable.

After that you can shorten the procedure and just do a few muscle groups at a time. You will probably have become much

---

SELF-INVENTORY—RELAXATION

1. Where in your body do you most commonly feel tension?

2. What situations are most likely to bring this on?

3. What changes can you make in your lifestyle that will help you cope with stress more effectively? Think about what you can do to decrease daily, as well as long-term, sources of ongoing stress.

4. How did you feel after practicing the relaxation exercises outlined in this chapter? What, if any, problems do you have in doing the exercises?

---

more aware of where in your body you tend to carry tension. Focus on those areas, as well as on such core muscle groups as the stomach, chest, shoulders, and face muscles.

USING RELAXATION THROUGHOUT YOUR DAY

Once you have increased your body awareness and taught yourself to relax your muscles at will, you are much better equipped to deal with tension as you go about your everyday routine. I suggest to my patients that they do periodic body scans and ask themselves, "Do I feel tight anywhere right now?"

If you feel your tension level rising, slow down your breathing for a few minutes and focus on each muscle group in turn, reminding yourself how it feels when it is relaxed. You may find it useful to concentrate on sensations such as heaviness, warmth, or a floating feeling. You can also let go of tension quickly by dropping your shoulders, letting your stomach relax outward, smoothing your brow and feeling it widen, and lowering your chin and letting your mouth drop open slightly. You can do these things in almost any situation without attracting notice—the changes are primarily on the inside.

As I point out in my groups, relaxation practice ultimately helps you realize that you do have a choice. You can't be tense and relaxed at the same time. And just as you can increase your tension, you can also make a choice to let it go—wherever you are.

21

Family Members, Friends, and Colleagues

BY NOW YOU'VE realized that your anxiety disorder affects not only you, but everyone around you as well:

- You get angry when your well-meaning friend or family member says, "Just go ahead and do it. Just try." And the person reaching out to help you experiences frustration or anger when you say, "I can't," and when you won't try.
- You become embarrassed when your boss sees you walking up ten flights of steps rather than taking the elevator. Your boss gets impatient when you waste valuable time taking a train, rather than flying, to an important meeting.
- You feel devastated when you miss your child's performance in his school play because you're afraid to be in a crowded auditorium. Your child feels neglected, regardless of the reason you give him.
- You feel lonely when you think no one understands what you are experiencing. Your family and friends feel helpless—they want to help but fear they may be doing or saying the wrong thing.

■ ■ ■

You may have noticed that your own difficulty in honestly confronting the existence and impact of your anxiety disorder has further complicated your home and/or work relationships. Perhaps you've tried to hide your problem but at the same time are disappointed when the people around you aren't sensitive to your needs and concerns. Maybe you've been too ashamed or embarrassed to ask for help. Yet those who are unaware of your problem are not only unable to help you, they are also likely to feel rejection or anger when they are disappointed by your behavior.

Or you may have actively reached out for help and been disappointed when even those around you who are well meaning gave you the misguided and frustrating "just pull yourself up by your bootstraps" response.

In order for people to better understand your problem and to be of help to you, they are going to need some education. It is important that they be educated about your condition and how they can be helpful to you, rather than reprimanded because they do not understand.

Many of my patients find it difficult to know where to begin, since they themselves are baffled by their phobic or panic disorder and its powerful impact on their day-to-day lives. So I suggest that prior to beginning a discussion with someone whom they want to tell about their problem, they give that person a copy of the "Dear Friend" letter on pages 232–34. I also recommend that they give a copy of this letter to anyone with whom they have already discussed their problem, as a way of shedding additional light on its confusing nature.

But asking someone who has never personally experienced a panic attack to read the letter is *only* a beginning. It may be quite a while before that person can appreciate the true complexity of your phobic or panic disorder. Rather than becoming angry and frustrated when he or she says or does the wrong thing, be patient. For example, when you tell someone about your panic

---

SELF-INVENTORY—RELATIONSHIPS

1. Describe a situation in which you manipulated someone because of your phobia or panic disorder. How did this affect your relationship?

2. Which of the people around you are most affected by your problem and your learning to overcome it?

3. What effect has your phobic/panic disorder had on your relationship with these people?

4. What effect has your learning to overcome it had on them?

5. What changes do you see and/or anticipate in these relationships as a result of successful treatment?

6. How can you best handle these changes so they have a positive effect on your relationships?

7. Imagine an "ideal support person" helping you in an "ideal practice session." What would this be like?

---

attacks and that person says something like "I know just how you feel. Last week I was stuck in traffic and was so afraid of being late for an appointment that I had a panic attack," your natural reaction might be to berate the person for having the nerve to compare the anxiety anyone might experience when stuck in traffic with that which you experience during a panic attack. Instead, let the person know that you don't expect him or her to understand what it feels like to have a panic attack any more than a man can be expected to know what it feels like to give birth to a child. And when someone *can* say to you, "I can't really understand what it feels like to have a panic attack, but I do know that what you experience is real and not trivial," recognize that attitude as an indication of the point at which an honest and trusting relationship can begin.

A Letter to a Friend

Dear Friend:

There is something about me that I would like to tell you about. I suffer from a phobia [or panic disorder], and I am currently learning techniques that are helping me overcome it.

Phobic and panic disorders are *not* associated with "insanity," nor are they the result of laziness, selfishness, or emotional weakness. They come from having repeated panic attacks: involuntary, frightening reactions that may either come "out of the blue" (indicative of panic disorder) or be provoked by specific situations (indicative of a phobia). These panic attacks cannot be reasoned away and often lead to avoidance of specific places or situations.

Imagine the terror you would feel if you were stuck standing in the middle of a six-lane highway with cars coming at you at one hundred miles an hour. Think of the physiological sensations you would experience: your heart would race, your muscles would tremble, and your chest would tighten and pound. You'd be weak at the knees, and break out in a cold sweat. During that split-second in which you thought you were going to be hit by a car, you would feel dizzy and disoriented—and you would *certainly* have an overwhelming desire to escape. All these physical sensations would come at once!

Now, imagine how you would feel if that same intensity of fear came upon you for absolutely no reason while you were standing in line to pay for your groceries, riding in an elevator, or just walking out of your house. Then imagine if the fear reoccurred each time you even thought about that situation. Imagine your embarrassment and humiliation if no one else felt as you do in these situations—and people told you, "Don't be silly, there is nothing wrong!" That's a scary and lonely feeling, isn't it?

If you are fortunate enough never to have had a panic attack, I cannot expect you really to understand the fear and shame I suffer as a result of it. But I do ask you to believe that what I feel is very *real* and *frightening* to me.

I know this seems irrational and unrealistic. Intellectually, it seems that way to me, too—and that makes it even more difficult. In the past I have tried to hide my fear from other people because I was afraid of being ridiculed and misunderstood. But I no longer feel I have to hide behind a mask. It is a tremendous relief for me to be able to share this with you.

You can help by simply "being with me" when I am feeling panicky. Knowing that I am with someone who will not laugh at me or force me into a situation that I feel I cannot handle is a great source of comfort to me. Once that pressure is removed, I am often more able to confront the anxiety-provoking situation step by step.

Knowing that I can leave a situation at any time also helps alleviate my anxiety and makes confronting my fears easier, so please allow me that option. And respect my efforts to face my fears, however small these efforts may seem.

I know that I have to face my fears to get over them, and I am being taught how to do this in a systematic way. At times, the ways in which I approach things may seem strange to you, but I am learning to use specific techniques that have helped others to cope with their panic attacks and lead normal lives.

I am excited about the positive changes that are taking place in my life, and greatly relieved to be actively working on my problem. And I am most appreciative to you for your support and understanding.

Sincerely,

WORKING WITH YOUR SUPPORT PERSONS

If you haven't yet told anyone about your problem, your first step is to identify someone with whom you feel comfortable talking. Don't worry about whether or not this person understands anything about anxiety disorders at this point. What's more important is that you identify someone whom you trust and who is willing and able to listen to you.

Most people find that when they first start talking to others about their phobic or panic disorder, they're often surprised at the response. Sometimes, after thinking that they've just shared their most personally embarrassing secret, the reaction they get is one of indifference or simple curiosity. At other times, the person in whom they are confiding interrupts to tell about a friend or colleague who has a similar problem. And in many instances, the person confided in reveals their own anxiety disorder, and a close bond is instantly formed.

Even if you receive a less-than-empathetic response, once you tell one person about your problem, you'll find it easier to talk to the next person about it. When describing your problem to others, keep in mind that you did not choose to have an anxiety disorder, it is not the result of some "personal weakness," nor is it something that you can simply "will" away. Think about how you might tell someone that you have diabetes, high blood pressure, or migraine headaches. Like these illnesses, anxiety disorders are real, not imagined—and are characterized by physiological as well as psychological and environmental factors.

Select one or several people with whom you feel safe and

comfortable who are willing to actively help you. They will become your "support" people—people you can count on to help you practice confronting anxiety-producing situations. Your support person or people need not fully understand your problem in order to effectively help you. They do need to understand, however, that what you experience during a panic attack or when you are struggling with anticipatory anxiety is *not* the same as the anxiety or fear that most people feel when confronted with a threatening situation.

You might ask them to imagine what it might feel like to see a speeding car heading directly at them. Then ask them to imagine experiencing that same intensity of panic and terror while waiting in line to buy groceries, signing their name in public, or simply leaving their home.

Describe to them the physical sensations as well as the feelings of loss of control. Then ask them to think how *inappropriate* this reaction might make them feel—and how this leads to feelings of shame, embarrassment, and fears of having something terribly wrong with you.

When you give them a copy of the "Dear Friend" letter, ask them to read it carefully, and then discuss it together.

LEARNING TO ASK FOR HELP

You have probably become a master at hiding your anxiety, having learned a variety of ways to manipulate situations so you won't be discovered. Yet at the same time you probably secretly wish that the people around you would be sensitive enough to realize when you are experiencing difficulties and would, in some magical way, be able to help you.

Just think of the dilemma people around you will experience if you expect them to know, intuitively, when you need their help. Even if they are very sensitive, it is not reasonable to expect them to be so tuned in to your feelings that they automatically know when you need help. If you assume that, everyone loses.

Instead, begin to think about your phobic or panic disorder as a problem shared by you and the people close to you. Your anxiety rarely manifests itself externally: Even though you may feel very anxious and nervous and think everyone can see your distress, *people usually are quite unaware.*

Make it your responsibility to tell your support people that you are having difficulties and would like help, making your request for the kind of help you might want or need as specific and concrete as possible. This may seem difficult at times; embarrassment and pride often stand in the way. But the results are *always* positive. Communication becomes more open, the need to hide and manipulate people and situations is no longer necessary, and the joint effort produces pride and feelings of accomplishment for you both.

In addition, when you tell those helping you how you're really feeling, the pressure to pretend no longer exists, making it easier for you to confront your anxiety-provoking situations.

When you're telling someone exactly what is helpful and what is not, be sure to explain that your needs may change from one time to the next. One time you may welcome being held or talked to; another time you may want to hold on to them or be the one to talk. And at still other times, you may prefer to be left alone.

It is helpful to explain that these inconsistencies have to do with the unpredictable, chameleonlike nature of the anxiety disorder itself, and should not be taken as personal rejections.

As discussed in Chapter 15, having an Out enables people with phobic and panic disorders to enter situations they may otherwise avoid. It is helpful to decide with a support person what your Out will be *prior* to entering the anxiety-provoking situation. For example, if you are hesitant to go into a crowded theater for fear of panicking and having to leave, you may say to someone who invites you to a show, "It will help me to know that *if* I want to leave at any time, it will be okay with you." Explain to the person that just knowing there is a way out—that you will not perceive yourself as being trapped—will enable you to enter and remain in the situation. And explain that it is important to you that he or she be willing to accept this even though it may seem irrational.

As you begin to progress and can do more things than you could previously, you might be concerned that more and more will be expected of you. Sometimes this does happen, because the people helping you do not understand the nature of the disorder.

It's important to explain to your support team that it's possible to do something ten times without any difficulty, then feel as if you can't possibly do it the eleventh time. Or just the opposite: You may be unable to do something, and then, suddenly, just go ahead and do it without any difficulty whatsoever.

Let your support person know that this is a common experience. And be sure to talk about it at a time when you are *not* feeling anxiety and can discuss it calmly. Explain that you want to take each situation as a separate event.

When someone is trying to help you, it is often difficult to know when he is being supportive and when he is pushing you too fast. There is a fine line between the two, and your support person can't know whether he is crossing that line unless you tell him. It is up to you to help clarify that distinction.

The following suggestions will enable you and your support people to get the most out of your practice sessions:

1. Set specific goals.
2. Approach each goal one step at a time.
3. Clearly define Outs prior to entering the anxiety-producing situation.
4. Reinforce each achievement by being specific about what worked.
5. Jointly acknowledge progress, no matter how small. If your support person isn't aware of your effort or success, call it to his or her attention.
6. Eliminate criticisms and blame. Stress patience and a sense of commitment.
7. Jointly test reality. If, for example, you are concerned that others can see you shaking or blushing when you are in a social situation, ask your support person to honestly assess whether or not you physically appear anxious.

8. Be specific and honest about what is helpful and what is not.

9. Work together to remain in situations until your high anxiety levels are diminished, focusing on the Six Points and doing manageable things in the present.

10. Allow for setbacks. They are always followed by growth (for both you and your support person).

11. Feel good about what you do, not bad about what you did not do. And especially feel good about what you did when you felt anxious.

HOW TO EXPLAIN YOUR PHOBIA OR PANIC DISORDER TO YOUR CHILDREN

Don't be afraid to tell your children about your anxiety-related problem. Our natural instinct is to hide problems from our children in order to "protect" them. Children, however, are extremely perceptive, and even though they may not understand the nature of a specific problem, they do recognize unusual behavior. They are far more likely to assume *they* did something wrong or that you don't love them anymore than to grasp that you don't take them to the amusement park because you're unable to drive, or that you didn't show up for their school play because of your fear of crowds.

I suggest to my patients that they explain their irrational fears and avoidance behavior to their children in a way that helps the children understand that sometimes people become afraid of things that aren't really scary, and that it's helpful to talk about their fears, even if they seem embarrassing or unjustified.

A good example to use in helping children understand irrational fear is that of monsters—those imaginary frightful beings of childhood. Most children can relate to a time when they were frightened of monsters, in spite of the reassurance of their parents that such things don't exist. They can usually remember checking under the bed and in the closet to see for themselves that none was there.

And they often recall how the night light or cup of warm milk "made the monsters go away."

I encourage parents to engage even their young children in their recovery process by having them participate in practice sessions. I remember one patient telling me that she overheard her six-year-old daughter telling her husband how much fun she had driving back and forth over a bridge that afternoon with her mother. "Every time Mommy got scared", she bragged, "I helped her count out loud or sing a song and then she wasn't scared anymore." In addition to being helpful to her mother, this child was learning at an early age that fear isn't something to be ashamed of and that one can do things to help make it go away.

Many parents are concerned that if they expose their child to their irrational fears, the child will learn the same fears. Certainly many fears are learned, but the fears generated by an anxiety disorder are not the same as regular fears. Anxiety-disorder fear reactions are the result of a combination of biological, biochemical, and psychological interactions and are different from ordinary learned behaviors. Since anxiety disorders do tend to run in families, however, the child of someone with an anxiety disorder is at a slightly higher risk for developing a similar problem. This makes it even more important that the child learn how to talk openly and honestly about frightening thoughts and feelings. Then, if the disorder should surface, it can be diagnosed and treated in its early stages.

CHANGING ROLES AND RELATIONSHIPS

You'll find that certain roles and relationships, at home and in the workplace, will begin to change as you recover from your anxiety disorder. When you're preoccupied with the frightening thoughts and feelings surrounding anticipatory anxiety and avoidance behavior, other feelings and emotions—anger, sadness, even happiness or love—may be overshadowed or ignored. As you recover, many of these feelings and emotions—or new ones—will begin to surface or resurface, often leaving you and those around you confused.

Also, it is probable that your behavior has directly or indirectly influenced your friends, family members, and coworkers repeatedly to alter their plans in order to accommodate your special needs. As a result, you may feel you no longer have the right to ask for other things you want or need. The frustration of not getting your emotional or everyday needs met may put additional strain on your interpersonal and/or collegial relationships.

BECOMING ASSERTIVE: GETTING YOUR NEEDS MET

It is also quite possible that as you become more aware of your emotional needs and more assertive about getting them met, people close to you will begin to feel uncomfortable and confused. As you work toward overcoming your anxiety disorder, they may begin to feel less needed. Even well-meaning people may unknowingly attempt to keep you passive and dependent because of their own particular needs. They don't do this intentionally, of course, but it may be difficult for them to adjust to the "new you."

It is important for you to be open and communicative and, at the same time, sensitive to the needs of those around you. If you previously were always at home when your spouse came home from work each night, and now you are out and around about, make sure you call or leave a note indicating that you are out and the approximate time that you will return.

If you've always asked a certain friend to accompany you to specific places, and are now able and wanting to go to those places on your own, make sure the friend understands that this change is part of your recovery, so the friend doesn't feel neglected.

If a coworker has usually waited by the elevator in the morning to accompany you to your office, let him know how much you have appreciated this in the past and share your new successes with him. Be careful not to just "stop needing" someone.

Often people with phobic or panic disorders are so concerned about not appearing "needy" that they will go to great lengths to suppress even healthy and appropriate needs and preferences—a kind of overcompensation. Thus, the phobic person may make exaggerated efforts to be well liked and nondemanding—in contrast to the times when he or she is avoiding confronting a phobic situation and then becomes *extremely* demanding.

It's not uncommon for someone with an anxiety disorder to put their healthy wants and needs on the back burner and become the "good little girl or boy who doesn't cause any waves." It is not unusual for such a person to assume the role of a hero: the one who holds everyone in the family or office together in times of crisis, always has a smile on his or her face, and is sensitive to everyone else's feelings and needs. The internal messages may go something like this: "By taking care of everyone around me, I'll be liked. If I let my own feelings show, I may not be liked, so I'll try even harder to please (I'll ignore my own feelings) and thus be more well liked."

You may notice yourself smiling more when you're angry or upset so that others won't "suspect" something is wrong. Or perhaps you act a bit detached, hoping others will magically guess or sense what you need and give it to you without your having to ask.

However you go about hiding your needs, the bottom line is that they remain unmet and you're left frustrated. To change this pattern you have to consciously change your behavior.

The best place to begin is by recognizing that *you have the right to ask for what you want*. As you practice and become more comfortable with this, you'll discover that it can be very satisfying to ask a direct question and get a direct response. Even though the response may be negative, it is not you who is being rejected; the focus is on the object of your request.

My patients have found the following list, "Your Rights," to be a helpful reminder that they can and deserve to have more than their phobic needs met!

241

"I" Statements—Your Rights

I have the right to make a mistake and be responsible for it.

I have the right to say No without feeling guilty.

I have the right to do what will make me happy, as long as it does not infringe upon another person's rights.

I have the right to ask for help.

I have the right to feel angry.

I have the right to feel confused.

I have the right not to care.

I have the right to offer no excuses for my behavior.

I have the right to have my needs respected.

I have the right not to know the answer.

I have the right to disagree.

I have the right to be weak.

I have the right to cry.

I have the right to be scared.

I have the right not to like everybody.

I have the right to get what I pay for.

I have the right to ask for what I want, knowing that it can be refused.

I have the right to be listened to; the right to be taken seriously.

I have the right to set my own priorities.

I have the right to change my mind.

I have the right to privacy.

I have the right to ask for help from professionals.

I have the bodily right to walk away.

I have the right to be nonassertive.

SELF-INVENTORY—NEEDS

1. Do you have emotional needs that you feel uncomfortable expressing? If yes, what are they?

2. What effect does this have on you and on your relationships with others?

3. What can you do to change this?

4. Which "rights" do you have the most difficulty claiming? Describe.

22

Overcoming Setbacks

ABOUT FOUR OR five weeks into treatment, invariably someone in my group who has been progressing very nicely will announce that he or she has had a terrible week and is right back at the beginning—all of the old feelings have returned: anticipatory anxiety, panic attacks, avoidance behavior.

Strange as this may sound, what this tells me is not that our work has failed, but that my patient is now ready to leap forward and make *significant progress*. This person has experienced a "setback," a critical part of the recovery process.

UNDERSTANDING SETBACKS

Setbacks, such as anticipatory anxiety about confronting situations you thought were no longer troublesome or having a panic attack after you haven't had one for a while, are an inevitable and essential part of your recovery. The sooner you understand and accept this, the more headway you will make in overcoming your phobia or panic disorder.

Let's look at what happens during a setback. As you begin to do things you haven't done for years, you feel terrific about yourself.

Along with your new accomplishments come increased self-esteem and elevated moods. You have magical thoughts of never having another panic attack.

Then, just as you become convinced that you've got the darn thing licked—whammo, it strikes again. And this time it seems worse than ever! This is partly because you are terrified that you are regressing, that the relief was just temporary, and partly because the symptoms *seem* more pronounced.

Neither is true. As a matter of fact, a setback is really a "springboard." Each setback moves you further along toward recovery. Why?

First of all, each setback is an opportunity for growth. Remind yourself of something you thought you couldn't do—perhaps only a few weeks ago—and then did. How did you feel afterward? Proud? Stronger? Did you feel a sense of accomplishment?

Second, each setback makes facing your fear the next time easier. You will notice that it doesn't take as long to get back to where you were. You never lose the ground you've already gained—it just seems like that, temporarily. You gain new confidence from confronting and coping with a difficult situation.

Finally, setbacks enable you to practice the techniques you have learned. Each opportunity to practice reinforces your understanding that no matter how frightening a situation may seem, nothing is going to happen to you, except that you may experience uncomfortable feelings and scary thoughts.

Each time you pass through a setback, think of this: The journey made *with* panic is even more successful than the journey made *without* panic. Focus on your gains and work from there.

The nature of setbacks is that they occur when you least want or expect them. You're driving on the highway, thinking about how terrific it is to be able to drive without having panic attacks, and up pops your anxiety level.

Or you're shopping in a crowded store, telling your friend how glad you are that your panic attacks are gone—and guess what? Panic shows its ugly face.

Part of this is because panic attacks "have no conscience." Even if you are "thinking positive thoughts" about your panic attacks, such as "I haven't had one in a long time," you may begin to experience anticipatory anxiety just because you're thinking about them.

Also, there may be stresses going on in your life that you may or may not be aware of. Some people find that when they are stressed, they are more likely to have a panic attack. Others find just the opposite. When they are preoccupied with "real-life" stresses, they are less aware of irrational or inappropriate fear reactions. Perhaps these people feel they have "permission" to be anxious when there is something really stressful going on, and therefore they don't worry about feeling that way. In any case, stress can affect your phobia or panic disorder. Recognizing and accepting this can save you a lot of futile "Why now?" thinking.

Furthermore, a setback is always an opportunity. As you move forward, you'll discover that the greatest growth experiences come *after* a setback. It's then that you realize and accept that while there is no "magic bullet" to cure an anxiety disorder, it is treatable—and your best weapon is your own hard work and practice.

As I mentioned earlier, Dr. Claire Weekes tells us that "peace is on the other side of fear—and only when you pass through your fears will you find comfort." Tell yourself this the next time you think you are having a setback, and you will understand why we call it a "springboard."

To "grow" from a setback, think about the following points

1. There are "good days" and bad days." A bad day or bad time does not mean "forever bad." It is simply a bad day or bad time. Isolate it as such. Accept that something is occurring, or has occurred, that you are reacting to in a negative way.

That is all that is happening. You aren't going back to square one. You haven't lost what you have gained. You're simply having a bad time. It will pass, just as the other bad times have.

2. If you are predisposed to having panic attacks, you are probably supersensitive to any out-of-the-ordinary bodily sensations or emotions, including some that most people would not be

aware of. Even normal feelings and movements—like becoming winded—may become worrisome. It doesn't take much to become overwhelmed.

When you do become overwhelmed, you are likely to become filled with unidentified feelings and racing, confused thoughts. This can be so frightening that there is a tendency to turn inward: Instead of trying to identify what is really happening or what the problem is, you focus on your feelings, which, given enough fuel, can easily escalate into panic.

If you give it free rein, this negative spiral is likely to arouse your old feelings of helplessness and your patterns of avoidance. *But now you know how to interrupt it.* Use the techniques you have learned to bring yourself back to the present. And notice how quickly you can lower your anxiety level.

3. Recovery and success do *not* mean that you will never have another anxiety or panic attack. Understandably, that's what you unconsciously want and expect, and you may therefore misinterpret anything short of "no anxiety" as failure. But when you think about it rationally, you know that it's just not possible or realistic never to experience anxiety again. However, it is possible to no longer let anxiety or panic attacks run your life!

4. Life changes affect everyone, but people prone to anxiety disorders are typically more sensitive and reactive than other people and, therefore, more strongly affected.

There is a sense of security in having everything familiar. Any major change—a move, a job change, personal loss or rejection—will generate strong emotions. Even positive changes can produce uncomfortable or frightening feelings.

Respect what you are feeling. It is normal, healthy, and perfectly okay to feel uneasy about change. The problems arise when you begin to confuse these feelings with old feelings of panic. Being apprehensive, uneasy, or anxious about a change does not mean you are going back to the way you were. It's simply how your mind and body react to "new information." Recognize it for what it is, and *move on.*

5. Strong feelings—anger, grief, disappointment, loneliness,

SELF-INVENTORY—SETBACKS

1. Describe a recent setback. How would you handle it differently if it happened again?

2. What strong feelings are most difficult for you to deal with? What, if any, effect does this have on your phobic or panic disorder?

3. In your own words, tell how you can *benefit* from a setback.

---

even pleasurable feelings such as love—often get lumped into one awareness: "anxiety," "panic," or "fear." When these feelings are not identified for what they are, extra anxiety is added to what is already there. As the anxiety builds up, things begin to feel out of control, and you think you are having a setback.

You can stop this spiraling by becoming aware of what your feelings really are. Allow them to surface. Don't run away from them, even if they're frightening.

Strong feelings, including "bad" feelings like anger and disappointment, are normal and useful. Learn to use all your feelings. It might help to write them down, or to talk about them with someone you feel close to and trust.

LETTING GO: RESISTANCE TO CHANGE

It is not uncommon for patients in the throes of a setback to wonder whether there may be some unconscious reason why they are not able or willing to let go of their anxiety disorder. What often comes up just as strongly during the group sessions, however, is how *enraging* it is when a friend or family member suggests this, since it implies that the panic attacks or the avoidance behavior is developed or maintained as an excuse to get out of undesirable activities. The suggestion that the person indirectly benefits from his or her negative behavior, a concept called "secondary gain," can be both painful and frustrating.

Although some patients are self-consciously concerned that their anxiety disorder may serve some unmet need, the only people who could really believe that it was *developed* for that purpose would be those who have never experienced a panic attack!

Anyone who has personally struggled with this problem knows that there isn't any "secondary gain" in the world that could possibly justify the emotional pain and humiliation endured as a consequence of having an anxiety disorder. (Furthermore, we now know that the onset of an anxiety disorder has a very strong biological component.)

Although you clearly did not develop your anxiety disorder as a means of getting your needs met or of having other people do things for you, once it has surfaced, it is almost inevitable that some secondary gains will develop. If you can't go shopping, someone else will have to do it for you. If you're unable to drive, a friend or family member will have to transport you. If you are phobic about public speaking, most likely a colleague will take over your speaking engagements.

Most of the time you will not see these as secondary gains because you would much prefer to do these activities for or by yourself. However, in some cases they do benefit you, and you have to address that. If your inability to drive means that your spouse takes over all of your child's carpooling activities—something you would be happy to give up even if you didn't have a driving phobia—getting better means driving the carpool yourself, no matter how inconvenient.

As you recover from your anxiety disorder you need to recognize the secondary gains that developed as a result of your anxiety problem. This is often scary. As desperately as you want to get rid of your problems, you may find yourself somewhat reluctant to identify them—and to let them go.

You know what it's like to have an anxiety disorder: You know your limitations, and you know what's expected and not expected of you. But you don't know what it will be like without it—especially if it's been with you for a long time.

Letting go is frightening. Think about how many people stay in marriages even though they may despise their partners. The "terrible known" is often more comfortable than the unknown, even if the unknown promises to be better.

What can you do about this? Use the self-inventory on page 251 to start getting some answers to this question.

Begin by making a list of all the advantages you get from your anxiety disorder. This may sound silly, but think about it. What obligations are you excused from? What do people do for you that you would have to do for yourself if you didn't have the problem. What difficult life changes have you put off because of the disorder?

After you have made your list, ask the people most affected by your condition to make a similar list. Ask them to put down all the things they feel they do for you because of your limitations.

There are likely to be some strong differences of opinion. There may even be some angry or embarrassing feelings. That is normal and to be expected.

Try not to be defensive. Just listen.

After you've gathered all your information, think about which secondary gains you are willing to give up. What are you willing to change? Begin with the easiest. If driving in your child's carpool three days a week feels like too much of a commitment at this time, agree to begin by driving one day a week. If you are not quite ready to do all the family shopping, agree to be responsible for purchasing all the dairy products. If you have gotten out of giving major presentations at the office, begin by giving talks as part of a panel or jointly with a colleague.

You will find that as you begin to give up "getting out of things" and other secondary gains, you will start to feel freer and more independent. You'll feel increased self-esteem—and that alone makes it worth giving up any secondary gain.

SELF-INVENTORY—SECONDARY GAINS

1. What secondary gains are you aware of getting as a result of your phobic or panic disorder?

2. What secondary gains do others think you get as a result of your phobic or panic disorder?

3. What are your concerns about giving up these secondary gains?

4. Give an example of breaking down the steps in giving up one of your secondary gains.

Keep in mind, however, that *all* change is difficult—anxiety-related or not. It is normal for anyone in transition to feel resistance, apprehension, and discomfort. The more you can accept these feelings, the less they will get in the way of your recovery.

23

Becoming Acquainted
with the New You

WHEN MOST PEOPLE with a phobic or panic disorder are asked what they would be like if they did not have the problem, they say that they would like to be "the way I used to be—free of fears and anxiety, happy and enjoying life to the fullest."

They forget having ever felt stress, fear, or anxiety prior to developing an anxiety disorder, and they often recall "pre-panic-attack" life as being perfect. It is common to hear someone with a phobia say, "If only my phobia would go away, everything would be wonderful. I could do everything—just like the good old days . . ."

Of course, this is not realistic thinking. Life was no more perfect before you developed an anxiety disorder than it is today. You had your stresses, worries, and bad days. For sure, there were times when you felt angry, lonely, or depressed. But you have probably forgotten about those times. Compared to suffering with an anxiety disorder, everything else seems tolerable.

There is a tendency to put other feelings on the "back burner," judging how you feel only by how anxious you feel. If you don't feel anxiety on a particular day, then that is considered a good day. Naturally, the assumption then becomes, "Before I became phobic or developed a panic disorder, *all* days were good days."

Another common reaction to the question of what you would be like if you didn't have a panic or phobic disorder is "I would go back to doing all the things I used to love to do—going shopping, going to parties, going to the theater . . ." However, most likely many of your interests have changed over the months or years you have been restricted because of your problem, and you may not enjoy the same things you did in the past.

There is nothing wrong with not wanting to go to a party if you don't enjoy the people who will be there. You may not wish to go shopping or to go to the theater as much as you thought you would—even though you once longed to do those things. Part of our natural maturation process leads us to outgrow old interests and develop new ones. Your phobic or panic disorder has been such a dominant part of your life—and has prevented you from enjoying so many activities—that it often becomes difficult to tell whether or not you are genuinely interested in doing something.

You have probably found that there are many things you used to enjoy that you no longer find enjoyable, but you feel guilty about it and blame your lack of enjoyment on your anxiety problem. When this happens, you're being much too hard on yourself!

It is often difficult to distinguish between something you really do not want to do and something you are avoiding because you are afraid of having a panic attack. When this happens, ask yourself, "If I weren't afraid of having a panic attack, would I want to ——?" If the answer is Yes, go ahead and do it, regardless of how anxious you feel. If the answer is No, don't do it. If going to a restaurant is a problem for you, and people whom you don't care for invite you to join them for dinner, you have every right not to want to go. You are not copping out.

It is perfectly normal and healthy not to want to do things for reasons other than your fear of having a panic attack. But if you are not sure whether you want to avoid something because you are afraid of having a panic attack or because you simply do not want to do it, do it anyway. Keep in mind your goal: to live a normal life without avoidance.

SELF-INVENTORY—CHANGE

1. Describe what you were like before you developed a phobic/panic disorder (personality, interests, pet peeves, etc.)

2. How has the disorder changed you?

3. Are there things you avoid, but can't tell whether it is because of your phobia or for some other reason? If yes, what are they and what other reasons might you have for not wanting to do them?

4. If your phobic/panic disorder disappeared completely tomorrow, how might your life change?

5. What are some things you would like to do if you had more time and energy?

As you begin to use the techniques that allow you to go anywhere and do things you want to do, a "new you" will begin to emerge—not someone from the past coming back, but a stronger, more confident person with a whole new set of likes, dislikes, and interests. Since less of your time will be taken up worrying about your problem, you will find yourself having a lot more time and energy to do other things. *Now* is the time to start thinking about what these other things are.

Respect yourself. Listen to what you *really want* and follow your instincts—they are usually right. The key to growth is moving forward, not looking back. This means accepting change. It is not an easy road to follow, but it is the one that will lead you to recovery.

Appendices

Research Update

Anxiety disorders are significantly better understood today than they were even a few years ago. And there continues to be ongoing research into causes, symptomatology, diagnoses, and treatments of the disorder, with new findings published almost weekly.

Here are brief descriptions of some new findings and hints of things to come:

- Panic disorder has long been anecdotally associated with gastrointestinal symptoms such as vomiting and diarrhea. Now a team of researchers led by Bruce Lydiard, M.D., Ph.D., of the Medical University of South Carolina, has found in a survey of more than thirteen thousand individuals that persons with panic disorder have significantly higher rates of gastrointestinal symptoms, including those typical of irritable bowel syndrome. This overlap, the researchers noted, should be considered in preparing treatment programs, and they cited the relationship between "the brain and the gut" as an important area for future study.

- Although young women are the prime candidates for the first episode of panic disorder, a recent study at the University of South Florida Medical College found that 5.7 percent of a group of 560 patients over 60 years old had experienced their first panic attack after the age of 59. The overall prevalence of panic disorder in the group was nearly 10 percent. The researchers concluded that, indeed, panic disorder "can have onset in late life." Stress, medical illness, and central nervous system disease appeared to be contributing factors, and the older-onset group had more breathing difficulties than those who had had their first attack as young people.

▪ In response to theories that chronic hyperventilation can induce panic attacks, a team of veteran anxiety-disorder researchers reviewed some three hundred articles and concluded that the cause is less likely hyperventilation than a subtle sensitivity to carbon dioxide, the respiratory gas exhaled in exchange with oxygen. Laszlo A. Papp, M.D., Donald F. Klein, M.D., and Jack M. Gorman, M.D., wrote in 1992 that "catastrophic interpretation" of the symptoms, a sense of needing air, can set off the panic attack.

▪ Panic disorder in African-Americans appears to be very little different from that in whites, according to an analysis of the interviews from the National Institute of Mental Health Epidemiological Catchment Area study. Researchers examined the interview responses of 4,287 African-Americans and compared them to 12, 142 white subjects. Comparisons revealed little difference in age at onset, years with panic disorder, and suicide attempts. The researchers warned, however, that "there is reason to believe that panic disorder is not adequately recognized and treated among African-Americans. The evidence for misdiagnosis and poor treatment outcome among African-Americans indicates the need for improved diagnosis and treatment of panic disorder in this population." The authors were Ewald Horwath, M.D., M.Sc., Christopher D. Hornig, and the late Jim Johnson, Ph.D.

▪ At least one study has suggested that a subgroup of women with panic disorder may improve when they are pregnant. James Ballenger, M.D., and his team at the Medical University of South Carolina mailed questionnaires to 129 women who had been patients at the university's anxiety disorders clinic over the last five years asking them about changes in their disorder when they subsequently became pregnant. Of the 22 who reported, a majority (14) said their symptoms had improved while they were pregnant.

▪ Individuals with Seasonal Affective Disorder (SAD), who become depressed when the days begin to shorten in the fall and do not recover, without treatment, until the spring, appear at risk for seasonal panic disorder as well, a study at Ohio State University has demonstrated. Researchers examined thirty-eight patients with recurrent winter depression and found that nearly one quarter of them also had panic attacks that went away when the depression lifted in the spring.

▪ Mitral valve prolapse (MVP) is a common heart condition, considered benign in most cases. This deformation of the mitral valve, one of the four valves of the heart, was at first believed to occur most often in individuals with panic disorder, leading to a hypothesis that the heart problem might have initiated the panic disorder. Some studies showed a high correlation between the existence of panic disorder and MVP, but this remains controversial—possibly because of the different criteria used to make the diagnosis.

The presence of MVP does not change the treatment of the panic disorder in any way. People with both conditions should not ascribe all of their symptoms to MVP or assume that treatment of MVP will eliminate their panic attacks.

■ A relatively new treatment approach known as Non-Prescriptive Treatment (NPT) has been developed by Katherine Shear, M.D., of the Western Psychiatric Institute and Clinic in Pittsburgh. Shear's treatment utilizes psychoeducation and reflective listening strategies to help patients increase their awareness of and acceptance of unacknowledged, negative feelings (such as anger and aggression) which may be contributing to the onset and maintenance of panic attacks.

■ EMDR (eye movement desensitization and reprocessing) is a new technique developed only in the last few years by Francine Shapiro, Ph.D. It has had reported success in desensitizing individuals with post-traumatic stress disorder, panic disorder, and agoraphobia. There are anecdotal reports of its power, but it has not yet been fully tested. It involves a therapist's engaging in hand movements that are tracked by the patient as he or she imagines scenes that would normally evoke panic or anxiety. In some patients it produces a sense of meditation or, as one patient put it, as though she had been on three Valiums, but without "feeling zonked."

In 1987, Dr. Shapiro accidentally found that she was able to dispel her own anxious thoughts by moving her eyes rapidly from side to side. Since then she and other therapists have achieved often dramatic results with victims of catastrophes, and with agoraphobics resistant to other therapies. Not all clinicians share her success and the procedure remains unexplained and controversial.

Medications Used in the Treatment of Anxiety Disorders

Many different medications have proven useful in the treatment of anxiety disorders. But finding the right medication and dosage for each individual may require some detective work on the part of the physician. Since medication therapy for anxiety disorders is a relatively new area, it is best to choose a physician who has specific knowledge and experience in prescribing and managing medication for people with anxiety disorders.

Each medication has advantages and disadvantages. Some work faster than others; some remain in the bloodstream longer. Some require several doses daily; others need to be taken only once a day. Dietary restrictions are necessary when taking some medications, and some may be off limits to avoid dangerous interactions with other medications a patient is taking.

Medication's effectiveness varies with each individual. People's nervous systems and metabolisms are unique, and so is their response to outside agents—be they food or medicine. Older people may react differently than younger individuals to the same medication; a woman may respond differently than a man.

Most people can take antianxiety medication without difficulty, but sometimes there are side effects. Side effects vary with the medication, but they can range from minor annoyances like dry mouth or drowsiness to more troubling reactions like irregular heartbeat or impaired sexual functioning.

Fortunately, most side effects disappear in the first week or two of treatment. If the side effects persist, or if they interfere with normal activities, the doctor may change dosages or try a different medication.

Using medication is more complicated for some groups of people than for others. Pregnant women and nursing mothers, for example, must avoid certain drugs because of possible danger to the fetus or infant. Women who are attempting to conceive should also avoid certain medications.

Young children and the elderly also need special attention. Because of their lower body weight, youngsters are generally given smaller dosages of medications than adults. Treatment of elderly patients may be complicated by other health problems and/or other medication regimens.

People with high blood pressure, kidney and liver ailments, or other chronic conditions may need to avoid certain medications.

Getting the best results from medication depends on taking the right amount at the right time. Dosages and their frequency are determined by the desire to assure a consistent and steady amount of medication in the system. Generally, this requires that the medication be taken at specified times throughout the day. If sticking to the schedule proves difficult, the patient should ask the doctor whether or not adjustments can be made. Although changes are not always possible, sometimes schedule options are available.

Patients should not deviate from prescribed dosages unless so instructed by their physician. If you feel you need more medication, discuss this with your doctor. People who have forgotten to take their medication at some point in the day are often tempted to "catch up" and take twice as much as prescribed at the next dose, but doubling up may increase the risk of an adverse reaction. Ask your physician what to do if you miss a dose, and follow his or her instructions explicitly.

Believing that more is better, some patients increase their dosage if their symptoms are not relieved immediately or because previously arrested symptoms have returned. Others undermedicate themselves because they fear side effects. Some patients err by cutting back or stopping medication on their own because their symptoms have disappeared. Cutting dosages or stopping medication too abruptly can cause symptoms to return. Concerns about a medication's effectiveness, the length of drug therapy, how to terminate usage, and all other questions should be discussed directly and candidly with the physician.

Following is a brief overview of some of the medications that have been demonstrated to be useful in the treatment of anxiety disorders:

• *High potency benzodiazepines.* These drugs, which include alprazolam (Xanax) and clonazepam (Klonopin), are part of the same family as diazepam (Valium), but they are more effective in treating panic disorder and have fewer side effects.

• *Tricyclic antidepressants.* These drugs, among the first to be used to treat anxiety disorders, include imipramine (Tofranil), desipramine (Norpramin, Pertofrane), nortriptyline (Aventyl, Pamelor), amitriptyline (Elavil), and clomipramine (Anafranil). Clomipramine has been found to be especially useful in the treatment of obsessive-compulsive disorder.

262

- *Serotonin specific reuptake inhibitors (SSRIs)* are drugs which enhance the presence of the neurotransmitter serotonin in the brain. They include fluoxetine (Prozac), sertraline (Zoloft), and paroxetine (Paxil). Fluvoxamine (Luvox) is a newcomer in this field, soon to be introduced commercially. SSRIs are particularly helpful in the treatment of panic disorder, social phobia, and OCD.

- *Monoamine oxidase inhibitors (MAOIs)* including phenelzine (Nardil) and tranylcypromine (Parnate) are useful in treating panic disorder and social phobia with or without a co-existing depression. These are generally used as a third line of treatment for patients who do not respond to other antidepressants, because MAOIs can be difficult to tolerate and require rigid dietary restrictions.

- *Azaspirones.* Buspirone (Buspar) enhances the activity of serotonin and is useful in treating generalized anxiety disorder.

- *Beta blockers* such as propranolol (Inderal) and atenolol (Tenormin), which are often prescribed to treat high blood pressure, are sometimes helpful in blocking the physiological symptoms of stage fright or performance anxiety, such as heart palpitations, tremor, or sweating.

Foods and Other Substances to Avoid

Many people who suffer from one or another of the anxiety disorders, and especially those for whom panic attacks are at least part of the problem, may be particularly sensitive to certain common foods.

Caffeine is a prime offender. It is found in coffee, tea, cocoa, chocolate, and virtually all cola drinks. Even some non-cola drinks contain added caffeine. Sensitivities vary, so whereas some people can consume these things without difficulty, others may react to even minute amounts. There are several theories, but no definitive explanation for this sensitivity.

Other stimulants should be avoided, such as pseudoephedrine, which is found in many over-the-counter medications for colds, allergies, and sinus problems (Sudafed, for example). Some prescription drugs, including several asthma medicines, may also precipitate panic attacks in some patients. These sensitivities vary from individual to individual, so each patient must use them with caution. Diet pills almost always contain stimulants of some sort. Aside from their highly dubious effectiveness for weight loss, they can initiate panic attacks.

Illicit drugs should be anathema to anyone with any sort of anxiety disorder. Stimulants such as cocaine or amphetamines will produce all the symptoms of a full-blown panic attack. Marijuana has been widely cited by people with panic disorder as the *single initiating factor* in their first attack.

Resources

BOOKS AND TAPES

PANIC DISORDER, AGORAPHOBIA, AND SIMPLE PHOBIAS

Barlow, D.H., and M.G. Craske. *Mastery of Your Anxiety and Panic*. Albany, N.Y.: Graywind Publications, 1988.

Beck, A.T., G. Emery, and R. Greenberg. *Anxiety Disorders and Phobias: A Cognitive Perspective*. New York: Basic Books, 1985.

Gold, M.S. *The Good News About Panic, Anxiety & Phobias*. New York: Bantam Books, 1989.

Greist, J.H., and J.W. Jefferson. *Panic Disorder and Agoraphobia: A Guide*. Madison, Wis.: Anxiety Disorders Center and Information Centers, University of Wisconsin, 1992.

Hecker, J.E., and G.L. Thorpe. *Agoraphobia and Panic: A Guide to Psychological Treatment*. Needham Heights, Mass.: Allyn and Bacon, 1992.

Kernodle, W.D. *Panic Disorder*. Richmond, Va.: William Byrd Press, 1993.

Leaman, T.E. *Healing the Anxiety Diseases*. New York: Plenum Press, 1992.

Peurifoy, Reneau. *Anxiety, Phobias & Panic: Taking Charge and Conquering Fear*, 2nd ed. Citrus Heights, CA: LifeSkills Publications, 1992.

Sheehan, D.V. *The Anxiety Disease*. New York: Bantam Books, 1986.

Tieger, M.E., and B. Elkus. *The Fearful Flyers Resource Guide*. Cincinnati, Ohio: Argonaut Entertainment, 1993. To order, call toll-free 1–800–776–9800.

Weekes, C. *Hope and Help for Your Nerves*. New York: Hawthorne Books, 1969.

————. *Peace from Nervous Suffering*. New York: Signet, 1972.

————. *Simple, Effective Treatment of Agoraphobia*. New York: Bantam Books, 1979.

Wilson, R. *Achieving Comfortable Flight*, Audio tape series available through Pathway Systems. To order, call toll-free 1–800–394–2299.

————. *Breaking the Panic Cycle: Self-Help for People with Phobias*. Anxiety Disorders Association of America, 1987. A self-help book available through ADAA (see address on page 270).

————. *Don't Panic: Taking Control of Anxiety Attacks*. New York: Harper and Row, 1986. Audio tape series available through Pathway Systems. To order, call toll-free 1–800–394–2299.

SOCIAL PHOBIA

Markway, B.G., C.N. Carmin, C.A. Pollard, and T. Flynn. *Dying of Embarrassment: Help for Social Anxiety & Phobias*. Oakland, Calif.: New Harbinger Publications, 1992.

Rubin, B.J. *Stage Fright Handbook*. Washington, D.C.: Decision-Making Systems, Ltd., 1986. To order, call 703–548–7972.

OBSESSIVE-COMPULSIVE DISORDER

Baer, L. *Getting Control: Overcoming Your Obsessions and Compulsions*. Boston, Mass.: Little, Brown and Company, 1991.

Foa, E.B., and R.R. Wilson. *Stop Obsessing!* New York: Bantam Books, 1991. A three-tape self-help supplement to the book is available from Pathway Systems. To order the book or the tapes, call toll-free 1–800–394–2299.

Greist, J.H. *Obsessive Compulsive Disorders: A Guide,* 3rd edition. Madison, Wis.: Obsessive Compulsive Information Center, University of Wisconsin; 1991.

Livingston, B. *Learning to Live with Obsessive-Compulsive Disorder*. New Haven, Conn.: Obsessive-Compulsive Foundation, 1989. A guidebook for families available through the OC Foundation (see address under Organizations listing on page 271).

Neziroglu, F. and J. Yaryura-Tobias. *Over and Over Again: Understanding Obsessive-Compulsive Disorder*. Lexington, Mass.; Lexington Books; 1991.

Obsessive Compulsive Disorder—A Survival Guide for Family and Friends. Send $10 (U.S. check or money order) to: Obsessive Compulsive Anonymous, P.O. Box 215, New Hyde Park, N.Y. 11040

Rapoport, J.L. *The Boy Who Couldn't Stop Washing*. New York: E.P. Dutton (Division of NAL Penguin Inc.), 1989.

Steketee, G., and K. White. *When Once Is Not Enough: Help for Obsessive Compulsives*. Oakland, Calif.; New Harbinger Press; 1990.

FURTHER READING

Benson, H. *The Relaxation Response.* New York: William Morrow & Co., 1975.

Burns, D.D. *Feeling Good: The New Mood Therapy.* Chicago, Ill: Signet, 1981.

————. *The Feeling Good Handbook: Using the New Mood Therapy in Everyday Life.* New York: William Morrow & Co., 1989.

Rosenthal, N.E. *Winter Blues.* New York: Guilford Press, 1992.

ORGANIZATIONS AND HELPLINES

Since 1980, many thousands of people with an anxiety disorder and their family members have benefited from the services and publications of the Anxiety Disorders Association of America (ADAA), a nonprofit membership organization that promotes the prevention and cure of anxiety disorders and works to improve the lives of all people who suffer from them. ADAA's dedicated board of directors, members, and staff include mental health professionals (researchers and clinicians), consumers, family members, and other interested individuals.

ADAA provides educational materials, a quarterly newsletter, and state-by-state listings of self-help groups and mental health professionals who specialize in treating anxiety disorders. Its annual national conference brings together clinicians, researchers, and consumers interested in learning more about the causes and latest methods of treating anxiety disorders. Cassette tapes from the conferences are available. ADAA membership dues help to support anxiety-disorders research and the association's efforts to educate health professionals, legislators, and consumers about the recognition and treatability of anxiety disorders.

To become a *Consumer* member of ADAA, please send $25 to the address below and include your name, address, and telephone number. Membership includes a State Listing of Professional Treatment Providers, a Self-Help Group State Listing, a Membership Card, and an annual subscription to the *Reporter* (ADAA's newsletter). *Consumer* membership is open to persons coping with an anxiety disorder, their family members, and all others who are interested in the well-being of people with anxiety disorders.

Professional membership is open to psychiatrists, psychologists, clinical social workers, counselors, psychiatric nurses, and other mental health professionals with a special interest in anxiety-disorder treatment and research. To become a *Professional* member of ADAA, please contact the association for details.

Anxiety Disorders Association of America (ADAA)
Dept. B
P.O. Box 96505
Washington, DC 20077-7140
301-231-9350

The following professional and consumer groups also offer information and help for people with anxiety disorders and related conditions:

American Psychiatric Association
1400 K Street, N.W.
Washington, DC 20005
202-682-6000

American Psychological Association
750 First Street, N.E.
Washington, DC 20002
202-336-5500

Association for the Advancement of Behavior Therapy (AABT)
305 Seventh Avenue
Suite 16A
New York, NY 10001
212-279-7970

National Alliance for the Mentally Ill (NAMI)
2101 Wilson Boulevard
Suite 302
Arlington, VA 22201
703-524-7600

National Depressive and Manic Depressive Association (National DMDA)
730 N. Franklin Street
Suite 501
Chicago, IL 60610
800-82-NDMDA

National Institute of Mental Health
National Panic Disorders Education Campaign
800-64-PANIC

National Institute of Mental Health
Information Resources and Inquiries Branch/Publications List
Room 15C–05
5600 Fishers Lane
Rockville, MD 20857
301–443–4513

National Mental Health Association (NMHA)
1201 Prince Street
Alexandria, VA 22314–2971
703–838–7500

Obsessive Compulsive Anonymous
P.O. Box 215
New Hyde Park, NY 11040
516–741–4901

Obsessive-Compulsive Foundation (OCF)
P.O. Box 70
Milford, CT 06460
203–878–5669
203–874–3843 (24-hour information line)

Obsessive Compulsive Information Center
8000 Excelsior Drive
Suite 203
Madison, WI 53717–1914
608–836–8070

Trichotillomania Learning Center, Inc. (TLC)
1215 Mission Street
Suite 2
Santa Cruz, CA 95060
408–457–1004

FINDING TREATMENT

Anxiety disorders are treated by a wide variety of health professionals, including psychiatrists, psychologists, clinical social workers, and psychiatric nurses. Finding the right treatment provider may involve meeting with more than one potential therapist to determine compatability. It is important that one feel personally comfortable with whomever he or she chooses.

This process may include talking for a few minutes on the telephone and then, ideally, having a longer meeting in the office. There will most likely be a charge for an in-office consultation; so be sure to ask about the cost of such a discussion and how much time will be alloted with the therapist.

Fees for anxiety-disorders treatment are set by individual therapists and will vary in different parts of the country. Insurance coverage will also vary depending on your policy, so it is recommended that you check with your insurer in advance to determine what portion of your costs will be covered.

Although there is no single, correct set of questions that should be raised during a phone or office consultation, the Anxiety Disorders Association of America suggests the following list of some inquiries you might make:

- What training and experience do you have in treating anxiety disorders?
- What is your basic approach to treatment?
- Can you prescribe medication or refer me to somebody who can, if that proves necessary?
- How long is the course of treatment?
- How frequent are treatment sessions and how long do they last?
- Do you include family members in therapy?
- Will you or a staff member go to a patient's home if necessary?
- What is your fee schedule?
- Are you qualified for reimbursement by insurance plans?

Most of the patients whose cases have been discussed in this book were treated at the Ross Center for Anxiety and Related Disorders in Washington, D.C. The Ross Center is a comprehensive, out-patient treatment center, specializing in short-term individual and group cognitive-behavioral therapy and medication management for people with anxiety disorders. Intensive one- and two-week treatment programs are available at the Ross Center for individuals living outside the metropolitan Washington area. For more information, write to the Ross Center for Anxiety and Related Disorders, 4545 42nd Street, N.W., Suite 311, Washington, D.C. 20016, or call (202)–363–1010.

You can obtain a list of additional treatment programs and individual therapists in your area by contacting the Anxiety Disorders Association of America (see address and phone number listed under Organizations above).

One way to receive a thorough diagnostic evaluation and treatment is to volunteer to participate in a research program. These are often conducted at departments of psychology or psychiatry in universities, medical schools, and hospitals, and at some private mental health facilities. Among these research programs are clinical trials whose purpose is to test whether a certain new or experimental psychological or pharmacological treatment works for patients with a specific disorder. *A major advantage of these studies is that eligible participants receive a free comprehensive evalua-*

tion and free or low-cost treatment. These trials are usually studying a particular type of problem or treatment and may exclude people with significant medical problems or coexisting psychiatric problems, women of childbearing potential, and people outside specified age limitations. Treatment in such programs may be provided by a qualified psychiatrist or psychologist or by a trainee who works under the direct supervision of a senior person.

Listed below are some of the universities, hospitals, or private research centers in the United States and Canada that are studying anxiety disorders and may be looking for people to participate in one clinical trial or another. You can find additional research programs by checking with the psychology or psychiatry department of your local university, the consumer or professional mental health organizations listed above, and by watching for advertisements in your local newspaper placed by researchers who are recruiting subjects for a particular study.

Arizona

Good Samaritan Regional Medical Center
925 East McDowell Road
4th Floor
Phoenix, AZ 85006
(602) 239–6999
Eric M. Reiman, M.D.

California

UCLA Anxiety Disorders Program
300 UCLA Medical Plaza
Los Angeles, CA 90024
(310) 206–5133
Director: Alexander Bystritsky, M.D.

UCLA Anxiety Disorders Behavioral Program
UCLA Department of Psychology
405 Hilgard Avenue
Los Angeles, CA 90024–1563
(310) 206–9191
Director: Michelle G. Craske, Ph.D.

University of California, San Diego
Psychopharmacology Research Program
8950 Villa La Jolla Drive #2243
La Jolla, CA 92037
(619) 622–6111
Codirectors: Lewis Judd, M.D.
               Mark Rapaport, M.D.

EMDR Research Center
Mental Research Institute
Palo Alto, CA 94301
(415) 321–3055
Director: Clifford Levin, Ph.D.

Connecticut

Yale Anxiety Research Clinic
34 Park Street
New Haven, CT 06519
(203) 789–7689
Director: Andrew W. Goddard, M.D.

Yale Trauma Clinic
Box 208308
New Haven, CT 06519
(203) 737–2776 or 785–7210
Director: Thomas H. McGlashan, M.D.

District of Columbia

Anxiety Disorders Research Program
Georgetown University Medical Center
Department of Psychiatry
Kober-Cogan, No. 315
3750 Reservoir Road, N.W.
Washington, DC 20007
(202) 687–2392
Director: Teresa Pigott, M.D.

Clinical Psychiatric Research Center
George Washington University
2300 Eye Street, N.W.
Washington, DC 22314
(202) 994–4079
Codirectors: Karen Weihs, M.D.
            Michael Silver, M.D.

The Agoraphobia and Anxiety Program
Department of Psychology
American University
Washington, DC 20016–8062
(202) 885–1743
Director: Dianne Chambless, Ph.D.

Florida

University of Florida
Shands Clinics
Psychiatric Specialty Clinics
Box 100256
Gainesville, FL 32610–0256
(904) 395–0162
Director: Wayne Goodman, M.D.

Anxiety Disorders Program
University of Miami
School of Medicine
1400 N.W. 10th Avenue (D-79)
Room 304-A
Miami, FL 33136
(305) 547–4060
Director: Thomas A. Mellman, M.D.

Clinical Research Center
University of Southern Florida
Institute for Research and Psychiatry
3515 E. Fletcher Avenue
Tampa, FL 33613
(813) 979–3500
Director: David V. Sheehan, M.D.

Georgia

Emory Clinic Anxiety Disorders Program
Emory University School of Medicine
1701 Uppergate Road
Atlanta, GA 30322
(404) 727–8968
Principal Investigator: Philip T. Ninan, M.D.

Illinois

Anxiety Disorders Clinic of the
University of Illinois
College of Medicine at Peoria
7725 North Knoxville Avenue
Peoria, IL 61614
(309) 671–2165
Director: David Spiegel, M.D.

Iowa

Anxiety Clinic
Department of Psychiatry
University of Iowa Hospitals and Clinics
200 Hawkins Drive
Iowa City, IA 52242
(319) 353–6314
Director: Russell Noyes, Jr., M.D.

Louisiana

Louisiana State University
Anxiety and Mood Disorders Clinic
Louisiana State University Medical Center
1542 Tulane Avenue
New Orleans, LA 70112
(504) 568–6201
Director: James G. Barbee, M.D.

Anxiety and Mood Disorders Program
Ochsner Clinic
1514 Jefferson Highway
New Orleans, LA 70121
(504) 842–3843
Medical Director: Charles K. Billings, M.D.

Maryland

Anxiety Disorders Research Center
Johns Hopkins Hospital
115 Meyer Building
Baltimore, MD 21287–7144
(410) 955–5653
Director: Rudolf Hoehn-Saric, M.D.

National Institute of Mental Health
NIMH Clinical Center
Building 10 3N234
Bethesda, MD 20892
(301) 496–1337
Contact: Nazli Haq, M.A., Office of the Clinical Director

Unit on Anxiety and Affective Disorders
(301) 496–7141
Contact: Barbara Scupi, L.C.S.W.

Institute for Behavior and Health
6191 Executive Boulevard
Rockville, MD 20852
(301) 231–9010
President: Robert L. DuPont, M.D.

Anxiety and Stress Disorders Institute of Maryland
6525 North Charles Street
Towson, MD 21204
(410) 938–8449
Codirectors: Sally Winston, Psy.D.
              Harold Steinitz, Ph.D.

Massachusetts

Anxiety Clinic and Research Program at
Massachusetts General Hospital
15 Parkman Street #815
Boston, MA 02114
(617) 726–3488
Codirectors: Mark Pollack, M.D.
              Michael Otto, Ph.D.

Center for Research on Anxiety Disorders
Boston University School of Social Work
264 Bay State Road
Boston, MA 02215
(617) 353–3750
Director: Gail Steketee, Ph.D.

Phobia Clinic
Massachusetts Mental Health Center
74 Fenwood Road
Boston, MA 02115
(617) 734–1300
Director: Robert Goisman, M.D.

Michigan

Anxiety Disorders Program
University of Michigan, Department of Psychiatry
1500 East Medical Center Drive
Ann Arbor, MI 48109–0840
(313) 764–5348
Director: George Curtis, M.D.

University Psychiatric Center
2751 East Jefferson
Suite 200
Detroit, MI 48207
(313) 993–3444
Director: Robert Pohl, M.D.

New Jersey

Princeton Biomedical Research
330 North Harrison Street
Princeton, NJ 08540
(609) 921–3555
Director: Jeffrey T. Apter, M.D.

New Mexico

Anxiety Disorders Research Program
Department of Psychiatry
University of New Mexico
School of Medicine
2400 Tucker, N.E., 4th Floor
Albuquerque, NM 87131
(505) 277–2281 or 277–5416
Director: E. H. Uhlenhuth, M.D.

New York

Phobia and Anxiety Disorders Clinic
1535 Western Avenue
Albany, NY 12203
(518) 456–4127
Director: David Barlow, Ph.D.

Anxiety Disorders Clinic at Columbia University
New York State Psychiatric Institute
722 West 168th Street
New York, NY 10032
(212) 960–2367
Codirectors: Michael Liebowitz, M.D.
             Abby Fyer, M.D.

Child Psychiatry Research Center
Anxiety and Mood Disorders Clinic
New York State Psychiatric Institute
722 West 168th Street
New York, NY 10032
(212) 960–2344
Director: Rachel Klein, Ph.D.

Staten Island Research Center
at Freedom From Fear
308 Seaview Avenue
Staten Island, NY 10305
(718) 351–1717
Director: Mary Guardino

North Carolina

Anxiety and Traumatic Stress Program
Box 3812
Durham, NC 27710
(919) 684–2880
Director: Jonathan R. T. Davidson, M.B., FRC Psych.

Duke University Medical Center
Program in Child and Adolescent Anxiety Disorders
D.U.M.C. Box 3527
Durham, NC 27710
(919) 684–4950
Director: John March, M.D.

Ohio

Phobia and Anxiety Disorders Clinic
Ohio State University Medical Center
456 West 10th Avenue
Columbus, OH 43210
(614) 293–5130
Director: Matig Mavassakalian, M.D.

Pennsylvania

The Beck Institute for Cognitive Therapy and Research
GSB Building
City Line and Belmont Avenues
Suite 700
Bala Cynwyd, PA 19004-1610
(610) 664–3020
Director: Judith S. Beck, Ph.D.

Agoraphobia and Anxiety Treatment Center
Temple University Medical School
Department of Psychiatry
112 Bala Avenue
Bala Cynwyd, PA 19004
(215) 667–6490
Director: Alan Goldstein, Ph.D.

Center for the Treatment and Study of Anxiety
Medical College of Pennsylvania
Department of Psychiatry
3200 Henry Avenue
Philadelphia, PA 19129
(215) 842–4010
Director: Edna B. Foa, Ph.D.

Emotion Focused Treatment (EFT)
Western Psychiatric Institute and Clinic
3811 O'Hara Street
Pittsburgh, PA 15213
(412) 624–5500
Director: Katherine M. Shear, M.D.

Stress and Anxiety Disorders Institute
Pennsylvania State University
Room 546
University Park, PA 16802
(814) 863–6019
Codirectors: Larry Michelson, Ph.D.
Tom Borkovac, Ph.D.

Rhode Island

Anxiety Disorders Program
Butler Hospital
345 Blackstone
Providence, RI 02906
(401) 455–6230
Director: Steven A. Rasmussen, M.D.

South Carolina

Institute of Psychiatry at the
Medical University of South Carolina
171 Ashley Avenue
Charleston, SC 29425
(803) 792–4032
Codirectors: Bruce Lydiard, M.D.
James Ballenger, M.D.

Anxiety Prevention and Treatment Research Center
Institute of Psychiatry at the
Medical University of South Carolina
615 Wesley Drive
Suite 200
Charleston, SC 29407
(803) 852–4190
Codirectors: Samuel M. Turner, Ph.D., ABPP
     Deborah C. Beidel, Ph.D.

Texas

U. T. Southwestern Medical Center
Psychopharmacology Study Group
5959 Harry Hines Boulevard, POB I 520
Dallas, TX 75235–9101
(214) 648–8348
Director: Rege Stewart, M.D.

Laboratory for the Studies of Anxiety Disorders
Department of Psychology
University of Texas
Austin, TX 78712
(512) 471–5177
Director: Michael Telch, Ph.D.

Mood and Anxiety Disorders Program
University of Texas Medical Branch, Galveston
Department of Psychiatry and Behavioral Sciences
301 University Boulevard
Galveston, TX 77555-1355
(409) 772–7533
18333 Egret Bay Boulevard
Suite 150
Houston, TX 77058
(713) 333–3058
Codirectors: Ruth Levine, M.D.
     Janice A. Blalock, Ph.D.

Richardson Medical Center
301 West Campbell Drive
Richardson, TX 75080
(214) 234–0489
Wayne C. Jones, M.D.

282

Washington

Harborview Medical Center
Department of Psychiatry
325 9th Avenue
Seattle, WA 98104
(206) 223-2503
Director: Dane Wingerson, M.D.

Wisconsin

Dean Foundation for Health, Education and Research
8000 Excelsior Drive
Suite 302
Madison, WI 52717
(608) 836-8030
Codirectors: John Greist, M.D.
           James W. Jefferson, M.D.

Anxiety Disorders Clinic
University of Wisconsin Hospitals and Clinics
Clinical Sciences Center
600 Highland Avenue
Madison, WI 53792
(608) 263-6056
Director: John Marshall, M.D.

CANADIAN ANXIETY-DISORDERS CLINICS

Calgary General Hospital
Calgary, Alberta G2E 0A1
(403) 268-9682
David Johnson, M.D.

McMaster Psychiatric Unit
St. Joseph's Hospital
50 Charlton Avenue East
Hamilton, Ontario L8N 4A6
(905) 521-6040
Michael Van Ameringen, M.D., F.R.C.P.C.

3G Outpatient Clinic
McMaster University Medical Centre
1200 Main Street West
Hamilton, Ontario L8N 3Z5
(905) 521–5018
Catherine Mancini, M.D., F.R.C.P.C.

The Clarke Institute of Psychiatry
250 College St.
Toronto, Ontario M5T 1R8
(416) 979–2221
Richard Swinson, M.D.

St. Mary's Hospital
Montreal, Quebec H3T 1M5
(514) 345–3584
Jacques Bradwejn, M.D.

Royal University Hospital
103 Hospital Drive
Saskatoon, Saskatchewan S7N 0W0
(306) 966–8223
Rudy Bowen, M.D.

Centre Hospitalier Universitaire de Sherbrooke
Sherbrooke (Quebec) Canada GEH 5M4
(819) 563–5555 Ext. 4433
Jean-Philippe Boulenger, M.D.

Douglas Hospital
6875 LaSalle Boulevard
Verdun, Quebec H4H 1R3
(514) 761–6131
John Pecknold, M.D., F.R.C.P.C.

St. Boniface Hospital
Winnipeg, Manitoba R2H 2A6
(204) 237–2606
John Walker, Ph.D.

References

Agras, W. S. "Treatment of Social Phobia." *Journal of Clinical Psychiatry* 51 (October 1990, suppl.): 52–55.

Ashok, B., M. H. Corvea, and E. M. Dagon. "The Clinical Characteristics of Panic Disorder in the Elderly." *Journal of Clinical Psychiatry* 54 (April 1993).

Ballenger, J. C., G. D. Burrows, R. L. DuPont, et al. "Alprazolam in Panic Disorders and Agoraphobia: Results from a Multicenter Trial." *Archives of General Psychiatry* 45 (May 1988): 413–22.

Barlow, D. H., and M. G. Craske. *Mastery of Your Anxiety and Panic*. Albany: Center for Stress and Anxiety Disorders, State University of New York at Albany, 1991.

Beck, A. T., G. Emery, and R. Greenberg. *Anxiety Disorders and Phobias: A Cognitive Perspective*. New York: Guilford Press, 1985.

Boyd, J. H., D. S. Rae, J. W. Thompson, et al. "Phobia: Prevalence and Risk Factors." *American Journal of Psychiatry* 143 (December 1986): 1569–74.

Butler, K. "Too Good to Be True." *Networker* (November/December 1993): 19–31.

Charney, D. S., S. M. Southwick, and J. H. Krystal. "The Psychobiology of PTSD." In *The Yearbook of the Encyclopedia of Neuroscience*, edited by G. Adelman and B. Smith. Boston: Birkhauser Boston Publishing Company, 1993.

Clark, D. M. "A Cognitive Approach to Panic." *Behavior and Research Therapy* 24 (1986): 461–70.

Coplan, D. J., L. A. Papp, D. L. King, and J. M. Gorman. "Amelioration of Mitral Valve Prolapse After Treatment for Panic Disorder." *American Journal of Psychiatry* 149 (1992): 1587–88.

DuPont, R. L., S. Shiraki, D. Rice, et al. "The Economic Costs of Anxiety Disorders." Presented at the Anxiety Disorders Association of America Annual Meeting, Charleston, S.C., March 19, 1993.

Eagle, K. A. "Medical Decision Making in Patients with Chest Pain." Editorial in *The New England Journal of Medicine* 324 (1991): 1282–83.

Edlund, M. J., and A. C. Swann. "The Economic and Social Costs of Panic Disorder." *Hospital and Community Psychiatry* 38 (December 1987): 1277–88.

Gelernter, C. S., M. B. Stein, M. E. Tancer, and T. W. Uhde. "An Examination of Syndromal Validity and Diagnostic Subtypes in Social Phobia and Panic Disorder." *Journal of Clinical Psychiatry* 53 (1992): 23–27.

Goisman, R. M., and T. G. Gutheil. "Risk Management in the Practice of Behavior Therapy: Boundaries and Behavior." *American Journal of Psychotherapy* 46 (October 1992): 532–43.

Halle, M. T., and S. C. Dilsaver. "Comorbid Panic Disorder in Patients with Winter Depression." *American Journal of Psychiatry* 150 (July 1993).

Heimberg, R. G., and D. H. Barlow. "New Developments in Cognitive-Behavioral Therapy for Social Phobia." *Journal of Clinical Psychiatry* 52 (1991, suppl.): 21–30.

Horwath, E., J. Johnson, and C. D. Hornig. "Epidemiology of Panic Disorder in African-Americans." *American Journal of Psychiatry* 150 (March 1993).

Katon, W. *Panic Disorder in the Medical Setting.* U.S. Department of Health and Human Services pub. no. (ADM) 92–1629. Washington, D.C.: Superintendent of Documents, Government Printing Office, 1992.

Katon, W., D. V. Sheehan, and T. W. Uhde. "Panic Disorder: A Treatable Problem." *Patient Care* (April 1992): 81–107.

Kessler, R. C., K. A. McGonagle, et al. "Lifetime and 12-Month Prevalence of DSM-III-R Psychiatric Disorders in the United States." *Archives of General Psychiatry* (January 14, 1994).

Kushner, M. G., K. J. Sher, and B. D. Beitmen. "The Relation Between Alcohol Problems and the Anxiety Disorders." *American Journal of Psychiatry* 147 (1990): 685–95.

Liebowitz, M. R., J. M. Gorman, A. J. Fyer, et al. "Social Phobia: Review of a Neglected Anxiety Disorder." *Archives of General Psychiatry* 42 (1985): 729–36.

Liebowitz, M. R., F. R. Schneier, E. Hollander, et al. "Treatment of Social Phobia with Drugs Other Than Benzodiazepines." *Journal of Clinical Psychiatry* 52 (November 1991, suppl.): 10–15.

Lydiard, B. R., S. Greenwald, M. M. Weissman, et al. "Panic Disorder and Gastrointestinal Symptoms: Findings from the NIMH Epidemiological Catchment Area Project." *American Journal of Psychiatry* 151 (January 1994).

Markowitz, J., M. M. Weissman, R. Ouellette, et al. "Quality of Life in Panic Disorder." *Archives of General Psychiatry* 46 (1989): 984–92.

Marks, I. M. *Living with Fear.* New York: McGraw-Hill, 1978.

Moreau, D., and M. M. Weissman. "Panic Disorder in Children and Adolescents: A Review." *American Journal of Psychiatry* 149 (1992): 1306–14.

National Institutes of Health. NIH Consensus Development Conference Statement, vol. 9, no. 2. *Treatment of Panic Disorder*. Bethesda, Md.: NIH, September 1991.

O'Brien, E. "The Enigma of EMDR: Pushing the Panic Button." *Networker* (November/December 1993): 33–39.

Regier, D. A., W. E. Narrow, D. S. Rae, et al. "The De Facto U.S. Mental and Addictive Disorders Service System." *Archives of General Psychiatry* 50 (1993): 85–94. Also, personal communication with Darrel A. Regier, M.D., M.P.H., Director, Division of Epidemiology and Services Research, National Institute of Mental Health, January 24, 1994.

Ross, J. "The Role of the Family Member in the Supported Exposure Approach to the Treatment of Phobias." In *Learning Theory Approaches to Psychiatry*, edited by J. Boulougouris. London: John Wiley & Sons, 1982.

————. "Social Phobia: The Consumer's Perspective." *Journal of Clinical Psychiatry* 54 (December 1993, suppl.).

————. "Social Phobia: The Anxiety Disorders Association of America Helps Raise the Veil of Ignorance." *Journal of Clinical Psychiatry* 52 (November 1991, suppl.): 43–47.

————. "The Use of Former Phobics in the Treatment of Phobias." *American Journal of Psychiatry* 137 (1980): 715–17.

Salkovskis, P. M., and D. M. Clark. "Cognitive Therapy for Panic Attacks." *Journal of Cognitive Psychotherapy: An International Quarterly* 5, no. 3 (1991).

Saylor, K. E., R. L. DuPont, and M. Brouillard. "Self-help Treatment of Anxiety Disorders." In *Handbook of Anxiety, vol. 4, The Treatment of Anxiety*, edited by R. Noyes, Jr., M. Roth, and G. D. Burrows. Amsterdam: Elsevier.

Schneier, F. R., J. Johnson, C. D. Hornig, M. R. Liebowitz, and M. M. Weissman. "Social Phobia: Comorbidity and Morbidity in an Epidemiological Sample." *Archives of General Psychiatry* 49 (1992): 282–88.

Schneier, F. R., L. Y. Martin, M. R. Liebowitz, et al. "Alcohol Abuse in Social Phobia." *Journal of Anxiety Disorders* 3 (1989): 15–23.

Schwartz, J. M., K. M. Martin, and L. R. Baxter. "Neuroimaging and Cognitive-Behavioral Self-treatment for Obsessive-Compulsive Disorder: Practical and Philosophical Considerations." In *Obsessive-Compulsive Disorders: New Research Results*, edited by I. Hand and W. K. Goodman. Berlin: Springer Verlag, 1992.

Sharfstein, S. S. "The Economics of Anxiety." In *The Economic Fact Book for Psychiatry*, 2nd ed. Office of Economic Affairs of the American Psychiatric Association. Washington, D.C.: American Psychiatric Press, 1987.

Shear, K. M., A. M. Cooper, G. L. Klerman, et al. "A Psychodynamic Model of Panic Disorder." *American Journal of Psychiatry* 150 (1993); 859–66.

Stein, M. B., M. E. Tancer, C. S. Gelernter, et al. "Major Depression in Patients with Social Phobia." *American Journal of Psychiatry* 147 (1990): 637–39.

Turner, S. M., D. C. Beidel, P. J. Long, et al.. "Reduction of Fear in Social Phobics: An Examination of Extinction Patterns." *Behavior Therapy* 23 (1992): 389–403.

Villeponteaus, V. A., B. R. Lydiard, M. T. Larala, et al. "The Effects of Pregnancy on Preexisting Panic Disorder." *Journal of Clinical Psychiatry* 53 (June 1992).

Weiss, K. J., and D. J. Rosenberg. "Prevalence of Anxiety Disorders Among Alcoholics." *Journal of Clinical Psychiatry* 46 (1985): 3–5.

Zane, M. D. *Your Phobia: Understanding Your Fears Through Contextual Therapy.* Washington, D.C.: American Psychiatric Press, 1984.

Index

About the Author

Jerilyn Ross, M.A., L.I.C.S.W., is one of the nation's leading experts on anxiety disorders. A psychotherapist, patient advocate, and author, Ms. Ross is Director of The Ross Center for Anxiety and Related Disorders, an outpatient multidisciplinary treatment center in Washington, D.C., and President of the Anxiety Disorders Association of America, a nonprofit organization which promotes the welfare of people with anxiety disorders.

Ms. Ross received her graduate training in psychology at the New School for Social Research in New York City and began her clinical practice and public advocacy activities in 1978. Since then she has appeared on over 100 television and radio shows, including "Nightline," "Oprah Winfrey," "Today," "Donahue," and "Larry King Live." From 1987 to 1992, she hosted her own award-winning Washington, D.C., talk show, which focused on psychological and related topics.

As President of the Anxiety Disorders Association of America, Ms. Ross has twice testified before Congress and currently serves on the Scientific Advisory Committee of the federal government's Panic Disorder Prevention and Public Education Program.

A member of the American Psychological Association, the D.C. Psychological Association, and the Association for the Advancement of Behavior Therapy, Ms. Ross frequently conducts public and professional lectures, seminars, and workshops on anxiety disorders. Her previous publications include chapters and articles in the *American Journal of Psychiatry*, the *Journal of Clinical Psychiatry*, and several textbooks. She is frequently quoted in such publications as *The New York Times, The Wall Street Journal*, and *Newsweek*.

Ms. Ross is the recipient of many honors, including media awards from the American Association of University Women and the Mental Health Association of Northern Virginia. She also serves on the board of the National Women's Health Resource Center in Washington, D.C., where she now resides.